REAL HAUNTINGS

REAL HAUNTINGS

True American Ghost Stories

HANS HOLZER

BARNES
& NOBLE

NEW YORK

Contents

Introduction

What Exactly Is a Ghost?

*G*reat American Ghost Stories dealt with the famous of the past—historical hauntings that I was able to verify and report on. However, there are hundreds of thousands of hauntings all over America involving neither the famous nor great moments in history. These ghostly encounters are experienced by people in all walks of life, and they are just as meaningful as a haunting in the White House.

Those who have read *Great American Ghost Stories* and *Hans Holzer's Haunted America* will find these additional accounts equally absorbing and thought provoking. It can happen to anyone: Ghosts are, after all, people who had unfinished business on their minds when they passed on.

In *Real Hauntings: America's True Ghost Stories*, I have selected cases from many areas of America that seem to be particularly interesting, and also convincing so that those who need persuading will see that life does go on beyond the veil.

When you look through the following pages you need to forget a popular notion about ghosts—that ghosts are dangerous, frightening, and evil. Nothing could be further from the truth. Ghosts are also not figments of the imagination or the product of motion-picture writers. Ghostly experiences are neither supernatural nor unnatural; instead they fit into the general pattern of the universe we live in, even though the majority of conventional scientists have not yet understood exactly what ghosts are. Those who have studied parapsychology have come to understand that human life does continue beyond what we commonly call death. Once in a while, there are extraordinary circumstances when death occurs, and these exceptional situations create what we popularly call ghosts and haunted houses.

Ever since the dawn of humankind, people have believed in ghosts. The fear of the unknown—the certainty that there is something somewhere out there, bigger than life, beyond its pale, and more powerful than anything walking the earth—has persisted throughout the ages. These fears had their origins in primitive people's thinking. To them, there were good and evil forces at work in nature, both ruled over by supernatural beings, and to some degree capable of being influenced by the attitudes and prayers of humans. The fear of death was, of course, one of the strongest human emotions. It still is.

Then what are ghosts—if indeed there *are* such things? To the materialist and the professional skeptic—that is to say, people who do not wish to be disturbed in their belief that death is the end of life as we know it—the notion of ghosts is unacceptable. No matter how much evidence is presented for the reality of the phenomena, they will argue against it and ascribe it to any of several "natural" causes. Either delusion or hallucination must be the explanation, or perhaps a mirage, if not outright trickery on the part of parties unknown. Entire professional groups who deal in the manufacture of illusions have taken it upon themselves to label anything that defies their ability to reproduce it artificially through trickery or manipulation as false or nonexistent. Especially among photographers and magicians, the notion that ghosts exist has never been a popular one. However, authentic reports of psychic phenomena along ghostly lines keep coming into reputable report centers such as the various societies for psychic research, or to people, like me, who are parapsychologists.

Granted that even though a certain number of these reports may be due to inaccurate reporting, self-delusion, or other errors of fact, there still remains an impressive number of cases that cannot be explained by any other means than that of extrasensory perception.

What exactly is a ghost? In terms of psychic research, as I have defined it a ghost appears to be a surviving emotional memory of someone who has died traumatically, and usually tragically, but is unaware of his or her death. Ghosts, then, in the overwhelming majority, do not realize that they have died. Those who do know they are "dead" are confused as to where they are and why they do not feel quite as they used to feel. When death occurs unexpectedly or unacceptably, or when a person has become very attached to a place he or she has lived in for a very long time, sudden, unexpected death may come as a shock. Unwilling to part with the physical world, such human personalities then continue to stay on in the very spot where their tragedy or their emotional attachment had existed prior to physical death.

Ghosts do not travel; they do not follow people home;

nor do they appear at more than one place. Nevertheless, there are also reliable reports of the apparitions of the dead having indeed traveled and appeared to several people in various locations. Those, however, are not ghosts in the sense that I understand the term. They are free spirits, or discarnate entities, who are inhabiting what Dr. Joseph B. Rhine of Duke University has called the "world of the mind." They may be attracted for emotional reasons to one or another place at a given moment in order to communicate with someone on the earth plane. But a true ghost is unable to make such moves freely. Ghosts by their very nature are not unlike psychotics in the flesh; they are quite unable to understand fully their own predicament. They are kept in place, both in time and space, *by* their emotional ties to the spot. Nothing can pry them loose from it so long as they are reliving over and over again in their minds the events leading to their unhappy deaths.

Sometimes this is difficult for the ghost, as he or she may be too strongly attached to feelings of guilt or revenge to "let go." Eventually, though, a combination of informative remarks by the parapsychologist and suggestions to call upon the deceased person's family will pry the ghost loose and send him or her out into the free spirit world.

Ghosts have never harmed anyone except through fear found within the witness. The harm results from the witness's own doing because of his or her ignorance as to what ghosts represent. In the few cases where ghosts have attacked people of flesh and blood, such as the ghostly abbot of Trondheim, it is simply a matter of mistaken identity, where extreme violence at the time of death has left a strong residue of memory in the individual ghosts. By and large, it is entirely safe to be a ghost hunter or to become a witness to phenomena of this kind.

In his chapter on ghosts in *Man, Myth, and Magic,* Douglas Hill examines all alternate hypotheses one by one. Having done so, he states, "None of these explanations is wholly satisfactory, for none seems applicable to the whole range of ghost lore." Try as they might, people can't explain away ghosts, nor will ghosts simply disappear. They continue to appear frequently all over the world to young and old, rich and poor, in old houses and new, in airports and streets, and wherever tragedy strikes. For ghosts are indeed nothing more or nothing less than a human being trapped by special circumstances in this world while already being in the next; or, to put it another way, ghosts are human beings whose spirits are unable to leave the earthly surroundings because of unfinished business or emotional entanglements.

But even if you do not encounter ghosts or have a psychic experience in the houses described here, you will find them fascinating places. As an adventure in historical research, haunted houses have no equal.

Finally, I would suggest to my readers not to argue the existence or nonexistence of ghosts and haunted houses. Everyone must find his or her own explanations for what he or she experiences, and *belief* has nothing to do with it. Belief is the uncritical acceptance of something you cannot prove one way or another, and the evidence for ghosts and hauntings is so overwhelming, so large, and so well documented, that arguing the existence of the evidence would be a foolish thing indeed. While there may be various explanations for what people experience in haunted houses, no explanation will ever be sufficient to negate the experiences themselves. Thus, if you are one of the many who enter a haunted house and have a genuine experience in it, be assured that you are a perfectly normal human being who uses a natural gift that is neither harmful nor dangerous.

—Prof. Hans Holzer, Ph.D.
New York City, July 1994

Part I

Ghosts in New England

1

A Ghost in New Hampshire

When I speak of Plymouth, I am not talking about *the* Plymouth where the Pilgrims landed. This Plymouth is located in New Hampshire, in a part of the state that is rather lonely and sparsely settled even today. If you really want to get away from it all—whatever it may be—this is a pretty good bet. I mention this because living in this rural area isn't likely to give you much choice in the way of entertainment, unless of course you provide it yourself. But I am getting ahead of my story.

I was first contacted about this case in August 1966 when a young lady named Judith Elliott, who lived at the time in Bridgeport, Connecticut, informed me of the goings-on in her cousin's country house located in New

Hampshire. Judith asked if I would be interested in contacting Mrs. Chester Fuller regarding these matters. What intrigued me about the report was not the usual array of footfalls, presences, and the house cat staring at someone unseen, but the fact that Mrs. Fuller apparently had seen a ghost and identified him from a book commemorating the bicentennial of the town of Plymouth.

When I wrote back rather enthusiastically, Miss Elliott forwarded my letter to her cousin, requesting more detailed and chronological information. But it was not until well into the following year that I finally got around to making plans for a visit. The medium Ethel Johnson Meyers and my ex-wife, Catherine, always interested in spooky houses since she used to illustrate some of my books, accompanied me. Mrs. Fuller, true to my request, supplied me with all that she knew of the phenomena themselves, who experienced them, and such information about former owners of the house and the house itself as she could garner. Here, in her own words, is that report, which of course I kept from the medium at all times so as not to influence her or give her prior knowledge of house and circumstances. Mrs. Fuller's report is as follows:

"The house is located at 38 Merrill Street in the town of Plymouth, New Hampshire. To reach the house, you leave Throughway 93 at the first exit for Plymouth. When you reach the set of lights on Main Street, turn right and proceed until you reach the blue Sunoco service station, then take a sharp left onto Merrill Street. The house is the only one with a white picket snow fence out front. It has white siding with a red front door and a red window box, and it is on the right-hand side of the street.

A Ghost in New Hampshire

1. The first time was around the middle of June—about a month after moving in. It was the time of day when lights are needed inside, but it is still light outside. This instance was in the kitchen and bathroom. The bathroom and dining room are an addition onto the kitchen. The doors to both rooms go out of the kitchen beside each other, with just a small wall space between. At that time we had our kitchen table in that space. I was getting supper, trying to put the food on the table and keep two small children (ages two and five) off the table. As I put the potatoes on the table, I swung around from the sink toward the bathroom door. I thought I saw someone in the bathroom. I looked and saw a man. He was standing about half-way down the length of the room. He was wearing a brown plaid shirt, dark trousers with suspenders, and he [wore] glasses with the round metal frames. He was of medium height, a little on the short side, not fat and not thin but a good build, a roundish face, and he was smiling. Suddenly he was gone, no disappearing act or anything fancy, just gone, as he had come.

2. Footsteps. There are footsteps in other parts of the house. If I am upstairs, the footsteps are downstairs. If I am in the kitchen, they are in the living room, etc. These were scattered all through the year, in all seasons, and in the daytime. It was usually around two or three and always on a sunny day, as I recall.

3. Winter—late at night. Twice we (Seth and I) heard a door shutting upstairs. (Seth is an elderly man who stays with us now. When we first moved here he was not staying with us. His wife was a distant cousin to my father. I got acquainted with them when I was in high school. I spent a lot of time at their house and his wife

and I became quite close. She died eleven years ago and since then Seth has stayed at his son's house, a rooming house, and now up here. He spent a lot of time visiting us before he moved in.) Only one door in the bedrooms upstairs works right, and that is the door to my bedroom. I checked the kids that night to see if they were up or awake, but they had not moved. My husband was also sound asleep. The door was already shut, as my husband had shut it tight when he went to bed to keep out the sound of the television. The sound of the door was very distinct—the sound of when it first made contact, then the latch clicking in place, and then the thud as it came in contact with the casing. Anything that was or could be loose and have blown and banged or anything that could have fallen down was checked out. Nothing had moved. The door only shut once during that night, but it happened again later on in the winter.

4. The next appearance was in the fall. I was pregnant at the time. I lost the baby on the first of November, and this happened around the first of October. Becky Sue, my youngest daughter, was three at the time. She was asleep in her crib as it was around midnight or later. I was asleep in my bedroom across the hall. I woke up and heard her saying, 'Mommy, what are you doing in my bedroom?' She kept saying that until I thought I had better answer her or she would begin to be frightened. I started to say, 'I'm not in your room,' and as I did I started to turn over and I saw what seemed to be a woman in a long white nightgown in front of my bedroom door. In a flash it was gone out into the hall. All this time Becky had been saying, 'Mommy, what are you doing in my room?' As the image disappeared out in the hall, Becky changed her question to, 'Mommy, what were

you doing in my bedroom?' Then I thought that if I told her I wasn't in her room that she would really be scared. All this time I thought that it was Kimberly, my older daughter, getting up, and I kept waiting for her to speak to me. Becky was still sounding like a broken record with her questions. Finally I heard 'It' take two steps down, turn a corner, and take three steps more. Then I went into Becky's room and told her that I had forgotten what I had gone into her room for and to lie down and go to sleep, which she did. All this time Kim had not moved. The next morning I was telling Seth (who was living with us now) about it, and I remembered about the footsteps going downstairs. I wondered if Becky had heard them too, so I called her out into the kitchen and asked her where I went after I left her room. She looked at me as if I had lost my mind and said, 'Downstairs!'

5. This was in the winter, around two. Seth was helping me make the beds upstairs as they had been skipped for some reason. We heard footsteps coming in from the playroom across the kitchen and a short way into the hall. We both thought it was Becky Sue, who was playing outdoors. She comes in quite frequently for little odds and ends. Still no one spoke. We waited for a while expecting her to call to me. Finally, when she did not call, I went downstairs to see what she wanted, and there was no one there. I thought that maybe she had gone back out, but there was no snow on the floor or tracks of any kind. This was also on a very sunny day.

6. This was also late at night in 1965, around eleven. I was putting my husband's lunch up when there was a step right behind me. That scared me, although I do not know why; up until that time I had never had any fear. Maybe it was because it was right behind my back

and the others had always been at a distance or at least in front of me.

"I cannot remember anything happening since then. Lately there have been noises as if someone was in the kitchen or dining room while I was in the living room, but I cannot be sure of that. It sounds as if something was swishing, but I cannot *definitely* say that it is not the sounds of an old house.

"The history of the house and its previous owners is very hard to get. We bought the house from Mrs. Ora Jacques. Her husband had bought it from their son, who had moved to Florida. The husband was going to do quite a bit of remodeling and then sell it. When he died, Mrs. Jacques rented it for a year and then sold it.

"Mr. Jacques's son bought it from a man who used to have a doughnut shop and did his cooking in a back room, so I have been told. There was a fire in the back that was supposedly started from the fat. They bought the house from Mrs. Emma Thompson, who, with her husband, had received the house for caring for a Mr. Woodbury Langdon, and by also giving him a small sum of money. Mrs. Thompson always gave people the impression that she was really a countess and that she had a sister in Pennsylvania who would not have anything to do with her because of her odd ways.

"Mrs. Thompson moved to Rumney, where she contracted pneumonia about six months later and died.

"Mr. and Mrs. Thompson moved in to take care of Mr. Woodbury Langdon after he kicked out Mr. and Mrs. Dinsmore. (Mr. Cushing gave me the following information. He lives next door, and has lived there since 1914 or 1918.)

"He was awakened by a bright flash very early in the morning. Soon he could see that the top room (tower room) was all afire. He got dressed, called the firemen, and ran over to help. He looked in the window of what is now our dining room but was then Mr. Langdon's bedroom. (Mr. Langdon was not able to go up and down stairs because of his age.) He pounded on the window trying to wake Mr. Langdon up. Through the window he could see Mr. and Mrs. Dinsmore standing in the doorway between the kitchen and the bedroom. They were laughing and Mr. Dinsmore had an oil can in his hand. All this time Mr. Langdon was sound asleep. Mr. Cushing got angry and began pounding harder and harder. Just as he began to open the window Mr. Langdon woke up and Mr. Cushing helped him out the window. He said that no one would believe his story, even the insurance company. Evidently Mr. Langdon did, because soon after he kicked the Dinsmores out, and Mr. and Mrs. Thompson came to take care of him. Around 1927 he came down with pneumonia. He had that for two days and then he went outdoors without putting on any jacket or sweater. Mrs. Thompson ran out and brought him back in. She put him back in bed and warmed him up with coffee and wrapped him in wool blankets. He seemed better until around midnight. Then he began moaning. He kept it up until around three, when he died.

"Mr. Langdon was married twice. His first wife and his eighteen-year-old son died [of] typhoid fever. He had the wells examined and found that it came from them. He convinced his father to invest his money in putting in the first waterworks for the town of Plymouth. At that time he lived across town on Russell Street.

"He later married a woman by the name of Donna. He

9

worshipped her and did everything he could to please her. He remodeled the house. That was when he added on the bathroom and bedroom (dining room). He also built the tower room so that his wife could look out over the town. He also had a big estate over at Squam Lake that he poured out money on. All this time she was running around with anyone she could find. Mr. Cushing believes that he knew it deep down but refused to let himself believe it. She died, Mr. Cushing said, from the things she got from the things she did! He insists that it was called leprosy. In the medical encyclopedia it reads, under leprosy, 'differential diag: tuberculosis and esp. syphilis are the two diseases most likely to be considered.' She died either in this house or at the estate on the lake. She was buried in the family plot in Trinity Cemetery in Holderness. She has a small headstone with just one name on it: DONNA. There is a large spire-shaped monument in the center of the lot, with the family's names on it and their relationships. The name of Woodbury, Langdon's second wife, is completely eliminated from the stone. There is nothing there to tell who she was or why she is buried there. This has puzzled me up to now, because, as she died around 1911, and he did not die until around 1927, he had plenty of time to have her name and relationship added to the family stone. Mr. Cushing thinks that, after her death, Mr. Langdon began to realize more and more what she was really like. He has the impression that Mr. Langdon was quite broke at the time of his death.

"I cannot trace any more of the previous owners, as I cannot trace the house back any further than around 1860. Mr. Langdon evidently bought and sold houses like other men bought and sold horses. If this is the house I believe it to be, it was on the road to Rumney and had to be moved in a backward position to where it is now. They had something like six months later to move the barn back. Then they had to put in a street going from the house up to the main road. They also had to put a fence up around the house. This property *did* have a barn, and there was a fence here. There is a small piece of it left. The deeds from there just go around in circles.

"The man who I think the ghost is, is Mr. Woodbury Langdon. I have asked people around here what Mr. Langdon looked like and they describe him *very much* as the man I saw in the bathroom. The man in the bicentennial book was his father. There is something in his face that was in the face of the 'ghost.'

"I have two children. They are Kimberly Starr, age nine years and Rebecca Sue, age six years. Kim's birthday is on April 2 and Becky's is on August 10.

"I was born and brought up on a farm four and one-half miles out in the country in the town of Plymouth. My father believes in spirits, sort of, but not really. My mother absolutely does not.

"I carried the business course and the college preparatory course through my four years of high school. I had one year of nurses' training. I was married when I was twenty, in June, and Kim was born the next April.

"We also have a black cat who has acted queer at times in the past:

1. He would go bounding up the stairs only to come to an abrupt halt at the head of the stairs. He would sit there staring at presumably empty space, and then take off as if he had never stopped.

11

2. Sometimes he stood at the bathroom door and absolutely refused to go in.

3. He had spells of sitting in the hallway and staring up the stairs, not moving a muscle. Then suddenly he would relax and go on his way."

We finally settled on August 12, a Saturday, in 1967, to have a go at Mr. Langdon or whoever it was that haunted the house, since Miss Elliott was getting married in July and Mrs. Fuller wanted very much to be present.

Eleanor Fuller greeted us as we arrived and led us into the house. As usual Ethel began to sniff around, and I just followed her, tape recorder running and camera at the ready. We followed her up the stairs to the upper floor, where Ethel stopped at the bedroom on the right, which happened to be decorated in pink.

"I get an older woman wearing glasses," Ethel said cautiously as she was beginning to pick up psychic leads, "and a man wearing a funny hat."

I pressed Ethel to be more specific about the "funny hat" and what period hat. The man seemed to her to belong to the early 1800s. She assured me it was not this century. She then complained about a cold spot, and when I stepped into it I too felt it. Since neither doors nor windows could be held responsible for the strong cold draft we felt, we knew that its origin was of a psychic nature, as it often is when there are entities present.

I asked Ethel to describe the woman she felt present. "She is lying down . . . and I get a pain in the chest," she said, picking up the spirit's condition. "The eyes are closed!"

12

We left the room and went farther on. Ethel grabbed her left shoulder as if in pain.

"She is here with me, looking at me," Ethel said.

"She's been here."

"Why is she still here?" I asked.

"I got a sudden chill when you asked that," Ethel replied.

"She tells me to go left. . . . I am having difficulty walking. . . . I think this woman had that difficulty."

We were walking down the stairs, when Ethel suddenly became a crone and had difficulty managing them. The real Ethel was as spry and fast as the chipmunks that used to roam around her house in Connecticut.

"I think she fell down these stairs," Ethel said and began to cough. Obviously, she was being impressed by a very sick person.

We had barely got Ethel to a chair when she slipped into full trance and the transition took place. Her face became distorted as if in suffering, and a feeble voice tried to manifest through her, prodded by me to be clearer.

"Lander . . . or something . . ." she mumbled.

What followed was an absolutely frightening realization by an alien entity inside Ethel's body that the illness she was familiar with no longer existed now. At the same time, the excitement of this discovery made it difficult for the spirit to speak clearly, and we were confronted with a series of grunts and sighs.

Finally, I managed to calm the entity down by insisting she needed to relax in order to be heard.

"Calm . . . calm . . ." she said and cried, "good . . . he knows . . . he did that . . . for fifty years . . . the woman!"

She had seized Mr. Fuller's hand so forcefully I felt embarrassed for her, and tried to persuade the spirit within Ethel to let go, at the same time explaining her true condition to her, gently but firmly.

After I had explained how she was able to communicate with us, and that the body of the medium was merely a temporary arrangement, the entity calmed down, asking only if he loved her, meaning the other spirit in the house. I assured her that this was so, and then called on Albert, Ethel's spirit guide, to help me ease the troubled one from Ethel's body and thus free her at the same time from the house.

And then the man came into Ethel's body, very emotionally, calling out "Sylvia," the name of the woman she had seen earlier, clairvoyantly.

Again I explained how he was able to communicate.

"You see me, don't you." he finally said as he calmed down. "I loved everyone. . . . I'll go, I won't bother you. . . ."

I called again for Albert, and in a moment his crisp voice replaced the spirit's outcries.

"The man is a Henry MacLellan . . . there stood in this vicinity another house . . . around 1810, 1812 . . . to 1820 . . . a woman connected with this house lies buried here somewhere, and he is looking for her. His daughter . . . Macy? . . . Maisie? About 1798 . . . sixteen or eighteen years old . . . has been done wrong . . . had to do with a feud of two families . . . McDern . . ."

Albert then suggested letting the man speak to us directly, and so he did in a little while. I offered my help.

"It is futile," he said. "My problem is my own."

"Who are you?"

14

"Henry. I lived right here. I was born here."

"What year? What year are we in now as I speak with you?"

"I speak to you in the year 1813."

"Are you a gentleman of some age?"

"I would have forty-seven years."

"Did you serve in any governmental force or agency?"

"My son . . . John Stuart Mc . . ."

"McDermot? Your son was John Stuart McDermot?"

"You have it from my own lips."

"Where did he serve?"

"Ticonderoga."

And then he added, "My daughter, missing, but I found the bones, buried not too far from here. I am satisfied. I have her with me."

He admitted he knew he was no longer "on the earth plane," but was drawn to the place from time to time.

"But if you ask me as a gentleman to go, I shall go," he added. Under these circumstances—rare ones, indeed, when dealing with hauntings—I suggested he not disturb those in the present house, especially the children. Also, would he not be happier in the world into which he had long passed?

"I shall consider that," he acknowledged, "You speak well, sir. I have no intention of frightening."

"Are you aware that much time has passed . . . that this is not 1813 any more?" I said.

"I am not aware of this, sir . . . it is always the same time here."

Again I asked if he served in any regiment, but he replied his leg was no good. Was it his land and house? Yes, he replied, he owned it and built the house. But

15

when I pressed him as to where he might be buried, he balked.

"My bones are here with me. . . . I am sufficient unto myself."

I then asked about his church affiliation, and he informed me his church was "northeast of here, on Beacon Road." The minister's name was Rooney, but he could not tell me the denomination. His head was not all it used to be.

"A hundred and fifty years have passed," I said, and began the ritual of exorcism. "Go from this house in peace, and with our love."

And so he did.

Albert, Ethel's guide, returned briefly to assure us that all was as it should be and Mr. McDermot was gone from the house; also, that he was being reunited with his mother, Sarah Ann McDermot. And then Albert, too, withdrew and Ethel returned to her own self again.

I turned to Mrs. Fuller and her cousin, Miss Elliott, for possible comments and corroboration of the information received through Mrs. Meyers in trance.

It appears the house that the Fullers were able to trace back as far as about 1860 was moved to make room for a road, and then set down again not far from that road. Unfortunately going further back proved difficult. I heard again from Mrs. Fuller in December of that year. The footsteps were continuing, it seemed, and her seven-year-old daughter, Becky, was being frightened by them. She had not yet been able to find any record of Mr. McDermot, but vowed to continue her search.

That was some time ago, and nothing further turned up, and I really do not know if the footsteps continued or

Mr. McDermot finally gave up his restless quest for a world of which he was no longer a part.

As for Mr. Langdon, whom Ethel Meyers had also identified by name as a presence in the house, he must by now be reunited with his wife Donna, and I hope he has forgiven her her trespasses—over there, even her sins do not matter any longer.

2

A Ghost on Cape Cod

Some of the best leads regarding a good ghost story come to me as the result of my having appeared on one of many television or radio programs, usually discussing a book dealing with the subject matter for which I am best known—psychic phenomena of one kind or another. So it happened that one of my many appearances on the Bob Kennedy television show in Boston drew unusually heavy mail from other New England states and even New York.

Now if there is one thing ghosts don't really care much about it is time—to them everything is suspended in a timeless dimension where the intensity of their suffering or problem remains forever constant and alive. After all, they are unable to let go of what it is that ties them to a

19

specific location, otherwise they would not be what we so commonly (and perhaps a little callously) call ghosts. I am mentioning this as a way of explaining why, sometimes, I cannot respond as quickly as I would like to when someone among the living reports a case of a haunting that needs to be looked into. Reasons were and are now mainly lack of time but more likely lack of funds to organize a team and go after the case. Still, by and large, I do manage to show up in time and usually manage to resolve the situation.

Thus it happened that I received a letter dated August 4, 1966, sent to me via station WBZ-TV in Boston, from the owner of Cap'n Grey's Smorgasbord, an inn located in Barnstable on Cape Cod. The owner, Mr. Lennart Svensson, had seen me on the show and asked me to get in touch.

"We have experienced many unusual happenings here. The building in which our restaurant and guest house is located was built in 1716 and was formerly a sea captain's residence," Svensson wrote.

I'm a sucker for sea captains haunting their old houses so I wrote back asking for details. Mr. Svensson replied a few weeks later, pleased to have aroused my interest. Both he and his wife had seen the apparition of a young woman, and their eldest son had also felt an unseen presence; guests in their rooms also mentioned unusual happenings. It appeared that when the house was first built the foundation had been meant as a fortification against Indian attacks. Rumor has it, Mr. Svensson informed me, that the late sea captain had been a slave trader and sold slaves on the premises.

Svensson and his wife, both of Swedish origin, had lived on the Cape in the early thirties, later moved back

20

to Sweden, to return in 1947. After a stint working in various restaurants in New York, they acquired the inn on Cape Cod.

I decided a trip to the Cape was in order. I asked Sybil Leek to accompany me as the medium. Mr. Svensson explained that the inn would close in October for the winter, but he, and perhaps other witnesses to the phenomena, could be seen even after that date, should I wish to come up then. But it was not until June 1967, the following year, that I finally managed to get our act together, so to speak, and I contacted Mr. Svensson to set a date for our visit. Unfortunately, he had since sold the inn and, as he put it, the new owner was not as interested in the ghost as he was, so there was no way for him to arrange for our visit now.

But Mr. Svensson did not realize how stubborn I can be when I want to do something. I never gave up on this case, and decided to wait a little and then approach the new owners. Before I could do so, however, the new owner saw fit to get in touch with me instead. He referred to the correspondence between Mr. Svensson and me, and explained that at the time I had wanted to come up, he had been in the process of redoing the inn for its opening. That having taken place several weeks ago, it would appear that "we have experienced evidence of the spirit on several occasions, and I now feel we should look into this matter as soon as possible." He invited us to come on up whenever it was convenient, preferably yesterday.

The new owner turned out to be an attorney named Jack Furman of Hyannis, a very personable man. When I wrote we would indeed be pleased to meet him, and the ghost or ghosts, as the case might be, he sent us all sorts of information regarding flights and offered to pick us up at the airport. Mr. Furman was not shy in reporting his own experiences since he had taken over the house.

There has been on one occasion an umbrella mysteriously stuck into the stairwell in an open position. This was observed by my employee, Thaddeus B. Ozimek. On another occasion when the Inn was closed in the evening early, my manager returned to find the front door bolted from the inside, *which appeared strange since no one was in the building. At another time, my chef observed that the heating plant went off at 2:30, and the serviceman, whom I called the next day, found that a fuse was removed from the fuse box. At 2:30 in the morning, obviously, no one that we know of was up and around to do this. In addition, noises during the night have been heard by occupants of the Inn.*

I suggested in my reply that our little team consisting, as it would, of medium (and writer) Sybil Leek, Catherine (my ex-wife), and myself, should spend the night at the inn as good ghost hunters do. I also requested that the former owner, Mr. Svensson, be present for further questioning, as well as any direct witnesses to phenomena. On the other hand, I delicately suggested that no one not concerned with the case should be present, keeping in mind some occasions where my investigations had been turned into entertainment by my hosts to amuse and astound neighbors and friends.

In the end it turned out to be best to come by car, as we had other projects to look into en route. The date for our visit was to be August 17, 1967—a year and two weeks after the case first came to my attention. But not much of a time lag, the way it is with ghosts.

When we arrived at the inn, after a long and dusty journey, the sight that greeted us was well worth the trip. There, set back from a quiet country road amid tall, aged trees, sat an impeccable white colonial house, two stories high with an attic, nicely surrounded by a picket fence, and an old bronze and iron lamp at the corner. The windows all had their wooden shutters opened to the outside and the place presented such a picture of peace it was difficult to realize we had come here to confront a disturbance. The house was empty, as we soon realized, because the new owner had not yet allowed guests to return —considering what the problems were!

Quickly, we unburdened ourselves of our luggage, each taking a room upstairs, then returned to the front of the house to begin our usual inspection. Sybil Leek now let go of her conscious self the more to immerse herself in the atmosphere and potential presences of the place.

"There is something in the bedroom . . . in the attic," Sybil said immediately as we climbed the winding stairs. "I thought just now someone was pushing my hair up from the back," she added.

Mr. Furman had, of course, come along for the investigation. At this point we all saw a flash of light in the middle of the room. None of us was frightened by it, not even the lawyer, who by now had taken the presence of the supernatural in his house in his stride.

We then proceeded downstairs again, with Sybil assuring us that whatever it was that perturbed her up in the attic did not seem to be present downstairs. With that we came to a locked door, a door that Mr. Furman assured us that had not been opened in a long time. When we managed to get it open, it led us to the downstairs office or the room now used as such. Catherine, ever the alert artist and designer that she was, noticed that a door had been barred from the inside, almost as if someone had once been kept in that little room. Where did this particular door lead to, I asked Mr. Furman. It appeared it led to a narrow corridor and finally came out into the fireplace in the large main room.

"Someone told me if I ever dug up the fireplace," Mr. Furman intoned significantly, "I might find something."

What that something would be was left to our imagination. Mr. Furman added that his informant had hinted at some sort of valuables, but Sybil immediately added, "bodies . . . you may find bodies."

She described, psychically, many people suffering in the house, and a secret way out of the house—possibly from the captain's slave trading days?

Like a doctor examining a patient, I then inspected the walls both in the little room and the main room and found many hollow spots. A bookcase turned out to be a false front. Hidden passages seemed to suggest themselves. Quite obviously, Mr. Furman was not about to tear open the walls to find them. But Sybil was right: the house was honeycombed with areas not visible to the casual observer.

Sybil insisted we seat ourselves around the fireplace, and I insisted that the ghost, if any, should contact us there rather than our trying to chase the elusive phantom from room to room. "A way out of the house is very important," Sybil said, and I couldn't help visualizing the unfortunate slaves the good (or not so good) captain had held captive in this place way back when.

But when nothing much happened, we went back to

24

the office, where I discovered that the front portion of the wall seemed to block off another room beyond it, not accounted for when measuring the outside walls. When we managed to pry it open, we found a stairwell, narrow though it was, where apparently a flight of stairs had once been. I asked for a flashlight. Catherine shone it up the shaft: We found ourselves below a toilet in an upstairs bathroom! No ghost here.

We sat down again, and I invited the presence, whomever it was, to manifest. Immediately Sybil remarked she felt a young boy around the place, a hundred and fifty years ago. As she went more and more into a trance state, Sybil mentioned the name Chet . . . someone who wanted to be safe from an enemy . . . Carson. . . .

"Let him speak," I said.

"Carson . . . 1858 . . ." Sybil replied, now almost totally entranced as I listened carefully for words coming from her in halting fashion.

"I will fight . . . Charles . . . the child is missing. . . ."

"Whom will you fight? Who took the child?" I asked in return.

"Chicopee . . . child is dead."

"Whose house is this?"

"Fort . . ."

"Whose is it?"

"Carson . . ."

"Are you Carson?"

"Captain Carson."

"What regiment?"

"Belvedere . . . cavalry . . . 9th . . ."

"Where is the regiment stationed?"

There was no reply.

"Who commanded the regiment?" I insisted.

"Wainwright . . . Edward Wainwright . . . commander."

"How long have you been here?"

"Four years."

"Where were you born?"

"Montgomery . . . Massachusetts."

"How old are you now?"

There was no reply.

"Are you married?"

"My son . . . Tom . . . ten . . ."

"What year was he born in?"

"Forty . . . seven . . ."

"Your wife's name?"

"Gina . . ."

"What church do you go to?"

"I don't go."

"What church do you belong to?"

"She is . . . of Scottish background . . . Scottish kirk."

"Where is the kirk located?"

"Six miles . . ."

"What is the name of this village we are in now?"

"Chicopee . . ."

Further questioning gave us this information: that "the enemy" had taken his boy, and the enemy were the Iroquois. This was his fort and he was to defend it. I then began, as I usually do when exorcism is called for, to speak of the passage of time and the need to realize that the entity communicating through the medium was aware of the true situation in this respect. Did Captain Carson realize that time had passed since the boy had disappeared?

"Oh yes," he replied. "Four years."

"No, a hundred and seven years," I replied.

Once again I established that he was Captain Carson, and there was a river nearby and Iroquois were the enemy. Was he aware that there were "others" here besides himself?

He did not understand this. Would he want me to help him find his son since they had both passed over and should be able to find each other there?

"I need permission . . . from Wainwright. . . ."

As I often do in such cases, I pretended to speak for Wainwright and granted him the permission. A ghost, after all, is not a rational human being but an entity existing in a delusion where only emotions count.

"Are you now ready to look for your son?"

"I am ready."

"Then I will send a messenger to help you find him," I said, "but you must call out to your son . . . in a loud voice."

The need to reach out to a loved one is of cardinal importance in the release of a trapped spirit, commonly called a ghost.

"John Carson is dead . . . but not dead forever," he said in a faint voice.

"You lived here in 1858, but this is 1967," I reminded him.

"You are mad!"

"No, I'm not mad. Touch your forehead . . . you will see this is not the body you are accustomed to. We have lent you a body to communicate with us. But it is not yours."

Evidently touching a woman's head did jolt the entity from his beliefs. I decided to press on.

"Go from this house and join your loved ones who await you outside. . . ."

A moment later Captain Carson had slipped away and a sleepy Sybil Leek opened her eyes.

I now turned to Mr. Furman, who had watched the proceedings with mounting fascination. Could he corroborate any of the information that had come to us through the entranced medium?

"This house was built on the foundations of an Indian fort," he confirmed, "to defend the settlers against the Indians."

"Were there any Indians here in 1858?"

"There are Indians here even now," Furman replied. "We have an Indian reservation at Mashpee, near here, and on Martha's Vineyard there is a tribal chief and quite a large Indian population."

He also confirmed having once seen a sign in the western part of Massachusetts that read "Montgomery"—the place Captain Carson had claimed as his birthplace. Also that a Wainwright family was known to have lived in an area not far from where we were now. However, Mr. Furman had no idea of any military personnel by that name.

"Sybil mentioned a river in connection with this house." Furman said, "And, yes, there is a river running through the house, it is still here."

Earlier Sybil had drawn a rough map of the house as it was in the past, from her psychic viewpoint, a house surrounded by a high fence. Mr. Furman pronounced the drawing amazingly accurate—especially as Sybil had not set foot on the property or known about it until our actual arrival.

"My former secretary, Carole E. Howes, and her family

occupied this house," Mr. Furman explained when I turned my attention to the manifestations themselves. "They operated this house as an inn twenty years ago, and often had unusual things happen here as she grew up, but it did not seem to bother them. Then the house passed into the hands of a Mrs. Nielson; then Mr. Svensson took over. But he did not speak of the phenomena until about a year and a half ago. The winter of 1965 he was shingling the roof, and he was just coming in from the roof on the second floor balcony on a cold day—he had left the window ajar and secured—when suddenly he heard the window sash come down. He turned around on the second floor platform and he saw the young girl, her hair windswept behind her. She was wearing white. He could not see anything below the waist, and he confronted her for a short period, but could not bring himself to talk—and she went away. His wife was in the kitchen sometime later, in the afternoon, when she felt the presence of someone in the room. She turned around and saw an older man dressed in black at the other end of the kitchen. She ran out of the kitchen and never went back in again.

"The accountant John Dillon's son was working in the kitchen one evening around ten. Now some of these heavy pots were hanging there on pegs from the ceiling. Young Dillon told his father two of them lifted themselves up from the ceiling, unhooked themselves from the pegs, and came down on the floor."

"Did any guests staying at the Inn during Svensson's ownership complain of any unusual happenings?" I asked.

"There was this young couple staying in what Mr. Svensson called the honeymoon suite," Mr. Furman replied. "At 6:30 in the morning, the couple heard three knocks at the door, three loud, distinct knocks, and when they opened the door, there was no one there. This sort of thing had happened before."

Another case involved a lone diner who complained to Svensson that "someone" was pushing him from his chair at the table in the dining room onto another chair, but since he did not see another person, how could this be? Svensson hastily had explained that the floor was a bit rickety and that was probably the cause.

Furman then recounted the matter of the lock: He and a young man who worked with him had left the inn to bring the chef, who had become somewhat difficult that day, home to his own place. When Mr. Furman's assistant returned to the inn at 2:30 in the morning, the door would not open, and the key would not work. After he had climbed into the house through an upstairs window, he found to his amazement that the door had been locked *from the inside.*

The story gave me a chill: That very day, after our arrival, nearly the same thing happened to us—except that we did not have to climb to the upper floor to get in but managed to enter through a rear door! Surely, someone did not exactly want us in the house.

The chef, by the way, had an experience of his own. The heating system is normally quite noisy, but one night it suddenly stopped and the heat went off. When the repair crew came the next day they discovered that a fuse had been physically removed from the fuse box, which in turn stopped the heating system from operating. The house was securely locked at that time so no one from the outside could have done this.

The famous case of an umbrella being stuck into the

ceiling of the upstairs hall was confirmed by the brother of the young man, Mr. Bookstein, living in the house. He also pointed out to us that the Chicopee Indians were indeed in this area, so Sybil's trance utterances made a lot of sense.

"There was an Indian uprising in Massachusetts as late as the middle of the nineteenth century," he confirmed, giving more credence to the date, 1858, that had come through Sybil.

Was the restless spirit of the captain satisfied with our coming? Did he and his son meet up in the Great Beyond? Whatever came of our visit, nothing further has been heard of any disturbances at Cap'n Grey's Smorgasbord in Barnstable.

3

The "Ship Chandler's" Ghost of Cohasset

There are many haunted houses people can visit if they so desire. However, just as many of these houses *used to have a ghost* that was dealt with by people like me whose work not only includes research and verification of events, but also the morally obligatory task of setting the unfortunate ghost free of whatever kept him or her in the place to begin with.

In some cases, an attempt may have been made to "de-ghost" a place, but for some reason the manifestations are still evident. Naturally, the real "ghost buff" will prefer such places to the ones where, at best, only the impression of past hauntings can be picked up. The following account is about a house that we tried to "de-ghost" and failed.

REAL HAUNTINGS

Moving an old house from its original location to a new spot frequently awakens the ghostly manifestations that may have been slumbering in it for a long time. Such was the case when the Historical Society of Cohasset, Massachusetts, moved the old ship's chandlery inland somewhat so that tourists could visit it more conveniently. About an hour's drive from Boston, Cohasset is a very old town that used to make its living mainly from the sea.

When we arrived at the wooden structure on a corner of the Post Road—it had a nautical look, its two stories squarely set down as if to withstand any gale—we found several people already assembled. Among them were Mrs. E. Stoddard Marsh, the curator of the museum (which is what the Ship's Chandlery is now) and her associate—lean, quiet Robert Fraser. The others were friends and neighbors. We entered the building and walked around the downstairs portion, admiring its displays of nautical supplies ranging from fishing tackle and scrimshaw made from walrus teeth, to heavy anchors, hoists, and rudders—all the instruments and wares of a ship chandler's business.

Built in the late eighteenth century by Samuel Bates, the building was owned by the Bates family, notably by one John Bates, second of the family to have the place, who had died seventy-eight years before our visit. Something of a local character, John Bates had cut a swath around the area as a gay blade. He could well afford the role, for he owned a fishing fleet of twenty-four vessels and business was good in those far-off days when the New England coast was dotted with major ports for fishing and shipping. A handwritten record of his daily catch can be seen next to a mysterious closet full of ladies' clothes. Mr. Bates led a full life.

I questioned Mrs. Marsh, the curator, about strange happenings in the house, especially after it was moved to its present site. "Two years ago we were having a lecture here. There were about forty people listening to Francis Hagerty talk about old sailing boats. I was sitting over here to the left—on this ground floor—with Robert Fraser, when all of a sudden we heard heavy footsteps upstairs and things being moved and dragged—so I said to Mr. Fraser, 'Someone is up there; will you please tell him to be quiet'—I thought it was kids."

There was a man who had helped them with the work at the museum who had lately stayed away for reasons unknown. Could he have heard the footsteps, too, and decided that caution was the better part of valor?

"The other day, just recently, four of us went into the room this gentleman occupies when he is here, and the door closed on us by itself. It had never done that before."

We decided to go upstairs now, and see if Mr. Bates— or whoever the ghost might be—felt like walking for us. We quietly waited in the semidarkness upstairs, near the area where the footsteps had been heard, but nothing happened.

"The steps went back and forth," Mrs. Marsh reiterated, "heavy, masculine steps, the kind a big man would make."

A year after my visit to the Ship's Chandlery of Cohassett, nothing further was heard from the curators. Evidently, John Bates must have simmered down after all. If you happen to be up near Boston and feel like visiting the house at Cohassett, do so by all means. Maybe you will be luckier than I was, and John Bates will put in an appearance.

4

Young Erlend and
the Ghost of the Admiral

*I*t is a known fact that children sometimes have ghostly encounters where adults cannot see or hear a thing. Perhaps this is so because young people are not yet conditioned to believe or disbelieve in things, and instead follow their own instincts more fully.

In any event, the following case occurred when our chief witness was still very young.

The Jacobsen family has a lovely summer home in Whitefield, New Hampshire. The house stands in a secluded part of the forest at the end of a narrow winding driveway lined by tall trees with a wooden porch surrounding it on three sides. The house itself rises up three stories and is painted white in the typical New England manner.

The house was called "Mis'n' Top" by its original owner and builder. I questioned Erlend Jacobsen, who was an instructor at Goddard College, about his experiences in the old house.

"When my parents decided to turn the attic into a club room where I could play with my friends," Jacobsen began, "they cut windows into the wall and threw out all the possessions of the former owner of the house they had found there. I was about seven at the time.

"Soon after, footsteps and other noises began to be heard in the attic and along the corridors and stairs leading toward it. But it wasn't until the summer of 1955 that I experienced my first really important disturbance. That summer we slept here for the first time in this room, one flight up, and almost nightly we were either awakened by noises or could not sleep, waiting for them to begin. At first we thought they were animal noises, but they were too much like footsteps and heavy objects being moved across the floor overhead and down the hall. We were so scared we refused to move in our beds or turn down the lights."

"But you did know of the tradition that the house was haunted, did you not?" I asked.

"Yes, I grew up with it. All I knew is what I had heard from my parents. The original owner and builder of the house, an admiral named Hawley, and his wife, were both most difficult people. The admiral died in 1933. In 1935 the house was sold to my parents by his daughter, who was then living in Washington. Anyone who happened to be trespassing on his territory would be chased off it, and I imagine he would not have liked our throwing out his sea chest and other personal possessions."

"Any other experience besides the footsteps?"

"About four years ago," Erlend Jacobsen replied, "my wife and I, and a neighbor, Sheppard Vogelsang, were sitting in the living room downstairs discussing interpretations of the Bible. I needed a dictionary at one point in the discussion and got up to fetch it from upstairs.

"I ran up to the bend here, in front of this room, and there were no lights on at the time. I opened the door to the club room and started to go up the stairs, when suddenly I walked into what I can only describe as a *warm, wet blanket*, something that touched me physically as if it had been hung from wires in the corridor. I was very upset, backed out and went downstairs. My wife took one look at me and said, 'You're white.' 'I know,' I said. 'I think I just walked into the admiral.'"

"Has anyone else had an encounter with a ghost here?" I asked.

"Well another houseguest went up into the attic and came running down reporting that the door knob had turned in front of his very eyes before he could reach for it to open the door. The dog was with him, and steadfastly refused to cross the threshold.

"Another houseguest arrived very late at night, about five years ago. We had already gone to bed, and he knew he had to sleep in the attic since every other room was already taken. Instead, I found him sleeping in the living room, on the floor, in the morning. He knew nothing about the ghost. 'I'm not going back up there anymore,' he vowed, and would not say anything further. I guess he must have run into the admiral."

39

REAL HAUNTINGS

Every member of the family had at one time or another had an encounter with the ghostly admiral.

Sybil Leek, my mediumistic friend, had come with us and she was quickly able to pick up the vibrations of the unseen visitor. As soon as she had gone into a trance state she made contact with the admiral. She even had the name right, although she had not been present when I had spoken to the owners of the house earlier!

It seemed that the admiral had resented the new owners throwing out all of his things. He did not like that the house was sold, he would have preferred it went to his son. I implored the ghostly admiral not to upset the family now living in the house and he replied, in rather a stiff navy manner, that he was a tidy person and would take care of himself. When we left Whitefield, it seems to me that the old sea dog must have felt a lot better; after all, how many New Yorkers would drive all the way up to New Hampshire to talk to him after all those years?

Part II

Ghosts in New York State

5

A Staten Island Ghost

Some of the best reporters of ghostly experiences are young people—anywhere from age ten on up. Teenagers—between twelve and eighteen—are also particularly likely to actually experience some phenomena, such as poltergeists or other ghostly manifestations, because of their physical energies.

Such was the case in a certain old house on Staten Island, New York. I received a letter from Carolyn Westbo, whose aunt, Mrs. Carol Packer, had lived in a house on Staten Island where a poltergeist had also taken up residence. Poltergeists are ghosts who like to make noises or move objects around.

Carolyn's aunt had since moved to upstate New York,

so I asked the new owners of the house, a family by the name of Goetz, for permission to visit.

What I liked about Carolyn Westbo, who was seventeen and very serious, was that she herself was doubtful about her experiences and wondered if they weren't all due to imagination or, as she put it, "self-delusion." But deep down she knew she was psychic, and had already accepted this knowledge.

"When was the last time you were at the house on Henderson Avenue, Carolyn?" I asked.

"The last time I was at the house was in January of 1965," she answered. "My aunt was in the process of moving out, and the house was in an uproar. I stood against the wall and watched the proceedings. My left side was turned to the wall, and I was reminiscing about the wonderful times I had had on New Year's Eve, and somehow smiled to myself. All of a sudden, my *right side,* the right side of my head, felt very depressed and a feeling of great despair came over me. I felt like wringing my hands and was very distraught. It only stayed with me a few moments, but I had the distinct feeling of a woman who was very worried, and I could almost feel something or someone pressing against the right side of my head. And then I saw a mist, in the large downstairs dining room of the house."

"A mist? What sort of mist?"

"It had a shape, rather tall and thin. It did not have a face, and looked kind of ragged. *But I did see hands wringing.*"

Carolyn had told her aunt about her uncanny experience, even though she was afraid she would be laughed at. Her own family had pooh-poohed the whole thing, and Carolyn did not like to be laughed at, especially when she *knew* she had seen what she had seen. But her aunt did not laugh. She, too, had observed the misty shape when she was alone in the house, yet she had always felt great comfort with the ghost, whoever it was.

It was then that Carolyn learned about the poltergeist on Henderson Avenue. Objects were moving by themselves, her aunt admitted, such as things falling from a table and other objects that hadn't been touched. On one occasion she heard a loud crash downstairs—the house had three stories—and found a freshly baked pie upside down on the floor. She had placed it far back on the shelf in the pantry. Pots and pans around the pie had not been touched, and no trucks were passing by outside that might account for the vibration that could have caused the pie to fall. There had been nobody else in the house at the time. The aunt, Carol Packer, had never accepted the idea of a ghost, and yet could not offer any explanation for the strange happenings in the house.

"Have you had other experiences of a psychic nature?" I asked the young girl.

"Nothing really great, only little things, such as knowing what my teacher would ask the next day, or what people are wearing when I talk to them on the telephone or dream about them. I see things happening and a week later or so, they do happen."

Carolyn and her aunt had looked into the history of the house. They found that three families had lived in the house prior to Mrs. Packer's stay, and a woman had even dropped dead on the front porch. They never knew her name or anything else beyond this bare fact.

There the matter stood when our little expedition consisting of Sybil Leek and myself, book editor Evelyn Grippo, and CBS newscaster Lou Adler and his wife arrived at the Victorian structure where the ghost was presumably awaiting us. Mr. Adler brought along a CBS radio car and an engineer by the name of Leon, who we almost lost on the way over the Verrazano Bridge. It was a humid Sunday evening in May of 1965. Fifteen people had assembled at the Goetzes' to celebrate some kind of anniversary, but I suspect they were very curious about our investigation as an added attraction. We could hear their voices as we mounted the steep wooden steps leading to the house from Henderson Avenue, a quiet street lined with shade trees.

While the CBS people set up their equipment, I politely put the celebrants into the front room and collected those directly concerned with the haunting around a heavy oak table in the dining room on the first floor of the sturdy old house. Carolyn Westbo, her younger sister Betsy, Mr. and Mrs. Goetz, their son and a married daughter, Mrs. Grippo of Ace Books, the Adlers, and I formed a circle around the table. I had asked Sybil to wait in another room, where she could not possibly overhear a single word that was said in the dining room. Afterward, skeptical reporter Lou Adler admitted that "unless she had some sort of electronic listening device by which she could listen through walls, or unless you and Sybil set this up to trick everybody—there is no alternative explanation for what occurred this evening." Needless to say, we did not use electronic devices. Sybil could not hear anything, and neither she nor I knew anything of what would happen later.

As soon as Sybil Leek was out of earshot, I started to question the witnesses among those present. Carolyn Westbo repeated her testimony given to me earlier. I then

46

turned my attention, and my microphone, to Betsy Westbo.

Betsy had been to the house a number of times. Had she ever felt anything unusual in this house?

"One time I walked in here," the serious young girl said in response, "my mother and my cousin were in the kitchen downstairs, in the rear of the house, and I walked into the hall. It was dark, about sunset, and I suddenly felt as if someone were staring at me, just looking at me. I was sure it was my cousin, so I asked him to come out. He had played tricks on me before. But he wasn't there, and I went into the kitchen, and he had not left it at all."

"Any other experiences bordering on the uncanny?" I asked.

This fifteen-year-old girl was calm and not at all given to flights of imagination, and she struck me as mature beyond her years.

"The time my aunt moved out, I was here, too. I felt as if someone were crying and I wanted to cry with them. I was just walking around then, and it felt as if someone were next to me crying and saying, 'What's going to happen to me?' "

Betsy had also had psychic experiences in her young life. Not long before in her family's house, just down the street from the haunted house her aunt used to call home, Betsy was asleep in bed around 11:00 P.M. when she awoke with a start.

"I heard a screech and a dog yelping, as if he had been hurt. I was sure there had been an accident, and we looked out the window, but there was nothing, no car, no dog."

"What did you do then?"

47

"We couldn't figure it out," Betsy answered, "but the very next evening, again at eleven o'clock, we heard the same noises—my sister was with me in the room this time. We checked again, and this time there was a dog. I had seen the entire accident happen, *exactly as it did, twenty-four hours before!*"

"Amazing," I conceded. "Then you are indeed clairvoyant."

Mrs. Mariam Goetz, a pleasant-looking, vivacious woman in her middle years, had been the lady of the house since February of 1965. She had not seen or heard anything uncanny, and she felt very happy in the house. But then there was strange business about the silver.

"My silver spoons disappeared, one by one, and we searched and searched, and we thought someone was playing a prank. Each blamed the other, but neither Mr. Goetz, nor my son, nor my young married daughter, Irene Nelson, who lives with us, had hidden the spoons. The wedding gifts were displayed in Grandmother's room upstairs, including some pretty silver objects. One evening, after about a week of this, we discovered in each bowl—a silver spoon! Of course we thought Grandmother had been playing a trick on us, but she assured us she had not."

The rest of the spoons turned up in the drawers of the room, carefully hidden in many places. Although the grandmother was quite aged, she was in good mental condition, and the Goetzes really had no proof that she hid the spoons.

"Irene, my married daughter, had come to sleep with me several nights, because she hadn't felt very secure in her own bedroom," Mrs. Goetz added.

Mrs. Irene Nelson, a young woman with dark eyes and

dark hair, was not the dreamer type but was rather factually minded and to the point. She had been in the house as long as her parents, four months to the time of my investigation.

Had she noticed anything unusual?

"Yes," the young woman said. "One night I was sitting at the kitchen table with two friends of mine, and as we sat there and talked, some screws were falling to the floor from the kitchen table, by themselves, one by one. My friends left. I got up to gather my things, and the table collapsed behind me. One of its legs had come off by itself. But the table was not wobbly, or any of the screws loose, just before we used it, or we would have noticed it. There was nobody else in the house who could have loosened the screws as a prank, either."

"And poor Grandmother can't be blamed for it, either," I added. The octogenarian did not get around very much anymore.

"Anything else?" I asked, crisply.

"One night, about four in the morning," Mrs. Nelson said, "I woke up with a sudden start and I opened my eyes and could not close them again. Suddenly, I felt pinprickles all over my body. I felt chilly. I felt there was someone in the room I could not see. I heard a strange sound, seemingly outside, as if someone were sweeping the sidewalk. This was in my bedroom directly above the living room. The feeling lasted about ten minutes, and I just lay there, motionless and frightened. I had several bad nights after that, but that first time was the worst."

"Have you ever felt another presence when you were alone?"

"Yes, I have. In different parts of the house."

The house, along with the building next door, was

built at the turn of the century. It was Victorian in architecture and appointments. Heavy wooden beams, many small rooms on the three floors, high ceilings, and solid staircases characterized the house on Henderson Avenue.

It was time to bring Sybil Leek into the dining room and start the trance.

Had anything happened to her while she was waiting outside in the kitchen? Sybil seemed somewhat upset, a very unusual state for this usually imperturbable psychic.

"I was standing by the refrigerator," she reported, "and the kitchen door opened about two inches. It disturbed me, for I did not want anyone to think I was opening the door to listen. There was someone there, I felt, and I could have easily gone into trance that moment, but fought it as I never do this without you being present."

Imagine—a ghost too impatient to wait for the proper signal!

"I wanted to run outside, but restrained myself," Sybil added. "I never moved from the spot near the refrigerator. I was terrified, which I rarely am."

We sat down, and soon Sybil was in deep trance. Before long, a faint voice made itself heard through Sybil's lips.

"What is your name?" I asked.

"Anne Meredith." It came with great difficulty of breathing.

"Is this your house?"

"Yes . . . I want to get in. I live here. *I want to get in!*"

"What's wrong?"

"I . . . have . . . heart trouble . . . I can't get up the steps."

A Staten Island Ghost

Sybil's breathing was heavy and labored.

"How long have you lived here?"

"Thirty-five."

"What year did you move in?"

" 'Twenty-two."

"Were you alone in this house?"

"No . . . James . . . these steps . . . James . . . son."

"What is it you want?"

"I can't stay here . . . want to get in . . . the steps
. . . can't get to the door . . . *door must be opened.*"

"How old are you?"

"Fifty-two."

"Where did you go to school?"

"Derby . . . Connecticut."

"Your father's name."

"Johannes."

"Mother's?"

"Marguerite."

"Where were you baptized?"

"Derby . . . my lips are sore . . . I bite them . . . I
have pain in my heart."

I started to explain her true status to her.

"You passed out of the physical life in this house," I
began. "It is no longer your house. You must go on and
join your family, those who have passed on before you.
Do you understand?"

She did not.

"I have to get up the stairs," she mumbled over and
over again.

As I repeated the formula I usually employ to pry an
unhappy ghost away from the place of emotional turmoil
in the past, Sybil broke out of trance momentarily, her
eyes wide open, staring in sheer terror and lack of under-

51

standing at the group. Quickly, I hypnotized her back into the trance state, and in a moment or two, the ghost was back in control of Sybil's vocal apparatus. Heavy tears now rolled down the medium's cheeks. Obviously, she was undergoing great emotional strain. Now the voice returned slowly.

"I want to come in . . . I have to come back!"

"You died on the steps of this house. You can't come back," I countered.

"Someone's there," the ghost insisted in a shaky voice. "I have to come back."

"Who is it you want to come back to?"

"James."

I assured her James was well taken care of, and she need not worry about him anymore.

"Don't leave me outside, I shall die," she said now.

"You *have* died, dear," I replied, quietly.

"Open the door, open the door," she demanded.

I took another tack. Suggesting that the door was being opened for her, I took her "by the hand" and showed her that someone else lived here now. No James. I even took her "upstairs" by suggestion. She seemed shocked.

"I don't believe you."

"This is the year 1965," I said.

" 'Fifty-five?"

"No, 'sixty-five."

There was disbelief. Then she complained that a dog kept her up, and also mentioned that her mother was living upstairs.

What was the dog's name?

"Silly dog . . . Franz." A dog named Franz was unusual even for a ghost, I thought. Still, people do like to give their pets strange names. The Goetzes had named their aged spaniel Happy, and I had never seen a more subdued dog in my life.

Why was she afraid of the dog? I asked the ghost.

"I fall over him," she complained. "My heart . . . dog is to blame."

"But this happened in 1955, you say."

"Happened *today,*" she answered. To a ghost, time stands still. She insisted this was 1955. I strongly insisted it was 1965. I explained once more what had happened to her.

"Not dead," she said. "Not in the body? That's silly."

Unfortunately, very few ghosts know that they are dead. It comes as a shock when I tell them.

"I'm going upstairs and neither you nor that dog will stop me," she finally said resolutely.

I agreed to help her up the stairs.

"Lift me," she pleaded.

Mentally, we opened the door and went upstairs.

"Where is my mother?" she said, obviously realizing that her mother was not there. I explained she had died. The truth of the situation began to dawn on Anne Meredith.

I took advantage of this state of affairs to press my point and suggest her mother was awaiting her outside the house.

"May I come back sometime?" the ghost asked in a feeble voice.

"You may if you wish," I promised, "but now you must join your mother."

As the ghost faded away, Sybil returned to her own body.

She felt fine, but, of course, remembered nothing of

what had come out of her mouth during trance. Just before awakening, tears once more rolled down her face.

I thought it rather remarkable that Sybil, in her trance state, had brought on a female personality who had died of a heart attack on the outside steps leading to the house. Sybil had no way of knowing that such a person actually existed and that her death had indeed taken place some years ago as described.

What about the names Anne Meredith and James?

Carolyn Westbo checked with the lady who had owned both houses and who lived in the one next door, a Miss Irving. Quite aged herself, she did not recall anyone with the name of Anne Meredith. By a strange coincidence, her own first names were Anne Adelaide. Derby, Connecticut, does exist.

Checking church registers is a long and doubtful job at best. Finding a record of Anne Meredith would be wonderful, of course, but if I didn't find such a record, it didn't mean she never existed. Many tenants had come and gone in the old house atop the hill on Henderson Avenue. Perhaps Anne and Meredith were only her first and middle names.

Time will tell.

Meanwhile, it is to be profoundly hoped that the hand-wringing lady ghost of Staten Island need not climb those horrible stairs any longer, nor cope with dogs who have no respect for ghosts—especially ghosts who once owned the house.

6

The Ghost of
the Lady Parishioner

*D*espite the fact that most religious faiths, and their clergy, take a dim view of ghosts and hauntings, there are many recorded cases of supernormal goings-on in churches and cemeteries. One such place of worship is New York's famed old St. Mark's-in-the-Bouwerie church, located at the corner of Second Avenue and Tenth Street.

Originally the site of a chapel erected in 1660 by Peter Stuyvesant for the Dutch settlers of New Amsterdam, it became the governor's burial ground in 1672. The Stuyvesant vault was permanently sealed in 1953, when the last member of the family died. A century after the death of the governor, the family had adopted the Episcopalian faith, and a grandson, also named Peter Stuyvesant, gave the land and some cash to build on the same spot the present church of St. Mark's. It was completed in 1799 and has been in service continuously since. No major repairs, additions, or changes were made in the building.

The surrounding neighborhood has changed a great deal, although it was once a highly-respected one. But even in the confines of the Bowery, there is a legend that St. Mark's is a haunted church. If nothing else, it effectively keeps the neighborhood's colorful alcoholics at a distance!

I talked to the Reverend Richard E. McEvoy, later Archdeacon of St. John's, but for many years rector of St. Mark's, about any apparitions he or others might have seen in the church. Legend, of course, has old Peter Stuyvesant rambling about now and then. The reverend proved to be a keen observer, and quite neutral in the matter of ghosts. He himself had not seen anything unusual. But there was a man, a churchgoer, whom he had known for many years. This man always sat in a certain pew on the right side of the church.

Queried by the rector about his peculiar insistence on that seat, the man freely admitted it was because from there he could see "her"—the "her" being a female wraith who appeared in the church to listen to the sermon, and then disappeared again. At the spot he had chosen, he could always be next to her! I pressed the rector about any *personal* experiences. Finally he thought that he had seen something like a figure in white out of the corner of one eye, a figure that passed, and quickly disappeared. That was ten years before.

On the rector's recommendation, I talked to Foreman Cole, the man who comes to wind the clock at regular intervals, and who had been in and around St. Mark's for the previous twenty-six years.

Mr. Cole proved to be a ready talker. Some years earlier Cole asked his friend Ray Bore, organist at a Roman Catholic church nearby, to have a look at the church organ. The church was quite empty at the time, which was 1:00 A.M. Nevertheless, Cole saw "someone" in the balcony.

About fifteen years before, Cole had another unusual experience. It was winter, and the church was closed to the public, for it was after 5:00 P.M. That evening it got dark early, but there was still some light left when Cole let himself into the building. Nobody was supposed to be in the church at that time, as Cole well knew, being familiar with the rector's hours.

Nevertheless, to his amazement, *he clearly saw a woman standing in the back of the church,* near the entrance door, in the center aisle. Thinking that she was a late churchgoer who had been locked in by mistake, and worried that she might stumble in the semidarkness, he called out to her, "Wait, lady, don't move till I turn the lights on."

He took his eyes off her for a moment and quickly switched the lights on. But he found himself alone; she had vanished into thin air from her spot well within the nave of the church.

Unnerved, Cole ran to the entrance door and found it firmly locked. He then examined all the windows and found them equally well secured.

I asked Cole if there was anything peculiar about the woman's appearance. He thought for a moment, then said, "Yes, there was. She seemed to ignore me, looked right through me, and did not respond to my words."

Six weeks later, he had another supernormal experience. Again alone in the church, with all doors locked, he saw a man who looked to him like one of the Bowery derelicts outside. He wore shabby clothes and did not seem to "belong" here. Quickly, Cole switched on the lights to examine his visitor. But he had vanished, exactly as the woman had.

Cole has not seen any apparitions since, but some pretty strange noises have reached his ears. For one thing, there is frequent "banging" about the church, and "uncanny" feelings and chills in certain areas of the old church. On one occasion, Cole clearly heard someone coming up the stairs leading to the choir loft. Thinking it was the sexton, he decided to give him a scare, and hid to await the man at the end of the staircase. But nobody came. The steps were those of an *unseen man!*

Cole has no idea who the ghosts could be. He is reluctant to discuss his experiences with ordinary people lest they think him mad, yet he is healthy and realistic and is quite sure of his memories.

Several days later, I asked Mary R. M., a singer and a gifted psychic, to accompany me to the church and see if she could get any "impressions." It turned out that my friend had been to the church once before, last November, when she was rehearsing nearby. At that time, she was *sure* the place was haunted. We sat in one of the right-hand pews and waited. We were quite alone in the church; the time was three in the afternoon, and it was quite still. Within a minute or so, Mary told me she felt "a man with a cane walking down the middle aisle behind us." Peter Stuvyesant, buried here, walked with a cane.

Then my friend pointed to the rear, and advised me that she "saw" a woman in wide skirts standing near the rear door of the church. She added, "I see a white shape floating away from that marble slab in the rear!"

So if you ever see someone dissolve into thin air at St. Mark's—don't be alarmed. It's only a ghost!

7

The Greenwich Village
Studio Ghosts

*U*ntil 1956, the ancient studio building at 51 West Tenth Street, in Greenwich Village, New York, was a landmark known to many connoisseurs of old New York, but it was demolished to make way for one of those nondescript, modern apartment buildings that are gradually taking away the charm of Greenwich Village and leaving doubtful comforts in its stead.

Until the very last, reports of an apparition, allegedly the ghost of artist John La Farge, who died in 1910, continued to come in. A few houses down the street is the Church of the Ascension; the altar painting, "The Ascension," is the work of John La Farge. Actually, the artist did the work on the huge painting in his studio, Number

61

22, at 51 West Tenth Street. He finished it, however, in the church itself, "in place." Having just returned from the Orient, La Farge used a new technique involving the use of several coats of paint, thus making the painting heavier than expected. The painting was hung, but the chassis collapsed; La Farge built a stronger chassis and the painting stayed in place this time. Years went by. Oliver La Farge, the great novelist and grandson of the painter, had spent much of his youth with his celebrated grandfather. One day, while working across the street, he was told the painting had fallen again. Dashing across the street, he found that the painting had indeed fallen, and that his grandfather had died *that very instant!*

The fall of the heavy painting was no trifling matter to La Farge, who was equally as well known as an architect as he was a painter. Many buildings in New York for which he drew the plans seventy-five years ago are still standing. But the construction of the chassis of the altar painting may have been faulty. And therein lies the cause for La Farge's ghostly visitations, it would seem. The artists at Number 51 insisted always that La Farge could not find rest until he had corrected his calculations, searching for the original plans of the chassis to find out what was wrong. An obsession to redeem himself as an artist and craftsman, then, would be the underlying cause for the persistence with which La Farge's ghost returned to his old haunts.

The first such return was reported in 1944, when a painter by the name of Feodor Rimsky and his wife lived in Number 22. Late one evening, they returned from the opera. On approaching their studio, they noticed that a light was on and the door open, although they distinctly remembered having *left it shut.* Rimsky walked into the studio, pushed aside the heavy draperies at the entrance to the studio itself, and stopped in amazement. In the middle of the room, a single lamp plainly revealed a stranger behind the large chair in what Rimsky called his library corner; the man wore a tall black hat and a dark, billowing velvet coat. Rimsky quickly told his wife to wait, and rushed across the room to get a closer look at the intruder. But the man *just vanished* as the painter reached the chair.

Later, Rimsky told his experience to a former owner of the building, who happened to be an amateur historian. He showed Rimsky some pictures of former tenants of his building. In two of them, Rimsky easily recognized his visitor, wearing exactly the same clothes Rimsky had seen him in. Having come from Europe but recently, Rimsky knew nothing of La Farge and had never seen a picture of him. The ball dress worn by the ghost had not been common at the turn of the century, but La Farge was known to affect such strange attire.

Three years later, the Rimskys were entertaining some guests at their studio, including an advertising man named William Weber, who was known to have had psychic experiences in the past. But Weber never wanted to discuss this "special talent" of his, for fear of being ridiculed. As the conversation flowed among Weber, Mrs. Weber, and two other guests, the advertising man's wife noticed her husband's sudden stare at a cabinet on the other side of the room, where paintings were stored. She saw nothing, but Weber asked her in an excited tone of voice, "Do you see that man in the cloak and top hat over there?"

Weber knew nothing of the ghostly tradition of the studio or of John La Farge; no stranger could have gotten by the door without being noticed, and none had been expected at this hour. The studio was locked from the *inside.*

After that, the ghost of John La Farge was heard many times by a variety of tenants at Number 51, opening windows or pushing draperies aside, but not until 1948 was he *seen* again.

Up a flight of stairs from Studio 22, but connected to it —artists like to visit each other—was the studio of illustrator John Alan Maxwell. Connecting stairs and a "secret rest room" used by La Farge had long been walled up in the many structural changes in the old building. Only the window of the walled-up room was still visible from the outside. It was in this area that Rimsky felt that the restless spirit of John La Farge was trapped. As Miss Archer puts it in her narrative, "walled in like the Golem, sleeping through the day and close to the premises for roaming through the night."

After many an unsuccessful search of Rimsky's studio, apparently the ghost started to look in Maxwell's studio. In the spring of 1948, the ghost of La Farge made his initial appearance in the illustrator's studio.

It was a warm night, and Maxwell had gone to bed naked, pulling the covers over himself. Suddenly he awakened. From the amount of light coming in through the skylight, he judged the time to be about one or two in the morning. *He had the uncanny feeling of not being alone in the room.* As his eyes got used to the darkness, he clearly distinguished the figure of a tall woman, bending over his bed, lifting and straightening his sheets several times over. Behind her, there was a man staring at a wooden filing cabinet at the foot of the couch. Then he opened a drawer, looked in it, and closed it again. Getting hold of himself, Maxwell noticed that the woman wore a light red dress of the kind worn in the last century, and the man a white shirt and dark cravat of the same period. It never occurred to the illustrator that they were anything but *people;* probably, he thought, models in costume working for one of the artists in the building.

The woman then turned to her companion as if to say something, but did not, and walked off toward the dark room at the other end of the studio. The man then went back to the cabinet and leaned on it, head in hand. By now Maxwell had regained his wits and thought the intruders must be burglars, although he could not figure out how they had entered his place, since he had locked it from the *inside* before going to bed! Making a fist, he struck at the stranger, yelling, "Put your hands up!"

His voice could be heard clearly along the empty corridors. *But his fist went through the man and into the filing cabinet.* Nursing his injured wrist, he realized that his visitors had dissolved into thin air. There was no one in the dark room. The door was still securely locked. The skylight, 150 feet above ground, could not very well have served as an escape route to anyone human. By now Maxwell knew that La Farge and his wife had paid him a social call.

Other visitors to Number 51 complained about strange winds and sudden chills when passing La Farge's walled-up room. One night, one of Maxwell's lady visitors returned, shortly after leaving his studio, in great agitation, yelling, "That man! That man!" The inner court of the building was glass-enclosed, so that one could see clearly across to the corridors on the other side of the building. Maxwell and his remaining guests saw nothing there.

But the woman insisted that she saw a strange man

under one of the old gaslights in the building; he seemed to lean against the wall of the corridor, dressed in old-fashioned clothes and *possessed of a face so cadaverous and death-mask-like, that it set her screaming!*

This was the first time the face of the ghost had been observed clearly by anyone. The sight was enough to make her run back to Maxwell's studio. Nobody could have left without being seen through the glass-enclosed corridors and no one had seen a stranger in the building that evening. As usual, he had vanished into thin air.

So much for Miss Archer's account of the La Farge ghost. My own investigation was sparked by her narrative, and I telephoned her at her Long Island home, inviting her to come along if and when we held a séance at Number 51.

I was then working with a group of parapsychology students meeting at the rooms of the Association for Research and Enlightenment (Cayce Foundation) on West Sixteenth Street. The director of this group was a phototechnician for the *Daily News,* Bernard Axelrod, who was the only one of the group who knew the purpose of the meeting; the others, notably the medium, Mrs. Meyers, knew nothing whatever of our plans.

We met in front of Bigelow's drugstore that cold evening, February 23, and proceeded to 51 West Tenth Street, where the current occupant of the La Farge studio, an artist named Leon Smith, welcomed us. In addition, there were also present the *News* columnist Danton Walker, Henry Belk, the noted playwright Bernays, Marguerite Haymes, and two or three others considered students of psychic phenomena. Unfortunately, Mrs. Belk also brought along her pet chihuahua, which proved to be somewhat of a problem.

All in all, there were fifteen people present in the high-ceilinged, chilly studio. Dim light crept through the tall windows that looked onto the courtyard, and one wished that the fireplace occupying the center of the back wall had been working.

We formed a circle around it, with the medium occupying a comfortable chair directly opposite it, and the sitters filling out the circle on both sides; my own chair was next to the medium's.

The artificial light was dimmed. Mrs. Meyers started to enter the trance state almost immediately and only the loud ticking of the clock in the rear of the room was heard for a while, as her breathing became heavier. At the threshold of passing into trance, the medium suddenly said—

"Someone says very distinctly, *Take another step and I go out this window!* The body of a woman . . . close-fitting hat and a plume . . . close-fitting bodice and a thick skirt . . . lands right on face. . . . I see a man, dark curly hair, *hooked nose, an odd, mean face . . .* cleft in chin . . . light tan coat, lighter britches, boots, whip in hand, cruel, mean. . . ."

There was silence as she described what I recognized *as the face of La Farge.*

A moment later she continued: "I know the face is not to be looked at anymore. It is horrible. It should have hurt but I didn't remember. Not long. I just want to scream and scream."

The power of the woman who went through the window was strong. "I have a strange feeling," Mrs. Meyers said, "I *have to go out that window* if I go into trance." With a worried look, she turned to me and asked, "If I stand up and start to move, *hold me.*" I nodded assurance and the séance continued. A humming sound came from her lips, gradually assuming human-voice characteristics.

The next personality to manifest itself was apparently a woman in great fear. "They're in the courtyard. . . . He is coming . . . they'll find me and whip me again. I'll die first. Let me go. I shouldn't talk so loud. Margaret! Please don't let him come. See the child. My child. Barbara. Oh, the steps, I can't take it. Take Bobby, raise her, I can't take it. He is coming . . . *let me go!* I am free!"

With this, the medium broke out of trance and complained of facial stiffness, as well as pain in the shoulder.

Was the frantic woman someone who had been mistreated by an early inhabitant of Number 22? Was she a runaway slave, many of whom had found refuge in the old houses and alleys of the Village?

I requested of the medium's "control" that the most prominent person connected with the studio be allowed to speak to us. But Albert, the control, assured me that the woman, whom he called Elizabeth, was connected with that man. "He will come only if he is of a mind to. He entered the room a while ago."

I asked Albert to describe this man.

"Sharp features, from what I can see. You are closer to him. Clothes . . . nineties, early 1900s."

After a while, the medium's lips started to move, and a gruff man's voice was heard: *"Get out . . . get out of my house."*

Somewhat taken aback by this greeting, I started to explain to our visitor that we were his friends and here to help him. But he didn't mellow.

"I don't know who you are . . . who is everybody here. Don't have friends."

"I am here to help you," I said, and tried to calm the ghost's suspicions. But our visitor was not impressed.

"I want help, but not from you. . . . *I'll find it!*"

He wouldn't tell us what he was looking for. There were additional requests for us to get out of his house. Finally, the ghost pointed the medium's arm toward the stove and intoned, "I put it there!" A sudden thought inspired me, and I said, lightly, "We found it already."

Rage took hold of the ghost in an instant. "You took it . . . you betrayed me . . . it is mine . . . I was a good man."

I tried in vain to pry his full name from him.

He moaned. "I am sick all over now. Worry, worry, worry. Give it to me."

I promised to return "it," if he would cooperate with us.

In a milder tone he said, "I wanted to make it so pretty. *It won't move.*"

I remembered how concerned La Farge had been with his beautiful altar painting, and that it should not fall *again.* I wondered if he knew how much time had passed.

"Who is president of the United States now?" I asked.

Our friend was petulant. "I don't know. I am sick. William McKinley." But then he volunteered—"I knew him. Met him. In Boston. Last year. Many years ago. Who are you? I don't know any friends. *I am in my house.*"

"What is your full name?"

"Why is that so hard? I know William and I don't know my *own* name."

I have seen this happen before. A disturbed spirit sometimes cannot recall his own name or address.

"Do you know you have passed over?"

"I live here," he said, quietly now. "Times changed. I know I am not what I used to be. *It is there!*"

When I asked what he was looking for, he changed the subject to Bertha, without explaining who Bertha was.

But as he insisted on finding "it," I finally said, "You are welcome to get up and look for it."

"I am bound in this chair and can't move."

"Then tell us where to look for it."

After a moment's hesitation, he spoke. "On the chimney, in back . . . it was over there. I will find it, but I can't move now. . . . *I made a mistake* . . . I can't talk like this."

And suddenly he was gone.

As it was getting on to half past ten, the medium was awakened. The conversation among the guests then turned to any feelings they might have had during the séance. Miss Archer was asked about the building.

"It was put up in 1856," she replied, "and is a copy of a similar studio building in Paris."

"Has there ever been any record of a murder committed in this studio?" I asked.

"Yes . . . between 1870 and 1900, *a young girl went through one of these windows.* But I did not mention this in my article, as it *apparently* was unconnected with the La Farge story."

"What about Elizabeth? And Margaret?"

"That was remarkable of the medium," Miss Archer nodded. "You see, Elizabeth was La Farge's wife . . . and Margaret, well, she also fits in with his story."

For the first time, the name La Farge had been mentioned in the presence of the medium. But it meant nothing to her in her conscious state.

Unfortunately, the ghost could not be convinced that

his search for the plans was unnecessary, for La Farge's genius as an architect and painter has long since belonged to time.

A few weeks after this séance, I talked to an advertising man named Douglas Baker. To my amazement, he, too, had at one time occupied Studio 22. Although aware of the stories surrounding the building, he had scoffed at the idea of a ghost. But one night he was roused from deep sleep by the noise of someone opening and closing drawers. Sitting up in bed, he saw a man in Victorian opera clothes in his room, which was dimly lit by the skylight and windows. Getting out of bed to fence off the intruder, he found himself alone, just as others had before him.

No longer a scoffer, he talked to others in the building, and was able to add one more episode to the La Farge case. It seems a lady was passing Number 51 one bleak afternoon when she noticed an odd-looking gentleman in opera clothes standing in front of the building. For no reason at all, the woman exclaimed, "My, you're a funny-looking man!"

The gentleman in the opera cloak looked at her in rage. "Madam—how dare you!"

And with that, *he went directly through the building— the wall of the building, that is!*

Passers-by revived the lady.

Now there is a modern apartment building at 51 West Tenth Street. Is John La Farge still roaming its ugly modern corridors? Last night, I went into the Church of the Ascension, gazed at the marvelous altar painting, and prayed a little that he shouldn't *have to.*

REAL HAUNTINGS

*   *   *

On July 30, 1988, the *New York Times* reported to readers interested in Little Old New York that the parishioners of the Church of the Ascension were finally doing something about the matter. Apparently the mural by John La Farge had gotten dirtier with time—darker, too—and desperately needed a good cleaning job. The experts hired to do the job, Holly Hotchner and Robert Sawchuck, spent the entire summer trying to clean the old painting while lying on their stomachs on a rickety scaffold that continuously threatened to collapse.

Apparently the job was greatly complicated by Mr. La Farge's unusual technique of using encaustic painting. This method, employed by the ancient Romans and not used too frequently since, involves mixing wax with pigment and fusing it to the canvas with hot irons. It imparts a sense of richness to the work, like a fresco painting, and while this makes the painting look more three-dimensional, it also makes restoration very difficult.

Nonetheless, the pair did clean the painting, proud of their job, and never once were they interrupted by a ghostly La Farge. Neither did the scaffolding fall, nor the painting, for that matter.

As of this writing, it is still in place at the church, to be admired by one and all. As for the artist, he's probably painting angels and cherubs by now.

8

The Carriage House Ghosts

*W*hile casually leafing through the pages of *Tomorrow* magazine, a periodical devoted to psychical research in which my byline appears on occasion, I noticed a short piece by Wainwright Evans called "Ghost in Crinoline." Written in the spring of 1959, the article told of a spectral inhabitant at 422½ West Forty-sixth Street, in New York City. It seemed that Ruth Shaw, an artist who had for years lived in the rear section of the old building, which she had turned into a studio for herself, had spoken to Mr. Evans about her experiences. He had come to see her at Clinton Court, as the building still is called. There is a charming iron gate through which you pass by the main house into a court. Beyond the court rises an arcaded rear section, three

stories high and possessed of an outdoor staircase leading to the top. This portion dates back to 1809 or perhaps
even before, and was at one time used as the coach house
of Governor DeWitt Clinton.

Miss Shaw informed Evans about the legends around
the place, and in her painstaking manner told him of her
conversations with ninety-year-old Mr. Oates, a neighborhood druggist. An English coachman with a Danish
wife once lived in the rooms above the stables. The first
ghost ever to be seen at Clinton Court was that of "Old
Moor," a sailor hanged for mutiny at the Battery and
buried in Potter's Field, which was only a short block
away from the house. Today, this cemetery has disappeared beneath the teeming tenement houses of the middle West side, Hell's Kitchen's outer approaches. But
"Old Moor," as it were, did not have far to go to haunt
anyone. Clinton Court was the first big house in his path.
The coachman's wife saw the apparition, and while running away from "Old Moor," fell down the stairs. This
was the more unfortunate as she was expecting a child at
the time. She died from the fall, but the child survived.

The irony of it was that soon the mother's ghost was
seen around the court, too, usually hanging around the
baby. Thus, ghost number 2 joined the cast at the governor's old house.

One of the grandchildren of the Clinton family, who
had been told these stories, used to play "ghost" the way
children nowadays play cops and robbers. This girl,
named Margaret, used to put on old-fashioned clothes
and run up and down the big stairs. One fine day, she
tripped and fell down the stairs, making the game grim
reality. Many have seen the pale little girl; Miss Shaw
was among them. She described her as wearing a white

blouse, full sleeves, and a crinoline. On one occasion, she saw the girl ghost skipping down the stairs *in plain daylight*—skipping is the right word, for a ghost need not actually "walk," but often floats just a little bit above ground, not quite touching it.

I thought it would be a good idea to give Miss Shaw a ring, but discovered there was no telephone at the address. Miss Shaw had moved away and even the local police sergeant could not tell me where the house was. The police assured me *there was no such number* as 422½ West Forty-sixth Street. Fortunately, I have a low opinion of police intelligence, so my search continued. Perhaps a dozen times I walked by numbers 424 and 420 West Forty-sixth Street before I discovered the strange archway at Number 420. I walked through it, somehow driven on by an inner feeling that I was on the right track. I was, for before me opened Clinton Court. It simply was tucked away in back of 420 and the new owners had neglected to put the 422½ number anywhere within sight. Now an expensive, remodeled apartment house, the original walls and arrangements were still intact.

On the wall facing the court, Number 420 proudly displayed a bronze plaque inscribed CLINTON COURT—CA. 1840 —RESTORED BY THE AMERICAN SOCIETY FOR PRESERVATION OF FUTURE ANTIQUITIES. The rear building, where Miss Shaw's studio used to be, was now empty. Apparently the carpenters had just finished fixing the floors and the apartment was up for rent. I thought that fortunate, for it meant we could get into the place without worrying about a tenant. But there was still the matter of finding out who the landlord was, and getting permission. It took me several weeks and much conversation, until I finally got permission to enter the place one warm evening in August 1960.

Meanwhile I had been told by the superintendent that an old crony by the name of Mrs. Butram lived next door, at Number 424, and that she might know something of interest. I found Mrs. Butram without difficulty. Having been warned that she kept a large number of pets, my nose led me to her door. For twenty-five years, she assured me, she had lived here, and had heard many a story about the ghost next door. She had never seen anything herself, but when I pressed her for details, she finally said, "Well, they say it's a young girl of about sixteen. . . . One of the horses they used to keep back there broke loose and frightened her. Ran down the stairs, and fell to her death. That's what they say!"

I thanked Mrs. Butram and went home. I called my good friend Mrs. Meyers and asked her to accompany me to a haunted house, without telling her any more than that.

To my surprise, Mrs. Meyers told me on the phone that she thought she could see the place clairvoyantly that very instant.

"There is a pair of stairs outside of a house, and a woman in white, in a kind of backyard."

This conversation took place on August 9, a week before Mrs. Meyers knew anything about the location or nature of our "case."

About a week later, we arrived together at Clinton Court, and proceeded immediately into the ground-floor studio apartment of the former coach house. In subdued light, we sat quietly on the shabby, used-up furniture.

"Let me look around and see what I get," Mrs. Meyers said, and rose. Slowly I followed her around the apartment, which lay in ghostly silence. Across the yard, the windows of the front section were ablaze with light and the yard itself was lit up by floodlights. But it was a quiet night. The sounds of "Hell's Kitchen" did not intrude into our atmosphere, as if someone bent on granting us privacy for a little while were muffling them.

"I feel funny in the head, bloated . . . you understand I am *her* now. . . . There are wooden steps from the right on the outside of the place—"

Mrs. Meyers pointed at the wall. "There, where the wall now is; they took them down, I'm sure." On close inspection, I noticed traces of something that may have been a staircase.

"A woman in white . . . young . . . teenager . . . she's a bride . . . she's fallen down those steps on her wedding night . . . her head is battered in—"

Horror came over Mrs. Meyers's face. Then she continued. "It is cold, the dress is so flimsy, flowing; she is disappointed, for someone has disappointed *her*."

Deep in thought, Mrs. Meyers sat down in one of the chairs in a little room off the big, sunken living room that formed the main section of the studio apartment now, as the new owners had linked two apartments to make one bigger one.

"She has dark hair, blue eyes, light complexion . . . I'd say she's in her middle teens and wears a pretty dress, almost like a nightgown, the kind they used to have seventy-five or a hundred years ago. But now I see her in a gingham or checkered dress with high neck, long sleeves, a white hat, she's ready for a trip, only someone doesn't come. There is crying . . . disappointment. Then there is a seafaring man also, with a blue hat with shiny visor, a blue coat. He's a heavy-set man."

I thought of "Old Moor." Mrs. Meyers was getting her impressions all at the same time. Of course, she knew nothing of either the young girl ghost or the sailor.

Now the medium told a lively tale of a young girl ready to marry a young man, but pursued by another, older man. "I can hear her scream!" She grabbed her own throat, and violently suppressed a scream, the kind of sound that might have invited an unwelcome audience to our séance!

"Avoiding the man, she rushes up the stairs, it is a slippery and cold day around Christmas. She's carrying something heavy, maybe wood and coal, and it's the eve of her marriage, but she's pushed off the roof. There are two women, the older one had been berating the girl, and pushed her out against the fence, and over she went. It was cold and slippery and nobody's fault. But instead of a wedding, there is a funeral."

The medium was now in full trance. Again, a scream is suppressed, then the voice changes and another personality speaks through Mrs. Meyers.

"Who are you?" I said, as I always do on such occasions. Identification is a must when you communicate with ghosts.

Instead, the stranger said anxiously, "Mathew!"

"Who is Mathew?" I said.

"Why won't he come, where is he? Why?"

"Who are you?"

"Bernice."

"How old are you?"

"Seventeen."

"What year is this?"

" 'Eighty."

But then the anguish came to the fore again.

78

The Carriage House Ghosts

"Where is he, he has the ring . . . my head . . . Mathew, Mathew . . . she pushed me, she is in hell. I'm ready to go, I'm dressed, we're going to father. I'm dressed. . . ."

As she repeated her pleas, the voice gradually faded out. Then, just as suddenly as she had given way to the stranger, Mrs. Meyers's own personality returned.

As we walked out of the gloomy studio apartment, I mused about the story that had come from Mrs. Meyers's lips. Probably servant girls, I thought, and impossible to trace. Still, she got the young girl, her falling off the stairs, the stairs themselves, and the ghostly sailor. Clinton Court is still haunted all right!

I looked up at the reassuringly lighted modern apartments around the yard, and wondered if the ghosts knew the difference. If you ever happen to be in "Hell's Kitchen," step through the archway at 420 West Forty-sixth Street into the yard, and if you're real, real quiet, and a bit lucky, of course, perhaps you will meet the teenage ghost in her white dress or crinoline—but beware of "Old Moor" and his language—you know what sailors are like!

9

Brooklyn Henny

Clinton Street, Brooklyn, is one of the oldest sections of that borough, pleasantly middle class at one time, and still among Brooklyn's best neighborhoods, as neighborhoods go. The house in question is in the 300 block, and consists of four stories. There was a basement floor, then a parlor floor a few steps up, as is the usual custom with brownstone houses, with a third and fourth floor above it. Each level was capable of serving as an apartment for those who wished to live there. The house was more than a hundred years old at the time of the events herein described, and the records are somewhat dim beyond a certain point.

In the 1960s, the house was owned by some offbeat people, about whom little was known. Even the Hall of

Records isn't of much help, as the owners didn't always live in the house, and the people who lived in it were "live-in guests" of the actual tenants. However, for the purpose of my story, we need only concern ourselves with the two top floors; the third floor contained two bedrooms and a bath, while the fourth floor consisted of a living room, dining room, kitchen, and second bath.

At the time my account begins, the first two floors were rented to an architect and his wife, and only the two top floors were available for new tenants.

It was in the summer when two young ladies in their early twenties, who had been living at the Brooklyn YWCA, decided to find a place of their own. Somehow they heard of the two vacant floors in the house on Clinton Street and immediately fell in love with it, renting the two top floors without much hesitation. Both Barbara and Sharon were twenty-three years old at the time, still going to college, and trying to make ends meet on what money they could manage between them. Two years later, Barbara was living in San Francisco with a business of her own, independently merchandising clothing. Brooklyn was only a hazy memory by then, but on August 1 of the year she and Sharon moved in, it was very much her world.

Immediately after moving in, they decided to clean up the house, which needed it indeed. The stairway to the top floor was carpeted all the way up, and it was quite a job to vacuum it because there were a lot of outlets along the way, and one had to look out for extension cords. Sharon got to the top floor and was cleaning it when she removed the extension cord to plug it in further up. Instead, she just used the regular cord of the vacuum cleaner, which was about twelve feet long, using perhaps

82

three feet of it, which left nine feet of cord lying on the floor.

All of a sudden, the plug just pulled out of the wall. Sharon couldn't believe her eyes; the plug actually pulled itself out of the socket, and flew out onto the floor. She shook her head and put it back in, and turned the vacuum cleaner on again. Only then did she realize that she had turned the switch on the cleaner back on, when she had never actually turned it off in the first place! She couldn't figure out how that was possible. But she had a lot more work to do, so she continued with it. Later she came downstairs and described the incident to her roommate, who thought she was out of her mind. "Wait till something happens to you," Sharon said, "there is something strange about this house."

During the next five months, the girls heard strange noises all over the house, but they attributed it to an old house settling, or the people living downstairs in the building. Five months of "peace" were rudely shattered when Sharon's younger brother came to visit from New Jersey.

He was still in high school, and liked to listen to music at night, especially when it was played as loud as possible. The young people were sitting in the living room, listening to music and talking. It was a nice, relaxed evening. All of a sudden the stereo went off. The music had been rather loud rock and roll, and at first they thought the volume had perhaps damaged the set. Then the hallway light went out, followed by the kitchen light. So they thought a fuse had blown. Barbara ran down four flights of stairs into the basement to check. No fuse had blown. To be on the safe side, she checked them anyway, and switched them around to make sure everything was fine.

Then she went back upstairs and asked the others how the electricity was behaving.

But everything was still off. At this point, Sharon's brother decided to go into the kitchen and try the lights there. Possibly there was something wrong with the switches. He went into the hallway where there was an old Tiffany-type lamp hanging at the top of the stairway. It had gone off, too, and he tried to turn it on and nothing happened. He pulled again, and suddenly it went on. In other words, he turned it off first, then turned it on, so it had been on in the first place.

This rather bothered the young man, and he announced he was going into the kitchen to get something to eat. He proceeded into the kitchen, and when he came back to join the others he was as white as the wall. He reported that the kitchen was as cold as an icebox, but as soon as one left the kitchen, the temperature was normal in the rest of the house. The others then got up to see for themselves, and sure enough, it was icy cold in the kitchen. This was despite the fact that there were four or five radiators going, and all the windows were closed.

That night they knew they had a ghost, and for want of a better name they called her Hendrix—it happened to have been the anniversary of Jimi Hendrix's death, and they had been playing some of his records.

Shortly afterward, Toby joined the other two girls in the house. She moved in on April 1. It had been relatively quiet between the incident in the kitchen and that day, but somehow Toby's arrival was also the beginning of a new aspect of the haunting.

About a week after Toby moved in, the girls were in the living room talking. It was about eleven o'clock at night, and they had dimmers on in the living room. Toby was sitting on the couch, and Barbara and some friends were sitting on the other side of the room, when all of a sudden Toby felt a chilly breeze pass by her. It didn't touch her, but she felt it nonetheless, and just then the lights started to dim back and forth, and when she looked up, she actually saw the dial on the dimmer moving by itself. As yet, Toby knew nothing about the haunting, so she decided to say nothing to the others, having just moved in and not wishing to have her new roommates think her weird.

But things kept happening night after night, usually after eleven o'clock when the two girls and their friends sat around talking. After a couple of weeks she could not stand it any longer, and finally asked the others whether they could feel anything strange in the room. Barbara looked at Sharon, and a strange look passed between them; finally they decided to tell Toby about the haunting, and brought her up to date from the beginning of their tenancy in the house.

Almost every day there was something new to report: cooking equipment would be missing, clothing would disappear, windows were opened by themselves, garbage cans would be turned over by unseen hands. Throughout that period, there was the continued walking of an unseen person in the living room located directly over the third-floor bedroom. And the girls heard it at any hour of the night, and once in a while even during the day. Someone was walking back and forth, back and forth. They were loud, stomping footsteps, more like a woman's, but they sounded as if someone were very angry. Each time one of them went upstairs to check they found absolutely nothing.

The girls held a conference, and decided that they had

a ghost, make no mistake about it. Toby offered to look into the matter, and perhaps find out what might have occurred at the house at an earlier age. Barbara kept hearing an obscure whistling, not a real tune or song that could be recognized, but a human whistle nevertheless. Meanwhile, Toby heard of a course on witchcraft and the occult being given at New York University, and started to take an interest in books on the subject. But whenever there were people over to visit them and they stayed in the living room upstairs past eleven o'clock at night, the ghost would simply run them out of the room with all the tricks in her ghostly trade.

"She" would turn the stereo on and off, or make the lights go on and off. By now they were convinced it was a woman. There were heavy shutters from the floor to the ceiling, and frequently it appeared as if a wind were coming through them and they would clap together, as if the breeze were agitating them. Immediately after that, they heard footsteps walking away from them, and there was an uncomfortable feeling in the room, making it imperative to leave and go somewhere else, usually downstairs into one of the bedrooms.

As yet, no one had actually seen her. That June, Bruce, Toby's boyfriend, moved into the house with her. They had the master bedroom, and off the bedroom was a bathroom. Since Barbara would frequently walk through in the middle of the night, they left the light on in the bathroom so that she would not trip over anything. That particular night in June, Toby and her boyfriend were in bed and she was looking up, not at the ceiling, but at the wall, when suddenly she saw a girl looking at her.

It was just like an outline, like a shadow on the wall, but Toby could tell that she had long hair arranged in braids. Somehow she had the impression that she was an Indian, perhaps because of the braids. Toby looked up at her and called the apparition to her boyfriend's attention, but by the time he had focused on it she had disappeared.

He simply did not believe her. Instead, he asked Toby to go upstairs to the kitchen and make him a sandwich. She wasn't up there for more than five or ten minutes when she returned to the bedroom and found her boyfriend hidden under the covers of the bed. When she asked him what was wrong, he would shake his head, and so she looked around the room, but could find nothing unusual. The only thing she noticed was that the bathroom door was now wide open. She assumed that her boyfriend had gone to the bathroom, but he shook his head and told her that he had not.

He had just been lying there smoking a cigarette, when all of a sudden he saw the handle on the door turn by itself, and the door open. When he saw that, he simply dove under the covers until Toby returned. From that moment on, he no longer laughed at her stories about a house ghost. The following night, her boyfriend was asleep when Toby woke up at two o'clock in the morning. The television set had been left on and she went to shut it off, and when she got back into bed, she happened to glance at the same place on the wall where she had seen the apparition the night before. For a moment or two she saw the same outline of a girl, only this time she had the impression that the girl was smiling at her.

Two weeks after that, Toby and her boyfriend broke up. She had come back home one day and didn't know that he had left, then she found a note in which he explained his reasons for leaving, and that he would get in touch with her later. Naturally, this upset her very much, so much so that her two roommates had to calm her down. Finally, the two other girls went upstairs and Toby was lying on the bed trying to compose herself.

In the quiet of the room, she suddenly heard someone sob a little and then a voice said, "Toby." Toby got up from bed and went to the bottom of the stairs and called up, demanding to know what Barbara wanted. But no one had called her. She went back to the room and lay down on the bed again. Just then she heard a voice saying "Toby" again and again. On checking, she found that no one had called out to her—no one of flesh and blood, that is.

Toby then realized who had been calling her, and she decided to talk to "Henny," her nickname for Hendrix, which was the name given by the others to the ghost since that night when they were playing Jimi Hendrix records. In a quiet voice, Toby said, "Henny, did you call me?" and then she heard the voice answer, "Calm down, don't take it so hard, it will be all right." It was a girl's voice, and yet there was no one to be seen. The time was about five o'clock in the afternoon, and since it was in June, the room was still fairly light.

Toby had hardly recovered from this experience when still another event took place. Sharon had moved out and another girl by the name of Madeline had moved in. One day her brother came to visit them from Chicago, and he brought a friend along who had had some experience of a spiritual nature. His name was Joey, and both boys were about twenty or twenty-one years old.

Madeline and her brother were much interested in the occult, and they brought a Ouija board to the house. On Saturday, December 19, while it was snowing outside and the atmosphere was just right for a séance, they decided to make contact with the unhappy ghost in the house. They went upstairs into the living room, and sat down with the board. At first it was going to be a game, and they were asking silly questions of it such as who was going to marry whom, and other romantic fluff. But halfway through the session, they decided to try to contact the ghost in earnest. The three girls and Madeline's brother sat down on the floor with their knees touching, and put the board on top. Then they invited Henny to appear and talk to them if she was so inclined. They were prepared to pick up the indicator and place their hands on it so it could move to various letters on the board.

But before their hands ever touched it, the indicator took off by itself! It shot over to the word yes on the board, as if to reassure them that communication was indeed desired. The four of them looked at each other dumbfounded, for they had seen only too clearly what had just transpired. By now they were all somewhat scared. However, Toby decided that since she was going to be interested in psychic research, she might as well ask the questions. She began asking why the ghostly girl was still attached to the house.

Haltingly, Henny told her sad story. It was a slow process, since every word had to be spelled out letter by letter, but the young people didn't mind the passage of time—they wanted to know why Henny was with them. It appears that the house once belonged to her father, a medical doctor. Her name was Cesa Rist and she had lived in the house with her family. Unfortunately she had fallen in love with a boy and had become pregnant by him. She wanted to marry him and have the baby, but her father would not allow it and forced her to have an abortion. He did it in the house himself, and she died during the abortion.

Her body was taken to Denver, Colorado, and buried in the family plot. She realized that her boyfriend was dead also, because this all happened a long time ago. Her reasons for staying on in the house were to find help; she wanted her remains to be buried near her lover's in New York.

"Do you like the people who live in this house?" "Yes," the ghost replied. "Is anyone who lives here ever in any danger?" "Yes, people who kill babies." This struck the young people as particularly appropriate: a close friend, not present at the time, had just had an abortion. "Will you appear to us?" "Cesa has," the ghost replied, and as if to emphasize this statement, there suddenly appeared the shadow of a cross on the kitchen wall, for which there was no possible source, except, of course, from the parapsychological point of view.

The girls realized they did not have the means to go to Denver and exhume Cesa's remains to bring to New York, and they told the ghost as much. "Is there anything else we can do to help you?" "Contact Holzer," she said. By that time, of course, Toby had become familiar with my works, and decided to sit down and write me a letter, telling me of their problem. They could not continue with the Ouija board or anything else that night; they were all much too shaken up.

On Monday, Toby typed up the letter they had composed, and sent it to me. Since they were not sure the letter would reach me, they decided to do some independent checking concerning the background of the house, and if possible, try to locate some record of Cesa Rist. But they were unsuccessful, even at the Hall of Records, the events having apparently transpired at a time when records were not yet kept, or at least not properly kept.

When I received the letter, I was just about to leave for Europe and would be gone two and a half months. I asked the girls to stay in touch with me and after my return I would look into the matter. After Toby had spoken to me on the telephone, she went back into the living room and sat down quietly. She then addressed Henny and told her she had contacted me, and that it would be a couple of months before I could come to the house because I had to go to Europe.

Barbara decided not to wait, however; one night she went upstairs to talk to Henny. She explained the situation to her, and why she was still hanging around the house; she explained that her agony was keeping her in the house, and that she must let go of it in order to go on and join her boyfriend in the Great Beyond. Above all, she should not be angry with them because it was their home now. Somehow Barbara felt that the ghost understood, and nothing happened, nothing frightening at all. Relieved, Barbara sat down in a chair facing the couch. She was just sitting there smoking a cigarette, wondering whether Henny really existed, or whether perhaps she was talking to thin air.

At the moment, an ethereal form entered the room and stood near the couch. It looked as if she were leaning on the arm of the couch or holding onto the side of it. She saw the outline of the head, and what looked like braids around the front of her chest. For half a minute she was there, and then she suddenly disappeared.

It looked to Barbara as if the girl had been five feet four inches, weighing perhaps 120 pounds. Stunned, Barbara sat there for another ten or fifteen minutes, trying to believe what she had seen. She then walked down-stairs to try to go to sleep. But sleep would not come; she kept thinking about her experience.

At the time Sharon left, they were interviewing poten-tial roommates to replace her. One particularly unpleas-ant girl had come over and fallen in love with the house. Both Barbara and Toby didn't want her to move in, but she seemed all set to join them, so Toby decided to tell her about the ghost. She hoped it would stop the girl from moving in. As Toby delineated their experiences with Henny, the would-be roommate became more and more nervous.

All of a sudden there was a loud crash in the kitchen, and they went to check on it. The garbage can had turned itself over and all the garbage was spilled all over the kitchen, even though no one had been near it. The new girl took one look at this and ran out as fast as she could. She never came back.

But shortly afterward, Toby went on vacation to Cali-fornia. There she made arrangements to move and found employment in the market research department of a large department store. Under the circumstances, the girls decided not to renew the lease, which was up in July, but to move to another apartment for a short pe-riod. That September, they moved to California. Under the circumstances, they did not contact me any further, and I assumed that matters had somehow been straight-ened out, or that there had been a change in their plans. It was not until a year later that we somehow met in California, and I could fill in the missing details of Henny's story.

On the last day of the girls' stay at the house on Clinton Street, with the movers going in and out of the house,

Brooklyn Henny

Toby went back into the house for one more look and to say good-bye to Henny. She went up to the living room and said a simple good-bye, and hoped that Henny would be all right. But there was no answer, no feeling of a presence.

For a while the house stood empty, then it was purchased by the father of an acquaintance of the girls. Through Alan, they heard of the new people who had moved in after the house was sold. One day when they had just been in the house for a few days, they returned to what they assumed to be an empty house.

They found their kitchen flooded with water: There were two inches of water throughout the room, yet they knew they had not left the water taps on. Why had Henny turned the water on and let it run? Perhaps Henny didn't like the new tenants after all. But she had little choice, really. Being a ghost, she was tied to the house.

Following her friends to San Francisco was simply impossible, the way ghosts operate. And unless or until the new tenants on Clinton Street call for my services, there is really nothing I can do to help Henny.

Part III

Ghosts from Pennsylvania
to the Midwest

10

The Restless Ghost of the Parish Priest

I had heard rumors for some time of a ghost parson in a church near Pittsburgh, and when I appeared on the John Reed King show on Station KDKA-TV in the spring of 1963, one of the crew came up to me after the telecast and told me how much he enjoyed hearing about ghosts.

"Have you ever visited that haunted church in M———?" he asked, and my natural curiosity was aroused. A ghost here in Pittsburgh, and I haven't met him? I couldn't allow that. But my stay was over and I had to return to New York.

Still, the ghostly person of M——— was very much on my mind. When I returned to Pittsburgh in September of 1963, I was determined to have a go at that case.

97

With the help of Jim Sieger and his roving reporter, John Stewart, at Station KDKA, we got together a car, a first-class portable tape recorder, and photographer Jim Stark. Immediately following my telecast, we set out for M———.

Fate must have wanted us to get results, for the attendant of the first gasoline station we stopped at directed us to the Haunted Church. The names of the church and of those involved must remain hidden at their own request, but the story is nevertheless true.

The Haunted Church is an imposing Romanesque stone building, erected at the turn of the century on a bluff overlooking the Pittsburgh River. It is attached to a school and rectory and gives a clean and efficient impression, nothing haunted or mysterious about it.

When I rang the doorbell of the rectory, a portly, imposing man in sweater and slacks opened the door. I asked to talk to him about the history of the church. Evidently he had more than a share of the Sixth Sense, for he knew immediately what I was after.

"I am priest," he said firmly, with a strong Slavic accent. I was somewhat taken aback because of his casual clothes, but he explained that even priests are allowed to relax now and then. Father X., as we shall call him, was a well-educated, soft-spoken man of about forty-five or fifty, and he readily admitted he had heard the rumors about "spirits," but there was, of course, nothing to it. Actually, he said, the man to talk to was his superior, Father H.

A few moments later, Father H. was summoned and introduced to me as "the authority" on the subject. When the good Father heard I was a parapsychologist and interested in his ghost, he became agitated. "I have nothing

The Restless Ghost of the Parish Priest

to say," he emphasized, and politely showed us the door. I chose to ignore his move.

Instead, I persisted in requesting either confirmation or denial of the rumors of hauntings in his church. Evidently, Father H. was afraid of the unusual. Many priests are not and discuss freely that which they know exists. But Father H. had once met with another writer, Louis Adamic, and apparently this had soured him on all other writers. It seems that Adamic, a fellow Croatian, had mentioned in one of his books the story about the ghost at the altar—and seriously at that—quite a feat for a nonbeliever as Adamic was said to have been. Father H. had nothing to say for publication.

"No, no, no—nothing. I bless you. Good-bye." He bowed ceremoniously and waited for us to depart. Instead, I turned and smiled at Father X., the assistant pastor.

"May we see the church?" I said and waited. They couldn't very well refuse. Father H. realized we weren't going to leave at once and resigned himself to the fact that his assistant pastor would talk to us.

"Very well. But without me!" he finally said, and withdrew. That was all Father X. had needed. The field was clear now. Slowly he lit a cigarette and said, "You know, I've studied parapsychology myself for two years in my native Croatia."

After his initial appearance, nothing about Father X. surprised me. As we walked across the yard to the church, we entered into an animated discussion about the merits of psychic research. Father X. took us in through the altar door, and we saw the gleaming white and gold altar emerging from the semidarkness like a vision in one of Raphael's Renaissance paintings.

99

There was definitely something very unusual about this church. For one thing, it was a typically European, Slavonically tinged edifice. The large nave culminated in a balcony on which an old-fashioned—that is, nonelectric, nonautomatic—organ was placed in prominent position. No doubt services at this church were imposing and emotionally satisfying experiences.

We stepped closer to the altar, which was flanked on either side by a large, heavy vigil light, the kind Europeans call Eternal Light. "See this painting?" said Father X., pointing at the curving fresco covering the entire inner cupola behind the altar, both behind it and above it. The painting showed natives of Croatia in their costumes, and a group of Croatians presenting a model of their church.

These traditional scenes were depicted with vivid colors and a charming, primitive style. I inquired about the painter. "Maxim Hvatka," the priest said, and at once I recognized the name as that of a celebrated Yugoslav artist who had passed on a few years before. The frescos were done in the early part of the century.

As we admired the altar, standing on its steps and getting impressions, Father X. must again have read my mind, for he said without further ado, "Yes, it is this spot where the 'spirits were seen.'"

There was no doubt in my mind that our assistant pastor was quite convinced of the truth of the phenomena.

"What exactly happened?" I asked.

"Well, not so long ago, Father H. and this painter Hvatka, they were here near the altar. Hvatka was painting the altar picture and Father H. was here to watch him. Suddenly, Hvatka grabbed Father's arm and said with great excitement, 'Look, Father—this person—there is someone here in the church, in front of the altar!'

"Father H. knew that the church was locked up tight and that only he and the painter were in the building. There *couldn't* be another person. 'Where? Who?' he said and looked hard. He didn't see anything. Hvatka insisted he had just seen a man walk by the altar and disappear into nothing. They stepped up to the vigil light on the left and experienced a sudden chill. Moreover, *the light was out.*

"Now to extinguish this light with anything less than a powerful blower or fan directly above it is impossible. Glass-enclosed and metal-covered, these powerful wax candles are meant to withstand the wind and certainly ordinary drafts or human breath. Only a supernormal agency could have put out that vigil light, gentlemen."

Father X. paused. I was impressed by his well-told story, and I knew at once why Father H. wanted no part of us. How could he ever admit having been in the presence of a spirit without having seen it? Impossible. We took some photographs and walked slowly toward the exit.

Father X. warmed up to me now and volunteered an experience from his own youth. It seems that when he was studying theology in his native Croatia, he lived among a group of perhaps a dozen young students who did not share his enthusiasm for psychic studies—who, in fact, ridiculed them.

One young man, however, who was his roommate, took the subject seriously, so seriously in fact that they made a pact—whoever died first would let the other know. A short time later, Father X., asleep on a warm afternoon, suddenly woke up. He *knew* his friend had

101

died that instant, for he saw him sitting on a chair near his bed, laughing and waving at him. It was more than a mere dream, a vividly powerful impression. Father X. was no longer asleep at that moment; the impression had actually awakened him.

He looked at his watch; it was just three in the afternoon. Quickly, he made inquiries about his friend. Within a few hours he knew what he had already suspected—his friend had died in an accident at precisely the moment he had seen him in his room back at the seminary!

"You're psychic then," I said.

Father X. shrugged. "I know many psychic cases," he said obliquely. "There was that nun in Italy, who left her hand prints on the church door to let her superiors know she was now in purgatory."

Father X. spoke softly and with the assurance of a man who knows his subject well. "There are these things, but what can we do? We cannot very well admit them."

A sudden thought came to my mind. Did he have any idea who the ghost at the altar was? Father X. shook his head.

"Tell me," I continued, "did anyone die violently in the church?"

Again, a negative answer.

"That's strange," I said. "Was there another building on this spot before the present church?"

"No," Father X. said nonchalantly.

"That's even stranger," I countered, "for my research indicates there was a priest here in the nineteenth century, and it is his ghost that has been seen."

Father X. swallowed hard.

"As a matter of fact," he said now, "you're right. There

was an earlier wooden church here on this very spot. The present stone building only dates back to about 1901. Father Ranzinger built the wooden church."

"Was that around 1885?" I inquired. That is how I had it in my notes.

"Probably correct," the priest said, and no longer marveled at my information.

"What happened to the wooden church, Father?" I asked, and here I had a blank, for my research told me nothing further.

"Oh, it burned down. Completely. No, nobody got hurt, but the church, it was a total loss."

Father Ranzinger's beloved wooden church went up in flames, it appeared, and the fifteen years he had spent with his flock must have accumulated an emotional backlog of great strength and attachment. Was it not conceivable that Father Ranzinger's attachment to the building was transferred to the stone edifice as soon as it was finished?

Was it his ghost the two men had seen in front of the altar? Until he puts in another appearance, we won't know, but Pittsburgh's Haunted Church is a lovely place in which to rest and pray—ghost or no ghost.

11

The Little Ghost Girl on Lansdowne Avenue

*E*d Harvey ran a pretty good talk show called "Talk of Philadelphia" on WCAU radio. It was the sort of program people listened to in their homes and cars. They listened in large numbers. I know, for the telephone calls came in fast and furious in the show's final half hour, when calls from the public were answered on the air.

One day in April 1965, Ed and his charming wife, Marion, went to a cocktail party at a friend's house. There he got to talking to Jack Buffington, who was a regional director of a worldwide relief organization and a pretty down-to-earth fellow, as Ed soon found out. Somehow the talk turned to ghosts, and Buffington had a few things to say on that subject, since he lived in a haunted house. At that point, Ed Harvey asked that Sybil Leek and I be permitted to have a go at the house.

We arrived at Buffington's house on Lansdowne Avenue, in Lansdowne, a Philadelphia suburb, around ten o'clock. It was a little hard to find in the dark, and when we got there it did not look ghostly at all, just a nice old Victorian house, big and sprawling. Jack Buffington welcomed us at the door.

As I always do on such occasions, I asked Sybil to wait in another room where she could not hear any of the conversation, while I talked to those who had had experiences in the house.

After Sybil had graciously left, we seated ourselves and took inventory. What I saw was a tastefully furnished Victorian house with several wooden staircases and banisters, and lots of fine small antiques. Our host was joined by his dark-haired Italian-born wife, and two friends from his office. My wife, Catherine, immediately made friends with Mrs. Buffington, and then we started to find out what this was all about.

The Buffingtons, who had a four-year-old daughter named Allegra, had come to the house just nine months before. A lot had happened to them in those nine months.

"We came home from a trip to Scranton," Jack Buffington began, "and when we got back and I inserted the key in the front door, the hall light went on by itself. It has two switches, one on the upstairs level, so I raced upstairs to see who was in the house, but there was no one there. Periodically this happens, and I thought it was faulty wiring at first, but it has been checked and there is nothing wrong with it. The cellar light and the light in the third floor bathroom also go on and off by themselves. I've seen it, and so have my wife and our little girl."

"Anything else happening here?" I asked casually.

"There are many things that go bump in the night here. The first noise that happened recurrently was the sound of an old treadle sewing machine, which is heard on the average of once every month. This happens in a small room on the second floor, which we now use as a dressing room, but which may well have been a sewing room at one time."

I walked up the narrow stairs and looked at the little room. It had all the marks of a Victorian sewing room where tired servants labored or a worried mother worked at the clothes for her child.

"It's always around three in the morning, and it awakens us," Mr. Buffington continued, "and then there are footsteps and often they sound like children's footsteps."

"Children's footsteps?"

"Yes, and it is rather startling," Mr. Buffington added, "since we do have a small child in the house and inevitably go and check that it isn't she who is doing it. It never is."

"Is it downstairs?"

"All over the place. There are two stories, or three flights, including the basement. And there are a front and back stairway. There is never any pattern about these things. There may be a lot of happenings at the same time, then there is nothing for weeks, and then it starts again."

"Outside of the child's footsteps, did you ever have any indication of a grown-up presence?" I asked.

"Well, I saw the figure of a woman in the doorway of the dining room, walking down this hall, and through these curtains here, and I heard footsteps in conjunction with it. I thought it was my wife, and I called to her. I was hanging a picture in the dining room at the time. No answer. I was getting annoyed and called her several times over, but there was no response. Finally she answered from the second floor—she had not been downstairs at all."

"What happened to the other woman in the meantime?"

"I walked in here—the hall—and there was no one here."

"How was she dressed?"

"She had on a long skirt, looking like a turn-of-the-century skirt, and she did have her hair on top of her head, and she was tall and slender."

Mrs. Buffington is not very tall, but she does wear dark clothes.

"It was a perfectly solid figure I saw—nothing nebulous or transparent," our host added. "The spring lock at the entrance door was locked securely."

"Did anyone else see an apparition here?"

"My brother met a woman on the stairway—that is, the stairway leading to the third floor. He was spending the night with us, around Thanksgiving time. There was a party that evening and he mistook her for a guest who had somehow remained behind after all the other guests had gone home. She passed him going *up* while he was coming *down,* and she walked into his room, which he thought odd, so he went back to ask if he could help her, but there wasn't anybody there!"

Jack Buffington gave a rather nervous laugh.

I took a good look at the upstairs. Nobody could have gotten out of the house quickly. The stairs were narrow and difficult to negotiate, and the back stairs, in the servants' half of the house, are even more difficult. Anyone descending them rapidly was likely to slip and fall. The two brothers hadn't talked much about all this, I was told, since that time.

"Our little girl must be seeing her, too, for she frequently says she is going up to play with her lady friend," Jack Buffington said.

I started to wander around the house to get the feeling of it. The house was built in 1876 to the specifications of George Penn, a well-known local builder. Although it was now a duplex, it was originally a townhouse for just one family.

The upper stories contained several small, high-ceilinged rooms, and there was about them the forbidding atmosphere of a mid-Victorian house in a small town. The Buffingtons had furnished their house with taste, and the Italian background of the lady of the house is evident in the works of art and antiques strewn about the house.

As I soon discovered, tragedy had befallen the house on Lansdowne Avenue at least twice as far as is known. The original builder had a sister who suffered from mental illness and was hospitalized many times. She also spent many years in this house. Then a family named Hopkins came to live in it, and it was at that time that the house was divided into two parts. Incidentally, no manifestations had been reported from the other half of the house. About six years before—the exact time was none too clear, and it may be further back—a family named Johnson rented the half now occupied by the Buffingtons. They had a retarded child, a girl, *who was kept locked up in a room on the third floor.* She died in her

109

early teens, they say, in a hospital not far away. Then the house stood empty, looking out onto quiet Lansdowne Avenue with an air of tragedy and secret passion.

Three years went by before the Buffingtons, returning from Italy, took over the house.

"Have there been any unusual manifestations on the third floor?" I asked Mr. Buffington.

"Just one. Something carries on in the trunk up on the third floor. The trunk is empty and there is no reason for those frightful noises. We have both heard it. It is above where the child sleeps."

Mr. Buffington added that a book he read at night in bed often disappeared and showed up in the most peculiar spots around the house—spots that their little four-year-old couldn't possibly reach. On one occasion, he found it in a bathroom; at least once it traveled from his room upstairs to the top bookshelf downstairs, all by itself.

"My impression of this ghost," Mr. Buffington said, "is that it means no harm. Rather, it has the mischievousness of a child."

I now turned my attention to Mrs. Buffington, who had been waiting to tell me of her own most unusual experiences in the house.

"On one occasion I was on the second floor with the child," she began. "It was about eleven in the morning, and I was taking some clothes out of a cabinet. The back staircase is very close to this particular cabinet. Suddenly, I very distinctly heard a voice calling 'Mamma,' a voice of a person standing close to the cabinet, and it was a girl's voice, a child's voice and quite distinct—in fact, my daughter, Allegra, also heard it, for she turned to me and asked 'Mammi, who is it?' "

110

The Little Ghost Girl on Lansdowne Avenue

"What did you do?" I asked.

"I pretended to be nonchalant about it, looked all over, went up the stairs, opened cabinets—but, of course, there was no one there."

"And your daughter?"

"When we did not find anyone, she said, 'Oh, it must be our lady upstairs.'"

"Any other experiences you can recall?"

"Yes, tonight, in fact," Mrs. Buffington replied. "I was in the kitchen feeding the child, and I was putting something into the garbage container, when I heard a child's voice saying, 'It's lower down'—just that, nothing more."

"Amazing," I conceded.

"It was a young girl's voice," Mrs. Buffington added. "I looked at Allegra, but it was obvious to me that the voice had come from the opposite direction. At any rate, Allegra was busy eating. I've been very nervous the past few days and about a week ago, when my husband was away in Washington, I spent the night alone, and having had some strong coffee, could not find sleep right away. I had moved the child in with me, so I did not have to stay by myself. I switched the light off, and the door to the landing of the second floor staircase was open. Just on that spot I suddenly heard those crashing noises as if somebody were rolling down. I was terrified. As soon as I switched the light back on, it stopped. There was nothing on the stairs. I sat on the bed for a moment, then decided it was my nerves, and turned the light off again. Immediately, the same noise returned, even louder. There was no mistaking the origin of the noises this time. They came from the stairs in front of the room. I switched the light on again and they stopped, and I left the lights

111

burning the rest of the night. I finally fell asleep from sheer exhaustion."

"One more thing," Jack Buffington broke in. "On the back staircase, there is an area about four feet long which is a terribly frigid area sporadically. My little girl wouldn't walk up that staircase if she could possibly help it. Both my wife and I felt the cold spot."

"Is this in the area of the room where the little child was kept?" I asked.

"It is one floor below it, but it is the area, yes," Mrs. Buffington admitted.

I had heard enough by now to call in Sybil Leek, who had been waiting patiently outside for the call to lend her considerable psychic talents to the case.

After she had seated herself in one of the comfortable leather chairs, and we had grouped ourselves around her in the usual fashion, I quickly placed her into trance. Within a few minutes, her lips started to quiver gently, and then a voice broke through.

"Can't play," a plaintive child's voice said.

"Why not?" I asked immediately, bringing the microphone close to Sybil's entranced lips to catch every word.

"No one to play with. I want to play."

"Who do you want to play with?"

"Anyone. I don't like being alone."

"What is your name?"

"Elizabeth."

"What is your family name?"

"Streiber."

"How old are you?"

"Nine."

"What is your father's name?"

"Joseph Streiber."

112

The Little Ghost Girl on Lansdowne Avenue

Now Sybil had no knowledge that a child's ghost had been heard in the house. Nor had she overheard our conversation about it. Yet, the very first to manifest when trance had set in was a little girl!

I continued to question her.

"Your mother's name?"

"Mammi."

"What is her first name?"

The child thought for a moment, as if searching, then repeated:

"Mammi."

With sudden impact, I thought of the ghostly voice calling for "Mamma" heard on the steps by Mrs. Buffington and her little daughter.

"Do you go to school?"

The answer was almost angry.

"No! I play."

"Where do you live in this house?"

"Funny house . . . I get lost . . . too big."

"Where is your room?"

"On the stairs."

"Who else lives in the house?"

"Mammi."

"Anyone else?"

"No one."

"Where were you born?"

"Here."

"What is your birthday?"

"Eight . . . Eighteen . . . twenty-one."

"What month?"

"March."

Did she mean that she was born in 1821? The house was built in 1876 and before that time, only a field ex-

113

isted on the site. Or was she trying to say: March 8, 1921? Dates always confuse a ghost, I have found.

"Are you feeling well?"

A plaintive "no" was the answer. What was wrong with her, I wanted to know.

"I slip on the stairs," the ghost said. "I slipped down the stairs. I like to do that."

"Did you get hurt?"

"Yes."

"What happened then?"

"So I sit on the stairs," the little girl ghost said, "and sometimes I run down one staircase. Not the other. Then I have fun."

"Is there anyone else with you?"

"Mammi."

Again I thought of the apparition in the Victorian dress Jack Buffington had seen in the hall.

"Do you see her now?" I asked.

An emphatic "no" was the answer.

"When have you seen her last?"

She thought that one over for a moment.

"Two days."

"Is she living?"

"Yes . . . she goes away, and then I'm lost."

"Does she come back?"

"Yes."

"What about your father?"

"Don't like my father. Not very nice time with my father. He shouts."

"What floor is your room on?"

"At the top."

I recalled that the retarded little girl had been kept in a locked room on the top floor.

"Do you ever go downstairs?"

"Of course I go downstairs. I play on the stairs. And I'm going to sit on the stairs all the time until somebody plays with me!"

"Isn't there any other little girl or boy around?" I asked.

"I don't get at him . . . they take him away and hide him."

"Who does?"

"People here."

"Do you see people?"

"Yes."

"Do people see *you?*"

"They think they do . . . they're not very nice, really."

"Do you talk to them?" She seemed to nod. "What do you tell them?"

"I want to play."

"Do you call out for anyone?" I asked.

"Mammi."

"Is there anyone else in this house you can see? Any children?"

"Yes, but they won't play."

"What sort of children are there in this house?"

"They won't play."

How do you explain to a child that she is a ghost?

"Would you like to meet some other children like yourself who do want to play?" I asked. She liked that very much. I told her to imagine such children at play and to think of nothing else. But she wanted to play in this house.

"I live here."

I persisted in telling her that there were children outside, in a beautiful meadow, just waiting for her to join them.

"My father tells me not to."

"But he is not here."

"Sometimes I see him."

"Come outside now."

"I don't go outside in the daytime."

"What do you do in the daytime then?"

"I get up early and play on the stairs."

She was afraid to go outside, she said, but preferred to wait for "them" in the house, so she would not miss them. I explained things to her ever so gently. She listened. Eventually, she was willing to go, wondering only, "When do I come back?"

"You won't want to come back, Elizabeth," I replied, and asked if she understood these things now.

She thought for a moment, then said:

"Funny man . . ."

"You see, something happened to you, and you are not quite the same as before," I tried to explain. "People in this house are not like you and that's why you can't play with them. But outside in the meadow there are many like you. Children to play with all your life!"

And then I sent her away.

There was a strange, rapping noise on the staircase now, as if someone were saying good-bye in a hurry. Abruptly, the noise ceased and I recalled Sybil, still entranced, to her own body.

I asked her to describe what she saw on her side of the veil.

"The child is difficult," she said. "Doesn't want to leave the house. She's frightened of her father. She's about ten. Died here, fell."

116

I instructed the medium to help the child out of the house and across the border. This she did.

"There is also a woman here," Sybil said. "I think she followed the child. She is tied to this house because the child would not go."

"What does she look like?"

"Medium fair, full face, not thin—she wears a green dress in one piece, dark dress—she comes and goes—she worries about the child—I think *she left the child.*"

Guilt, I thought, so often the cause of a haunting!

"When she came back, something had happened," Sybil continued. "The child had been injured and now she keeps coming back to find the child. But the child only wants to play and sit on the stairs."

"Can you contact the woman for us?" I asked.

"The woman is not a good person," Sybil replied slowly. "She is sorry. She listens now."

"Tell her we've sent the child away."

"She knows."

"Tell her she need no longer haunt this house; her guilty feelings are a matter of the past."

"She wants to follow the child. She wants to go now."

"She should think of the child with love, and she will join her."

"She doesn't love the child."

"She will have to desire to see her family again, then, to cross over. Instruct her."

In a quiet voice, Sybil suggested to the ghost that she must go from the house and never return here.

"She won't upset the house, now that the child is gone," Sybil assured us. "The search for the child was the cause of it all."

"Was the child ill?" I asked.

"The child was difficult and lonely, and she fell."

Again I heard rapping noises for a moment.

"Was there anything wrong with this child?"

"I'm not so sure. I think she was a little *fou*. She was florid, you know, nobody to look after her, looking for things all the time and frightened to go out."

"Did she die in this house or was she taken somewhere?"

"She died here."

Sometimes the ghost reattaches himself to the last refuge he had on the earth plane, even though the body may expire elsewhere, and instantly returns to that place, never to leave it again, until freed by someone like myself.

"The woman is gone now," Sybil mumbled. "The child went a long way, and the woman is gone now, too."

I thanked Sybil and led her back to consciousness, step by step, until she woke up in the present, fully relaxed as if after a good night's rest, and, of course, not remembering a thing that had come through her entranced lips the past hour.

Mr. Buffington got up, since the spell of the foregoing had been broken, and motioned me to follow him to the next room.

"There is something I just remembered," he said. "My daughter, Allegra, took a fall on the staircase on the spot where those chills have been felt. She wore one of her mother's high heels and the likelihood of a spill was plausible—still, it was on *that* very spot."

The next morning, I called a number of people who knew Lansdowne's history and past residents well enough to be called experts. I spoke to the librarian at the Chester County Historical Society and the librarian at

Media, and to a long-time resident Mrs. Susan Worell, but none of them knew of a Joseph Streiber with a little girl named Elizabeth. The records back into the twenties or even earlier are pretty scanty in this area and research was almost hopeless. Quite conceivably, the Streibers were among the tenants who had the house in a transitory way during the years of which Jack Buffington had no records—but then again, there are certain parallels between fact and trance results that cannot be dismissed lightly.

Jack Buffington thought the description of the woman he saw and that given by the medium did not fully correspond, but then he did not see the specter long enough to be really sure.

The retarded child Sybil Leek brought through had an amazing similarity to the actual retarded girl of about ten who had lived in the house and died in a nearby hospital, and the word "Mamma" that Mrs. Buffington had heard so clearly was also close to what the ghost girl said she kept calling her mother.

There was some mystery about the dates—and even the long-time residents of the area I interviewed could not help me pin down the facts. Was there a man by that name with a little girl?

Records were not well kept in this respect and people in America could come and go far more easily than in some European countries, for instance, where there was an official duty to report one's moves to either the police or some other government office.

A day or two after our visit, Jack Buffington reported that the noises were worse than ever! It was as if our contact with the wraiths had unleashed their fury; having been told the truth about their status, they would

119

naturally have a feeling of frustration and resentment, or at least the woman would. This resentment often occurs after an investigation in which trance contact is made. But eventually things quiet down and I had the feeling that the woman's guilty feelings would also cease. That the little girl ghost had been sent out to play, I have no doubt. Perhaps that aftermath was the mother's fury at having her no longer in her sight. But then I never said that ghosts were the easiest people to live with.

12

A Minnesota Theater Ghost

*F*or this account, I am indebted to a creative production assistant in a Minneapolis advertising agency, by the name of Deborah Turner Miss Turner got hooked on some of my books, and started to look around in the Twin Cities for cases that might whet my appetite for ghost hunting. Being also musically inclined with an interest in theater, it was natural that she should gravitate toward the famed Guthrie Theater, named after the famous director, which is justly known as the pride of Minneapolis. At the theater she met some other young people, also in their early twenties, with whom she shared her interest in psychic phenomena. Imagine her surprise when she discovered that she had stumbled upon a most interesting case.

REAL HAUNTINGS

Richard Miller was born in Manhattan, Kansas, in 1951. Until age ten, he lived there with his father, a chemist in government service. Then his father was transferred to England, and Richard spent several years going to school in that country. After that, he and his family returned to the United States and moved to Edina. This left Richard not only with a vivid recollection of England, but also somewhat of an accent which, together with his childhood in Kansas, gave him a somewhat unusual personality.

His strange accent became the subject of ridicule by other students at Edina Morningside High School where he went to school, and it did not go down well with the shy, introspective young man. In the tenth grade at this school, he made friends with another young man, Fred Koivumaki, and a good and close relationship sprang up between the two boys. It gave Fred a chance to get to know Richard better than most of the other fellows in school.

As if the strange accent were not enough to make him stand out from the other boys in the area, Richard was given to sudden, jerky movements, which made him a good target for sly remarks and jokes of his fellow students. The Millers did not have much of a social life, since they also did not quite fit into the pattern of life in the small town of Edina.

During the years spent in an English school, Richard had known corporal punishment, since it is still part of the system in some English schools. This terrified him, and perhaps contributed toward his inability to express himself fully and freely. Somehow he never acquired a girlfriend as the other students did, and this, too, bothered him a lot. He couldn't for the world understand why people didn't like him more, and often talked about it to his friend Fred.

When both young men reached the age of sixteen, they went to the Guthrie Theater, where they got jobs as ushers. They worked at it for two years. Richard Miller got along well with the other ushers, but developed a close friendship only with Fred Koivumaki and another fellow, Barry Peterson. It is perhaps a strange quirk of fate that both Richard Miller and Barry Peterson never reached manhood, but died violently long before their time.

However, Richard's parents decided he should go to the university, and quit his job. In order to oblige his parents, he gave up the job as usher and moved into Territorial Hall for his first year at the university.

However, the change did not increase his ability to express himself or to have a good social life. Also, he seemed to have felt that he was catering to his parents' wishes, and became more antagonistic toward them. Then, too, it appears that these students also made him the butt of their jokes. Coincidentally, he developed a vision problem, with cells breaking off his retinas and floating in the inner humor of the eye. This caused him to see spots before his eyes, a condition for which there is no cure. However, he enjoyed skiing because he knew how to do it well, and joined the university ski club.

But Richard's bad luck somehow was still with him. On a trip to Colorado, he ran into a tree, luckily breaking only his skis. When summer came to the area, Richard rode his bike down a large dirt hill into rough ground and tall weeds at the bottom, injuring himself in the process. Fortunately, a motorcyclist came by just then, and got Richard to the emergency ward of a nearby hospital. All this may have contributed toward an ultimate breakdown; or, as the students would call it, Richard just "flipped out."

He was hospitalized at the university hospital and was allowed home only on weekends. During that time he was on strong medication, but when the medication did not improve his condition, the doctor took him off it and sent him home.

The following February 4, he decided to try skiing again, and asked his father to take him out to Buck Hill, one of the skiing areas not far from town. But to his dismay Richard discovered that he couldn't ski anymore, and this really depressed him. When he got home, there was a form letter waiting for him from the university, advising him that because he had skipped all the final exams due to his emotional problems at the time, he had received F's in all his classes and was on probation.

All this seemed too much for him. He asked his mother for forty dollars, ostensibly to buy himself new ski boots. Then he drove down to Sears on Lake Street, where he bought a high-powered pistol and shells. That was on Saturday, and he killed himself in the car. He wasn't found until Monday morning, when the lot clearing crew found him with most of his head shot off.

Richard Miller was given a quiet burial in Fort Snelling National Cemetery. His parents, Dr. and Mrs. Byron S. Miller, requested that memorials to the Minnesota Association for Mental Health be sent instead of flowers. Richard's mother had always felt that her son's best years had been spent as an usher at the Guthrie Theater; consequently he was cremated wearing his Guthrie Theater blazer. The date was February 7, and soon enough the shock of the young man's untimely death wore off, and only his immediate family and the few friends he had made remembered Richard Miller.

A few weeks after the death of the young usher, a woman seated in the theater in an aisle seat came up to the usher in charge of the aisle and asked him to stop the other usher from walking up and down during the play. The usher in charge was shocked, since he had been at the top of the aisle and had seen no one walk up and down. All the other ushers were busy in their respective aisles. However, the lady insisted that she had seen this young man walk up and down the aisle during the play. The usher in charge asked her to describe what she had seen. She described Richard Miller, even to the mole on his cheek. The incident is on record with the Guthrie Theater. Minneapolis Tribune columnist Robert T. Smith interviewed Craig Scherfenberg, director of audience development at the theater, concerning the incident. "There was no one in our employ at the time who fit the description," the director said, "but it fit the dead young man perfectly."

In the summer several years later, two ushers were asked to spend the night in the theater to make sure some troublesome air conditioning equipment was fully repaired. The Guthrie Theater has a thrust stage with openings onto the stage on all three sides; these openings lead to an actors' waiting area, which in turn has a door opening onto an area used as a lounge during intermissions.

The two young men were sitting in this waiting area with both doors open, and they were the only people in the building. At one o'clock in the morning, they suddenly heard the piano onstage begin to play. Stunned by this, they watched in silence when they saw a cloudlike form floating through the lounge door and hover in the center of the room. One of the ushers thought the form was staring at him. As quickly as they could gather their wits they left the room.

One of Deborah Turner's friends had worked late one evening shortly after this incident, repairing costumes needed for the next day's performance. She and a friend were relaxing in the stage area while waiting for a ride home. As she glanced into the house, she noticed that the lights on the aisle that had been the dead usher's were going on and off, as if someone were walking slowly up and down. She went to the Ladies' Room a little later, and suddenly she heard pounding on one wall, eventually circling the room and causing her great anxiety, since she knew that she and her friend were the only people in the house.

When the Guthrie Theater put on a performance of *Julius Caesar,* one of the extras was an older woman by the name of Mary Parez. She freely admitted that she was psychic and had been able to communicate with her dead sister. She told her fellow actors that she could sense Richard Miller's presence in the auditorium. Somehow she thought that the ghost would make himself known during Mark Antony's famous speech to the Romans after Caesar's death.

The scene was lit primarily by torches when the body of Julius Caesar was brought upon the stage. Jason Harlen, a young usher, and one of his colleagues, were watching the performance from different vantage points in the theater. One boy was in one of the tunnels leading to the stage, the other in the audience. Both had been told of Mary Parez's prediction, but were disappointed when nothing happened at that time. In boredom, they began to look around the theater. Independently of each other, they saw smoke rising to the ceiling, and shaping itself into a human form. Both young men said that the form had human eyes.

The aisle that the late Richard Miller worked was number eighteen. Two women in the acting company of *Julius Caesar*, named Terry and Gigi, complained that they had much trouble with the door at the top of aisle eighteen for no apparent reason. Bruce Benson, who now worked aisle eighteen, told that people complained of an usher walking up and down the aisle during performances. Bruce Margolis, who works the stage door, leaves the building after everyone else. When he was there one night all alone, the elevator began running on its own.

All this talk about a ghost induced some of the young ushers to try and make contact with him via the Ouija board. Dan Burg, head usher, took a board with him to the stage, and along with colleagues Bruce Benson and Scott Hurner tried to communicate with the ghost. For a while nothing happened. Then all of a sudden the board spelled TIPTOE TO THE TECH ROOM. When they asked why, the board spelled the word GHOST. They wanted to know which tech room the ghost was referring to: downstairs? "No," the communicator informed them, "upstairs." Then the board signed off with the initials MIL. At that, one of the men tipped over the board and wanted nothing further to do with it.

In November of the next year, an usher working at the theater told columnist Robert Smith, "It was after a night performance. Everyone had left the theater but me. I had forgotten my gloves and returned to retrieve them. I glanced into the theater and saw an usher standing in one of the aisles. It was him. He saw me and left. I went around to that aisle and couldn't find anything."

There is also an opera company connected with the Guthrie Theater. One night, one of the ladies working for the opera company was driving home from the Guthrie Theater. Suddenly she felt a presence beside her in the car. Terrified, she looked around, and became aware of a young man with dark curly hair, glasses, and a mole on his face. He wore a blue coat with something red on the pocket—the Guthrie Theater blazer. With a sinking feeling, she realized that she was looking at the ghost of Richard Miller.

For the past few years, however, no new reports have come in concerning the unfortunate young man. Could it be that he has finally realized that there await him greater opportunities in the next dimension and though his life on earth was not very successful, his passing into the spiritual life might give him most of the opportunities his life on earth had denied him? At any rate, things have now quieted down in aisle eighteen at the Guthrie Theater, in Minneapolis.

Part IV

Ghosts in the American South

13

The Phantom Grandfather

*G*rover C. was one of those colorful old-timers you hardly see anymore these days, not even in the Deep South. It wasn't that Grover had any particular background in anything special, far from it; he was an untutored man who owed his success solely to his own willpower and an insatiable curiosity that led him places his education—or lack of it—would have prevented him from ever reaching.

He saw the light of day just before the turn of the century in rural North Carolina. At the age of nineteen he married for the first time, but his wife, Fannie, and the child she bore him both died from what was then called "childbed fever," or lack of proper medical treatment. He had not yet chosen any particular career for himself, but was just "looking around" and did odd jobs here and there. A year later he was married again, to a lady from Georgia. After their first girl was born, they moved to Columbus, Georgia, and Mr. C. worked in a local mill for a while. This didn't satisfy his drive, however, and shortly afterward he and his brother Robert opened a grocery store. The store did right well until "the Hoover panic," as they called it, and then they managed to sell out and buy a farm in Harris County.

Life was pretty placid, and after an accident in which he lost his daughter, Mr. C. moved back to Columbus and tried his hand at the grocery business once more. About this time, the restless gentleman met a lady from Alabama, as a result of which he became the father of an "extracurricular" little girl, in addition to his own family, which eventually consisted of a wife and nine children.

When his second-born child died of an infectious disease, Mr. C. had his long-delayed breakdown, and for several years he was unable to cope with his life. During those rough years of slow, gradual recuperation, his daughter Agnes ran the store for him and supported the family.

As his health improved and he began to return to a happier and more constructive outlook on life, he developed an interest in real estate. With what money he could spare, he bought and sold property, and before long, he did so well he could dispense with the grocery store.

Soon he added a construction business to his real estate dealings and was considered a fairly well-to-do citizen in his hometown. This status naturally attracted a variety of unattached women and even some who were

132

attached, or semidetached, as the case may have been, and Mr. C. had himself a good time. Knowledge of his interest in other ladies could not fail to reach his wife and eventually he was given a choice by his wife: It was either her or them.

He picked them, or, more specifically, a lady next door, and for thirteen years he was reasonably faithful to her. Eventually she disliked living with a man she was not married to, especially when he happened to be married to someone else, even though he had bought her a cute little house of her own in Columbus. Mr. C. was not particularly happy about this state of affairs either, for he developed a penchant for drinking during those years. After they separated, the lady next door left town and got married.

Far from returning to the bosom of his family, now that the Other Woman had given him the gate, Grover looked elsewhere and what he found apparently pleased him. By now he was in his late sixties, but his vigorous personality wasn't about to be slowed down by so silly a reason as advancing age!

About 1962 he met a practical nurse by the name of Madeline, who turned out to be the opposite of what the doctor had ordered. After a particularly heavy argument, she kicked him in the nose. When it did not stop bleeding, she became alarmed and took him to the hospital. The family went to see him there even though his wife had not exactly forgiven him. But at this point it mattered little. Mr. C. also complained of pain in his side, and the children firmly believed that the practical nurse had also kicked him in that area. Since he died shortly afterward, it was a moot question whether or not she had done so because Mrs. C.'s abilities no longer corresponded to her amorous expectations. The old gent certainly did not discuss it with his family. He was seventy when he died and Madeline was a mere sixty. Death was somewhat unexpected despite the fact Mr. C. had suffered from various ailments. At first, he shared the hospital room with another older man, but several days later a young man was sent in to be with him. The young man's complaint was that he had a lollipop stick stuck in his throat. There probably aren't too many young men with such a predicament in medical annals, and even fewer in Columbus, Georgia. The family found this mighty peculiar, even more so since the young man was a close relative of Madeline, the very practical nurse.

They complained to the hospital authorities and the young man was moved. It is not known whether the lollipop stick was ever removed from his throat, but chances are it was or we would have heard more of it. Young men with lollipop sticks in their throats either die from them or become sideshow attractions in the circus; the records show neither so it must be assumed that the lollipop stick got unstuck somehow somewhere along the line. At any rate, Mr. C. was now guarded by one of his children each night, the children taking turns.

They are firmly convinced that the practical nurse slipped her erstwhile benefactor some poison and that perhaps the boy with the lollipop stick stuck in his throat might have done her bidding and administered it to the old gent. This is a pretty sticky argument, of course, and hard to prove, especially as no autopsy was ever performed on Mr. C. But it is conceivable that Madeline made a discovery about her friend that could have induced her to speed his failure to recover and to do so by any means at her command. She knew her way around the hospital and had ready access to his room. She also had equally ready access to his office and thereby hangs a strange tale.

On one of the infrequent occasions when Mr. C. slept at home, his estranged wife was making up the bed. This was five months before his demise. As she lifted the mattress, she discovered underneath it a heavy envelope, about six by ten inches in size, crammed full with papers. She looked at it and found written on it in Mr. C.'s large lettering: THIS IS NOT TO BE OPENED UNTIL I AM DEAD. I MEAN GOOD AND DEAD. DADDY.

She showed the envelope to her daughter Agnes, but put it back since she did not wish to enter into any kind of controversy with her husband. Evidently the envelope must have been taken by him to his office sometime later, for when she again made his bed two weeks before his passing, when he was still walking around, she found it gone. But there was a second, smaller envelope there, this one not particularly marked or inscribed. She left it there. A short time later Mr. C. was taken to the hospital. When Mrs. C. made the bed she found that the small envelope had also disappeared.

While the C.'s house in Columbus was not exactly a public place, neither was it an impregnable fortress, and anyone wishing to do so could have walked in at various times and quickly removed the envelope. As far as the office was concerned, that was even easier to enter and the family had no doubt whatever that Madeline took both envelopes for reasons best known to herself, although they could not actually prove any of it. At no time did the old gent say an unkind word about his Madeline, at least not to his children, preferring perhaps to take his troubles with him into the Great Beyond.

After his death, which came rather suddenly, the family found a proper will, but as Mr. C. had generously built homes for most of his children during his lifetime, in the 1950s, there was only a modest amount of cash in the bank accounts, and no great inheritance for anyone.

The will named Mrs. C. as executor, and as there was nothing to contest, it was duly probated. But the family did search the office and the late Mr. C.'s effects at the house for these two envelopes that were still missing. Only the wife and daughter Agnes knew of them, even though "nobody and everybody" had access to the house. The servants would not have taken them, and the safe was empty. As the old gent had occasionally slept in his office on a couch, the family looked high and low in his office but with negative results. The only thing that turned up in addition to the will itself was the neatly typed manuscript of a book of Biblical quotations. Mr. C. had been a serious Bible scholar, despite his uneducated status, and the quotes arranged by subject matter and source represented many thousands of hours of work. When his daughter Marie had seen him working on this project in 1962, she had suggested he have the scribbled notes typed up and she had prevailed upon her Aunt Catherine to undertake the job, which the latter did. Somewhat forlornly, Marie picked up the manuscript and wondered whether someone might not buy it and put a little cash into the estate *that* way.

The mystery of the disappearing envelopes was never solved. Even greater than the puzzle of their disappearance was the question about their content: What was in

The Phantom Grandfather

them that was so important that the old gent had to hide them under the mattress? So important that someone took them secretly and kept them from being turned over to the family, as they should have been?

Although there is no evidence whatever for this contention, Marie thinks there might have been some valuables left to Grover C.'s love child, the one he had with the lady from Alabama early in his romantic life.

At any rate, after several months of fruitless searches, the family let the matter rest and turned to other things. Grover C. would have gone on to his just reward, especially in the minds of his family, if it weren't for the matter of some peculiar, unfinished business.

About a year after Grover's death, Lewis C., one of the sons of the deceased, as they say in the police records, was busy building a brick flower planter in his home in Columbus. This was one of the houses his father had erected for his children, and Mr. C., the son, had been living in it happily without the slightest disturbance. Lewis was thirty years old and the mystery of his father's disappearing envelopes did not concern him very much at this point. Here he was, at four o'clock in the afternoon, on a brisk March day in 1967, working on his planter. Giving him a hand with it, and handing him one brick after another, was a professional bricklayer by the name of Fred, with whom he had worked before. They were in the living room and Lewis was facing the back door, Fred the front door.

"A brick, please" said Lewis, without turning around.

No brick came. He asked again. Still no brick. He then looked up at his helper and saw him frozen to the spot, gazing at the front door.

137

"What's the matter, Fred?" he inquired. He had never seen Fred so frightened.

Finally, as if awakening from a bad dream, Fred spoke. "I've just seen Mr. C.," he said, "big as life."

"But Mr. C. has been dead for a year," the son replied. Fred had worked for Grover for many years and he knew him well.

"What did he look like?" the son inquired.

"White . . . light," Fred replied and then went on to describe the figure in white pants he had seen at the door. Although it was only the bottom half of a man, he had instantly recognized his late employer. Grover was bowlegged and the white pants facing him surely were as bowlegged as old Grover had been. There was no doubt about whose lower half it was that had appeared and then gone up in a puff again.

Lewis shook his head and went on with his work. But a short time later he began to appreciate what Fred had experienced. In the middle of the night he found himself suddenly awake by reason of something in the atmosphere—undefinable, but still very real.

The lights in his bedroom were off, but he could see down the hallway. And what he saw was a man wearing a white shirt, dark pants . . . and . . . with no head. The headless gentleman was tiptoeing down the hallway toward him.

Lewis could only stare at the apparition, which he instantly recognized as his late father, head or no head. When the ghost saw that Lewis recognized him, he took three leaps backward and disappeared into thin air.

Unfortunately, Catherine, Lewis's wife, did not believe a word of it. For several months the subject of Father's headless ghost could not be mentioned in conversation.

The Phantom Grandfather

Then in December 1968 Lewis and Catherine were asleep one night, when at about 2:30 A.M. they were both roused by the sound of heavy footsteps walking down the hall from the bedrooms toward the living room. As they sat up and listened with nary a heartbeat, they could clearly hear how the steps first hit the bare floor and then the carpet, sounding more muffled as they did. Finally, they resounded louder again as they reached the kitchen floor. Lewis jumped out of bed, ready to fight what he was sure must be an intruder. Although he looked the house over from top to bottom he found no trace of a burglar, and all the doors were locked.

In retrospect they decided it was probably Grover paying them a visit. But why? True, he had built them the house. True, they had some of his effects, especially his old pajamas. But what would he want with his old pajamas where he *now* was? Surely he could not be upset by the fact that his son was wearing them. They decided then that Grover was most likely trying to get their attention because of those envelopes that were still missing or some other unfinished business, but they didn't like it, for who would like one's headless father popping in in the middle of the night?

But apparently Grover did not restrict his nocturnal visits to his son Lewis's place. His granddaughter Marie, who lived in Atlanta, had come to visit at her grandfather's house in the spring of 1968. The house had no city water but used water from its own well system. It was therefore necessary to carry water into the house from outside. On one such occasion, when she had just done this and was returning with an *empty* basin, Marie

139

stepped into what looked like a puddle of water. She started to mop up the puddle only to find that the spot was actually totally dry. Moreover, the puddle was ice cold, while the water basin she had just carried was still hot. She found this most unusual but did not tell anyone about it. Within a matter of hours eight-year-old Randy reported seeing a man in a dark suit in the bathroom, when the bathroom was obviously empty.

Apparently the old gent liked children, for little Joel was playing the piano in his Atlanta home in February 1969 when he heard the sound of shuffling feet approach. Then there was the tinkling of glasses and all this time no one was visible. Grover had always liked a drink and a little music.

Soon Marie began to smell carnations in her house when no one was wearing them or using any perfume. The aroma lingered for a moment and then disappeared, as if someone wearing this scent was just passing through the house.

In 1967, her Aunt Mary came to visit her in Atlanta and the conversation turned to the mysterious scent. "I'm glad you mentioned this," the aunt exclaimed, and reported a similar problem: Both she and her husband would smell the same scent repeatedly in their own house, sometimes so strongly they had to leave the house and go out for some fresh air. But the scent followed them, and on one occasion "sat" with them in their car on the way to church on Sunday morning!

They weren't too sure whether it was more like carnations or just a funeral smell, but it surely was a smell that had no rational explanation. Then in 1968, Mary informed her niece that a new perfume had suddenly been

140

added to their list of phenomena: This one was a spicy scent, like a man's aftershave lotion.

Not long after this report, Marie smelled the same sharp men's perfume in her own house in Atlanta, in her den. This was particularly upsetting, because they had shut off that room for the winter and no perfume or anyone wearing it had been in it for months.

In 1969, she had occasion to visit her grandfather's house in Columbus once again. She found herself wandering into her late grandfather's old bedroom. She stopped at his dresser and opened the drawer. There she found her spicy scent: a bottle of Avon hair lotion he had used. None of her husband's eau de cologne bottles had a similar smell. This was it. But how had it traveled all the way to Atlanta? Unless, of course, Grover was wearing it.

Marie was upset by her grandfather's insistence on continuing to visit his kinfolk and not staying in the cemetery as respectable folk are supposed to do, at least according to the traditional view of the dead. But evidently Grover was far from finished with this life, and judging from the lively existence he had led prior to his unexpected departure from this vale of tears, he had a lot of energy left over.

That, combined with a genuine grievance over unfinished business—especially the missing two envelopes—must have been the cause for his peripatetic visits. Marie decided not to wait for the next one, and went to see a card reader in Columbus. The card reader could tell her only that she had a restless grandfather who wished her well.

Unfortunately, even if the cause for Grover's continued presence could be ascertained, there was no way in which the missing envelopes could be legally recovered.

Marie tried, in vain, to get a local psychic to make contact with her grandfather. Finally, she turned her attention to the manuscript of Bible quotes. Perhaps it was the book he wanted to see published.

Whatever it was, she must have done the right thing, or perhaps all that talk about the headless grandfather had pleased the old gent's ego enough to pry him loose from the earth plane. At any rate, no further appearances have been reported and it may well be that he has forgotten about those envelopes by now, what with the attractions of his new world absorbing his interest.

Unless, of course, he is merely resting and gathering strength!

14

The Ghost of the British Spy

Spy drops, or secret meeting places where spies may meet and more or less freely exchange information—for which of course they are highly paid—must exist in quite a number in Washington, D.C. But how many of them are ghostly spy drops? Not one of them, I'd wager—except, of course, possibly the one in Arlington I know about.

It all started when Ruth Montgomery, a journalist for the Hearst syndicate and then still officially a skeptic in matters psychic, called my attention to a friend's plight. Would I please help and look into the matter of a haunting in suburban Arlington? This particular friend was a rather important man and a little nervous about the wrong kind of publicity.

I can be the soul of discretion when properly asked, and I assured Ruth that I would do everything in my power to prevent information about the investigation she asked me to undertake from leaking to the press, at least in such a manner that it would hurt anyone's standing in a community.

The gentleman in question was Bob Gray, an official with a large advertising agency who worked out of Washington, D.C. Until recently he had been in government. In fact, he was Secretary to the Cabinet in the Eisenhower administration. I was somewhat surprised by a column in which Ruth Montgomery heralded my coming to Washington to look into the matter of Bob Gray's haunted house. I am quite sure that Sybil Leek, my English friend who had then just begun to work with me as a medium, had never read that particular column. For one thing, newly arrived in this country, she was not aware of the identity of Ruth Montgomery, nor was she in the habit of picking up local newspapers and reading gossip columns.

Later I questioned Sybil about it—even showed her the column in question—and was assured that she had never seen it or been told about it. I have no reason to doubt Sybil's honesty and, under the circumstances, am confident that the little that Ruth Montgomery did publish about the case never reached Sybil Leek's knowledge.

Here is Ruth Montgomery's own summation of what had happened until May 1965 that had caused Bob Gray to seek my help:

Bob bought the rambling house on a wooded hillside three years ago, from a foreign official who seemed so re-

144

The Ghost of the British Spy

luctant to give possession that it took Gray six months to get him out. Almost immediately afterwards, neighbors began calling to tell him that the house was haunted, and to report rumors of a secret panel within.

Gray, a leader in the Eisenhower "Great Crusade," merely scoffed, but while doing some yard work he discovered a mysterious tunnel leading from the hillside to a bedroom on the ground floor. It divided into two passageways, and several empty cement sacks were found inside.

When the new owner got around to painting the walls of the bedroom he says he distinctly heard his name called twice, but no earthly visitors were present. Fearing that his driveway might cave into the tunnels, he prosaically had them filled in with cement.

Shortly afterwards he agreed to keep a big dog belonging to the widow of Chicago Tribune *publisher, Robert R. McCormick, while she went abroad. To his chagrin, Gray was awakened every 4:00 A.M. by the barking of the dog in a corner of the library.*

The dog eventually returned home, and gave up his 4:00 A.M. barking. Eerie happenings continued, however, at Gray's residence. In the middle of the night he heard music coming from the living room, and on going downstairs to investigate he discovered that the player piano had turned itself on.

He mentioned it a few evenings later; and immediately after a guest proclaimed that he did not believe in ghosts "a thirty-mile-an-hour wind whooshed through the closed room," according to Gray and his friends.

At a recent dinner party Bob again spoke of the alleged haunting, the mysterious panel which had not come to light, and the dog's nocturnal barking in the same spot

145

each night. One of the women slipped into the library, and in a few minutes excitedly shouted that she had "found it."

The other guests sprinted into the room, and there it was. By removing books and pushing on a panel that looked like all the others, an aperture to a closet appeared. Behind it was a five-foot-high block of cement to bar whatever lay on the other side. An architect who came to inspect the secret closet said the cement had obviously been spread by an amateur.

As no one was paying us to come down and look into the matter, I had to wait until I was sent down to publicize one of my books. The date was June 15, 1965, and Sybil Leek and I had rooms at the Washington Hilton Hotel. Even if Sybil had no knowledge of this column, apparently the Washington newspaper fraternity did indeed. During our stay, we learned to our surprise that everyone in Washington knew about our coming to look into a haunted house. Fortunately, I was always present when the question, "Where are you going to go to look for a ghost?" was asked. In one or two cases, I was able to prevent the name of Bob Gray being mentioned in front of Sybil. This was not as difficult as it seems since I never left her side during the interviews.

When the newspapermen had left, I breathed a little easier. Sybil was still in the dark about the whole thing. She knew we had come down to look into a haunted house, but she knew nothing further. For that matter, neither did the newspapermen, except for what Ruth Montgomery had prematurely disclosed in her column.

Immediately after our arrival I had telephoned Ruth and received exact instructions on how to get to the

146

house in Arlington. That very evening we drove out in a taxicab, almost got lost en route, and when we finally arrived at the house, we realized why it was so difficult to find. Situated in the most expensive section of Arlington, the house was located on a secluded hillside and was surrounded by trees and bushes. The nearest house was visible, but there must have been considerable privacy at all times for those in the Grays' house. On first inspection, the house itself appeared perhaps forty or fifty years old and seemed solid and somewhat imitative of European country houses.

Apparently we were the last ones to arrive, for I noticed several cars parked about the front and back entrances. At the door we were greeted by Bob Gray and Ruth Montgomery, and after an exchange of polite greetings, we were led into the living room on the ground floor of the house. There we met another five or six people, including Arthur Ford, who had come as an observer and not in his capacity as a renowned medium. He and Ruth Montgomery had been friends for years, and she had invited him to witness the investigation.

I decided first to let Sybil look around the place and to stay close to her, at the same time requesting that no one talk to her or say anything about the experiences they might have had in the house. Afterward, we returned to the living room, and Sybil sat down in a comfortable large chair in the middle of the room, with me in a chair next to her and the others loosely grouped around. There was expectation in the air, for Ruth Montgomery had assured Bob Gray that Sybil Leek and I would surely get to the heart of the matter.

I knew from experience that Sybil would at first give me her clairvoyant impressions about the house before going into full trance. There was, incidentally, nothing about the house or the room we were in that was in the slightest bit disturbing or eerie. It seemed a pleasant, relaxed atmosphere, and if I had not known that there was something strange about the house, I would have taken it for just another suburban residence.

I tapped Sybil on the hand and looked at her expectantly. "Sybil, do you feel anything in the atmosphere of this downstairs room that seems out of the ordinary?"

"Not particularly in this room. I feel it much more in the region of the doorway as you come in the house—I think that must be the front door—and at the room on the right as you come in. That gives me a much stronger atmosphere."

"Is there any disturbed feeling in this room we are in now?"

"I am disturbed now, but I'm more disturbed since I went in the other room."

"What is it that seems to disturb you?"

"Something very restless, and also very excited."

"Man or woman?"

"Well, I don't know. I just know there's something very restless that has probably been here for some time. I don't really think it's too long. But something very, very restless, and inclined to be *noisy.*"

"And you don't know what it wants?"

"No, I don't know what it wants."

"All right, let us try and see whether we can get it to make contact directly."

"Who are you?" I said as soon as Sybil was entranced.

"Peter Ellis."

The Ghost of the British Spy

The voice, very masculine and not at all like Sybil's own, was very British.

"Is this your house?"

"No."

"Do you live here?"

"No."

"What are you doing here?"

"Hiding."

"Why are you hiding?"

"I have to get something. Something from the girl."

"Who is the girl? What's her name?"

"Marilyn."

"Marilyn what?"

"Wade."

"Marilyn Wade? Does she live here?"

In an almost indistinguishable voice, the entranced medium mentioned "some children living here." Evidently Marilyn had some working connection with those children.

"Whose children are they?"

"Wassir's."

"Does he live in the house?"

"Lives here."

"Who owns the house?"

"DeVasser."

"Can I help you in any way?"

"Find the papers."

"Well if you don't tell me anything about them, how will I recognize them?"

"They're here. She said they were here."

"Who said? What has Marilyn got to do with the papers?"

"She wrote part of them."

149

"For whom?"

"For me."

"What is in the papers?"

"I don't know."

"Who gave you the papers?"

"Lord Case."

"Lord Keyes?" The British pronunciation of the name would sound as if spelled "Case," I realized.

"Case. Case. Case."

"Did you work for him?"

"Don't ask questions. . . ."

"Did you work for Lord Keyes?"

"Yes."

"In what capacity?"

"I'm not answering questions."

"Is he alive?"

"No."

"What were the papers concerned with?"

"I don't know."

"What profession do you have?"

"I am a grayhound."

"You're a *what?*"

"Grayhound."

"Grayhound? What does that mean?"

"Find out."

"How long are you in this house now?"

"Three weeks."

"What date did you come here?"

"May twenty-six."

"What year?"

"Nineteen thirty-five."

"Nineteen thirty-five. Did anything happen to you in this house?"

"I—I got—I got lost."

"You got lost? In which way did you get lost?"

"I—I don't know. I got confused."

"Whom did you meet outside of Marilyn? Did you meet anyone else in this house?"

"DeVasser."

"Would you spell that name for me?"

"D-E-V-A-S-S-E-R."

"Devasser?"

"Yes."

"What did you do with him? What was the reason for meeting this person?"

"I shan't tell you."

"You must tell me if I am to help you."

"Find the papers."

"If you will tell me why, I can help you; not any other way."

"She is not to be helped."

"Who are the papers for?"

"Everyham."

"Who is he?"

"He was here."

"Repeat that name."

"Ev-ry-ham."

"Abraham?"

"No. I, not A."

"Ibraham? Ebrehem?"

"Ebreham."

"Where does he live?"

"I don't know."

"Did you meet him?"

"Yes."

"Here in this house?"

"Upstairs."

"And what happened during your meeting?"

"I—nearly—hit him."

"Why did you nearly hit him?"

"He was not a gentleman."

"In which way was he not a gentleman?"

"He lost his temper."

"Why did he lose his temper?"

"Because he asked questions, and I didn't answer."

"What did he want to know of you?"

"Questions like you."

"About the papers?"

"Yes."

"And why couldn't you tell him?"

"I'm a grayhound."

"You are a grayhound. For which government?"

"British."

"Did anyone hurt you in this house?"

"Yes."

"Who?"

"Ebreham."

"Who does he work for?"

"Why do you ask?"

"Because I'd like to help you. I'm on your side, remember? I've come a long way to help you. Now I'm here; that is proof enough that I'm on your side, is it not?"

"No."

"You're speaking to me and I'm listening. What would you like us to do?"

"Find the papers."

"Well, where would I find them?"

"Where the hell is Marilyn?"

"Are they in this house?"

"Yes."

"Are they hidden in this house?"

"Yes."

"Where are they hidden?"

"In the wall."

"In the wall?"

Suddenly the voice grew angry and desperate. "No . . . I'm not telling you."

"I'm on *your* side, my friend. I will help you carry out your plans. You have my word of honor."

"I'll get them myself."

"You cannot. You are not what you used to be. Something has happened to you."

"Go away!"

"Then you'll be alone again, and it will be many, many years before anyone will find you. Tell me, is there anything in the wall?"

"I'm not telling you if he kills me."

"No one is going to touch you. I will protect you."

"Oh?" A dog barks faintly in the background. "The dog."

"What about the dog? . . . What about the dog? Is there anything about the dog you want to tell me?"

"No—no—no." Agitated breathing.

"Tell me, why are you upset? Why are you upset? I'm here to help you. You've been hurt."

"Let me go outside."

"I'll help you. Do you want to stay in this house or do you wish to leave?"

"I want to go outside."

"What would you do outside?"

"Get some air."

"Is there an errand you wish to make outside?"

"Yes. Yes."

"Can I make it for you?"

"I want some—air."

"Why do you want some air? Has someone hurt you?"

"Breathe."

"Tell me, what is there downstairs? What is downstairs in this house?"

"He sleeps there."

"Who does sleep there?"

"Ebreham."

"Then why does he sleep there? What does he do in this house?"

"Works and works and works."

"What is his profession, his work? What does he do?"

"Steals papers." The voice had a tinge of sarcasm now mixed in with the anguish and bitterness.

"How did he get into this house?"

"Visited."

"Did you see him visit?"

"Yes."

"What were you doing here?"

"Watching."

"Watching what?"

"People lying—"

"Who were you watching?"

"Ebreham."

"What is in those papers?"

"Don't ask."

"I have to ask if I am to help you."

"I shan't tell you."

"Do you realize that this house is no longer in the same hands? That time has gone on?"

"Time?"

"What year do you think this is?"

" 'Thirty-five."

"No. This is 'sixty-five."

" 'Sixty-five?"

"Nineteen sixty-five."

"No."

"Yes. You have been asleep for a long time; you have been ill; something has happened to you. Do you understand? That is why you are confused."

"I'm confused." The voice sounded very tired now.

"Someone hurt you. Now you must tell us exactly who hurt you and what happened, and we will be able to help you. Do you understand? It is thirty years since 1935. You have—what is commonly called—'died.' You are no longer in the flesh. It is your mind that speaks to us. Do you understand that? There has been a change. It is your memory that keeps you in this house, but you are in no danger. No one can hurt you ever again. We are your friends. We have come to help you find peace. Now you must tell us what you want done."

"The papers."

"Whom do you wish to have them delivered to?"

"Keyes."

"Keyes? Is it 'Keyes,' a name, or do you mean the keys?"

"Lord Keyes."

"Lord Keyes. Is he your—employer?"

"Room 1216."

"Room 1216—where?"

"In London."

"Where in London? Where?"

"Admiralty."

"Admiralty?"

"London."

"London. You want the papers delivered in London? But Lord Keyes is dead, too. He's gone. You need not keep your secret any longer."

"Has he died?" Genuine surprise filled the voice now.

"You are free to divulge your secret now. Thirty years have gone on; you are free to speak."

"I'm a grayhound. You don't understand."

"Then how can we locate these papers if we don't know where to look?"

"I can't find them either. So I'll keep on looking."

"Tell me, what is this house like? Is there anything underneath this house that is unusual?"

"I could hide outside if you'll take me out."

"How would you get out from this house?"

"I won't tell you. I've been hidden and I want to go back. There's not much room."

"There's not much room *where?* Where are you hiding?"

"Outside."

"Where outside?"

"Why do you want to know?"

"So I can help you."

"How?"

"Protect you."

"Too late."

"Don't you want to be helped?"

"It's too late."

"Why is it too late?"

"Something's gone wrong."

"What has gone wrong?"

"I don't know."

"Can you guess what has gone wrong?"

The Ghost of the British Spy

"No."

"Did someone kill you?"

"What's 'kill you'?"

"Has someone killed you? Taken your life?"

"Yes. Hit me."

"Someone hit you? Who hit you?"

"Ebreham."

"Did he take the papers from you?"

"No. Some of them."

"Where did he hit you? What part of the house?"

"By the fire."

"Upstairs or downstairs?"

"Downstairs. By the door."

"And then what did he do with you?"

"I fell asleep."

"Yes. You fell asleep. And then what happened?"

"Then I came back to find the papers."

"Did you find them?"

"But my head's bad."

"And then what happened?"

"She said she'd let me in."

"Who let you in?"

"Marilyn."

"What did she do in this house? What was her position?"

"She was looking after the children."

"Did she know you?"

"Yes."

"So she let you in. What did she do then?"

"No, she didn't let me in."

"Why didn't she let you in?"

"She wasn't faithful. She played."

"Did she see you?"

157

"She knew I was there. She played, and I knew it was wrong."

"What was wrong?"

"That she played. She wasn't safe."

"What did she play?"

"She played 'Moonlight and Roses.'"

"On what instrument?"

"A piano."

"What happened after that?"

"She played, but I came in."

Evidently Marilyn's playing the song was a prearranged signal.

"Where did you go?"

"I went to his bedroom."

"Whose bedroom?"

"Ebreham."

"All right, you went to his bedroom. What happened then?"

"We talked. And then we came to the door and then we went to the fireplace. And then I made him angry."

"What did you make him angry with?"

"About half the papers."

"You mean you had half the papers? Or did he have them?"

"He had half."

"Who had the other half?"

"I did."

"And you didn't want to give him the other half?"

"No."

"Where was the other half?"

"Marilyn hid them."

"Where did she hide them?"

"In the house."

The Ghost of the British Spy

"Where in the house?"

"I don't know. She was going to tell me, and *then I went to sleep.*"

"And she never told you? What did *he* do with *his* half of the papers? . . . Can you hear me? Can you hear my voice? Can you hear my voice?"

But apparently the "grayhound" had slipped away. Still, I needed more information. I decided to let Sybil look for it.

"Sybil," I suggested, *"stay on your side* of the veil and before you awaken, answer me. Is there anything about this house that involves violence of any kind?"

"Yes."

"Can you tell me what you feel?"

"Very confused. Two people—two people tried to come through."

"Who are they?"

"A man and a woman. I can see the man. I can't see the woman."

"Did he die in this house?"

"He was hurt. I think he died outside."

"Why was he hurt?"

"Let me look around. . . . I don't like this place."

"Why don't you like this place?"

"It has got so many people coming and going."

"What is going on in this place that is unusual?"

"People come for a little while, and then they go away. They leave very bad vibrations."

"What sort of business is going on in this place?"

"Business."

"What sort of business? What are they doing here, these people? What is their business in coming here?"

"I don't know. It's some exchange."

159

"Exchange of what?"

"Of—books, or something like that."

"Books. Is there anything underneath this house that needs explanation? Is there anything unusual about the structure of this house?"

"He hid there."

"You mean after he was killed?"

"No, before he was killed—and after."

"And whom did he hide from?"

"A man in the bedroom."

"Why did he hide from him?"

"I think he was watching him."

"Whom was he watching him for, and why?"

"I don't know."

"Do you know what is in those papers that he seems to have told me about?"

"He wants the papers, but I don't—"

"What is *in* the papers?"

"The papers are in the book room."

"The book room? Are they in a book?"

"Behind a book."

"Are they still there?"

"Deep down, though."

"Deep down?"

"Deep down; not where you'd put your hand on them. You have to—"

I had to change tapes at this moment and the entranced Sybil mentioned something about "a wall."

"What do you mean a wall?" I continued my line of questioning.

"There're *two* walls."

"And what is in back of those two walls?"

"A cavity."

"What is in back of the cavity?"
"Another wall."
"What is the cavity for?"
"Books and papers, and that sort of thing. I can't see; hard . . ."
"Try."
"I can't get in very well."
"Try again."
"This is so dusty."
"But it is still there now, is it?"
"Still there, but it's dusty, and the dust comes into my throat."
"What sort of dust?"
"Thick dust, like flour."
"Is there anything behind those two walls?"
"Papers."
"Outside of the papers, what else is there?"
"I can't see because the wall goes on."
"Where does it lead to?"
"Wait a minute, don't rush me."
"All right, take your time."
"He came this way."
"He came this way? From where?"
"From the woods."
"Who came this way, the man who was killed?"
"Peter. This is where he hid. How can I prove he was not? I'm in the house; and now I'm out. What's in between? There's something in between."
"All right, let us say there's something in between that wasn't always there. But try to see what there is now, at this moment, behind the wall. Papers and what else?"
"Papers."
"Is there anything else there?"

"It's deep. I can only see papers. I don't like going outside. I'm not going outside."

"Is there a man or a woman behind there—?"

"I'm not going outside."

"Is there a body in there?"

"I'm not going outside." The voice sounded positively agitated now.

"Why don't you want to go outside? Why are you afraid?"

"I'm not afraid."

"Well, why is it that you don't like going outside? Is it you, or do you feel this man who doesn't wish to go outside?"

"He had to go outside, but I don't."

"Well then, stay inside and tell us what you see in the cavity. What you call the cavity."

"He's still there."

"Who is?"

"That man."

"He is still there?"

"You said you'd do something about it. Don't leave him there."

"We have no intention of leaving him there. Is he there alone?"

"Yes. You shouldn't leave anyone there."

"Would you tell this man, Peter, that there's no reason for him to stay in this house; that his mission has been accomplished and he may leave."

"He's not in the house."

"Where do you sense him?"

"He's outside."

"Is he free to go?"

"He comes in. Now, let me go."

"All right. Is there anything else you want to tell me?"

"I want to go. I don't like this room. I don't like that wall."

"What is in the papers. Look at the papers. What is in those papers? Quick, look."

"If I look you'll come?"

"Yes. You must look. What are the papers about?"

"Ships."

"Ships? What sort of ships?"

"I don't know."

"Go and look at the papers and report back to me what you see."

"I can't read the writing; they're handwritten, not typed, and it's very difficult to read."

"Can you read any of it? Can you read the signatures?"

"The signature is King KR. . . ."

"King?"

"Royalty . . . R-O something . . . R-O-G-"

"R-O-G?"

"Eight papers."

"What do they concern themselves with?"

"I can't see. The writing is big, and I can't read them very well."

"Is there anything printed on top of the pages that you can easily read?"

"It's written."

"Nothing official, no seal, no printing?"

"Seal."

"Whose seal is it?"

"R.K."

"What language are they in?"

"English."

"Look at the first line of some of the papers and see who they are addressed to."

"Just wait a minute. . . . They're not letters."

"What are they?"

"Ah—about some ship business."

"Specifically, what sort of ship business?"

"I think it's some naval thing. I can't read this writing."

"Can you make out any words at all? Try."

"Make out Devasser. D-E-V-A-S-S-E-R."

"Who is Devasser?"

"He is an Admiral."

"All right, I will call you back."

"I *hate* things in walls. Two walls. Who wants two walls?"

"What should we do with those walls?"

"I would take them away. But don't let *him* know."

"Don't let who know?"

"Peter."

"Peter? But he's not there anymore."

"Oh yes he is."

"If we open those walls, would we find his body?"

"Body. He's there."

"With those papers?"

"Not with the papers!"

"But you said they were there, too."

"Papers in the house."

"Where in the house?"

"In there. Behind the books; behind the wall. Behind *another* wall. And then there's another wall. And *he's outside.*"

"But his body is in that cavity, is it?"

"His body is *outside.*"

"Where outside?"

"From the paper you go through the drains."

"The drains. And in there?"

"To the woods."

"To the woods?"

"Where he is hiding."

"Where will we find the body, exactly?"

"I'm *not* going to go down that drain."

"I don't want you to go down the drain, but *look.*"

"I am *not* going down that drain. I'm in the place where the books are, and there's a big slope. A big slope. And then there's a straight piece to some trees; three trees and you dig in there."

"Near the trees?"

"In the trees!"

"You mean underneath?"

"There's a long tunnel."

"Long tunnel."

"It's a drain or something. I don't know."

"And that is where he is?"

"That's where he is, poor man."

"All right, Sybil. I want you to come away from this wall. Come back to your own body, to the present."

But Sybil was still fascinated by the past. "Who put the wall there? Why did he have *three* walls?"

"Never mind, don't worry about it. Come back."

And back she came, waking up, rubbing her eyes, and remembering absolutely nothing of the past hour. Everyone was very quiet, still under the impact of what they had heard. I decided to question Bob Gray about his experiences now.

*   *   *

"Would you bring me up to date on what you *personally* have experienced in this house that you might classify as unusual?"

"Shortly after coming into the house," Bob Gray began, "I was fixing up one of the rooms, and thought I heard my name called. There was no one else around at that particular time. One other evening, in the middle of the night, *the player piano began to play.* But it is electric and plays on a switch."

"What did it play? Did you recognize the tune?"

"Whatever the roll that was on the piano, it finished the roll and automatically shut itself off."

"Can the piano be played manually, too?"

"Oh yes."

"Go on."

"One evening a group of us were talking about ghosts and someone said they didn't believe in ghosts, and *a wind went whistling through the room.* We checked, and on the lowest level of the house a door which is never opened—it has an air conditioner in the door and a dehumidifier in front of it and a latch on it—was nevertheless *fully open.*"

"By itself, somehow?"

"By itself."

"Is there anything unusual about the structure of the house?"

"Well, it roams all over the countryside a little. It's been added to and added to, that's the only thing that's unusual."

"Is there anything unusual about the library?"

"Well, there is this panel in the wall."

"Tell me about the panel, and how it was found."

"Well, it was found just very recently."

"How long ago did you get the house?"

"Two and a half years."

"And when did you get to the panel?"

"I *got* to the panel just three months ago but had the *idea* shortly after I came to the house. A woman who had lived here at one time stopped by and wanted me to identify the location of the panel. She said she'd been told by the owner at the time of her tenancy here that there was a panel, but he didn't want to tell her where the panel was unless she *bought* the house. She was curious to know if there were one and where it was. I denied its existence, not having located it at that point. I was telling this story one night at a party some months ago. One of the couples went up to the library and the girl just went right to the wall and started pulling books away and discovered the panel."

"This girl—was she any way psychic or unusual?"

"Not to my knowledge, but she said later that she felt she knew right where it was."

"What did it look like?"

"It was wide enough to be a *passage*, and the passageway itself was blocked with a piece of concrete; maybe twenty-five inches wide and thirty inches long."

"Did you try to remove the cement?"

"No."

"Did you have any desire to see what was in back of that?"

"A curiosity that didn't match the desire to tear the wall apart."

"Is there anything underneath the house, or outside the house, that you found that was unusual for a dwelling of this kind?"

"Well—at the time we first came into the house, there

was a passageway, or cave, tunnel, call it what you will, leading from one of the bedrooms out into the hillside. It went back about fifteen feet and then branched off in a T. It was shored up by four-by-fours on the side, but with very thin boards on the top; and dirt and water was trickling down through these broken boards at the top. I was afraid to have anyone go in, and I simply had a man come with a claw digger and pull the dirt away and clear the top away and fill it in. It took a couple of loads before it stopped settling, and *that was the end of the tunnel.*"

"Were the tunnels high enough for a man to go through?"

"Yes, from the room side. It was only about four feet above the floor level, but if you stepped across down into the tunnel itself it was about seven feet tall. It was quite tall."

"So one could use it as an escape hatch?"

"One could. This was obviously—to my eye at least—a very recent construction, and the tenant—the colonel—a Canadian Air Force colonel, who had had the house before me, had admitted later that he had built the tunnel. He said he did it because President Kennedy had told him to build an air-raid shelter."

"How long had the colonel been in this house?"

"Around three years."

"Did any of the previous tenants, before the colonel, talk about the tunnels?"

"No. The only previous tenant I've ever talked to was the woman who stopped by and wanted to know where the passageway was, or the panel."

"You have no idea how old the house is, then?"

"No. It's thirty years or so."

"Can you recognize the spot described by Sybil in

trance as the likely spot—the trees—where one might find the body?"

"No, the place is surrounded with trees, and I have no idea where any group of trees is."

"At the end of the tunnel, I believe."

"Well, this particular tunnel I've described to you is one that went toward the drive rather than toward trees in any area. In fact, one of the reasons that prompted me to have it filled in so quickly was that I was afraid the drive would collapse."

"Are there other tunnels going in other directions?"

"There may be, but I don't know of any."

"Have you lived in Washington a long time?"

"Eight years."

A close associate of Bob Gray's, who has lived at the house for a long time also, then requested to be heard. "I heard some noises," the gentleman said gravely, "last winter."

"What exactly did you hear?"

"I heard something that could have passed as a knock or a rattling at the door. I went to the door and though there was fresh snow outside there were *no tracks.*"

"Was this the door upstairs, or downstairs?"

"Actually, I went to each of the doors, because I thought that it was someone at the door."

"Did anyone else outside yourself hear those noises?"

"Yes, one other in the house."

"Another gentleman in the house."

"Yes."

"You have a lovely dog. What is his name?"

"Well, his name is so *distinctive* I'd like to skip that."

"All right, all right. Doggie then. Did Doggie have any unusual experiences in this house?"

169

"Yes—as a matter of fact the dog is only here on loan; he's not mine. But the last time I had him here was for a matter of ten days or so, while his owner was away. Every night, at exactly the same time, around four o'clock in the morning, the dog would start barking. Really barking up quite a storm. Always against the wall down here, just against the living room wall."

"In this room?"

"Yes. Rather than against, or at, a door. He would always be *barking at the wall.*"

"Is the wall in any way connected with the panel?"

"It's on the other side of the panel area."

I thanked the young man, who preferred that his name be withheld for personal reasons.

Ruth Montgomery, the columnist for the Hearst papers who was then already very much interested in psychic research even though she had not yet written her books along those lines, looked up with a serious expression. I asked her who knew enough about Washington to be able to fill us in on the background of this house, and with her help, and that of others in the room, I was able to piece together a most unusual account.

The house had been built about thirty years before by a man named Smith who had been working with the OSS, the Office of Strategic Services. That agency was the forerunner of the CIA, a kind of secret super-spy agency of the United States Government. He was a man of taste, who collected artistic glass with a vengeance. Ostensibly to enrich his collection, he traveled around the world, although in reality he was gathering information for the OSS.

The song that had been the signal for the spy to come

in out of the damp was still on the old player piano roll. With a nervous laugh, Bob Gray switched it on and the roll played "Moonlight and Roses" exactly as it had back in the 1930s when "the grayhound" had met his doom because of it.

I checked the data out with the librarian at the British Information Service in New York:

Lord Keyes died December 26, 1945. His full name was Roger John Brownlow Keyes. He had been an Admiral of the Fleet, who had retired in 1935, become a Member of Parliament until 1943, although in 1940 he returned to active duty, again with the Royal Navy.

At first his job was special liaison with the king of Belgium, and it is interesting to note that Sybil Leck mentioned the words "Royalty . . . King . . ." prior to disclosing Roger Keyes's other functions. After serving as Director of Combined Naval Operations in 1940 and 1941, he became Naval Attaché in various European capitals. That post is often used as a cover for the Naval Intelligence operative. Quite plainly, Lord Keyes was a Naval Intelligence officer, though not in America.

It is here that the spy's role becomes clear: He came from Keyes, either in his employ or on his orders, to seek out a contact in Washington. He mentioned the year 1935. Curiously, that was the year Keyes retired for the first time—to set up the intelligence service perhaps? At the time of sudden death, important dates sometimes become fixed in the mind of the victim and are remembered rather than a less impressive later date.

I still wondered about the term *grayhound*. But what I had suspected about its true meaning was confirmed by

171

REAL HAUNTINGS

A Dictionary of Slang and Unconventional English (Eric Partridge, 1938):

"GRAYHOUND: A HAMMOCK WITH LITTLE BEDDING, UNFIT FOR STORAGE IN THE NETTINGS; A NAUTICAL TERM."

Was that it? Not quite.

"OCEAN GRAYHOUND: A FAST ATLANTIC LINER."

That was it, then. The spy was a fast courier between Europe and America, truly a grayhound—quiet and fast, bent on his mission.

The missing papers, of course, were never found nor did Bob Gray make any attempt to locate the body, if there was one, in the closed-off tunnel. He was too fond of his beautiful house in the woods to start tearing down the wall just because a lowly British courier had met his death somewhere in it.

I suppose the "grayhound" isn't running anymore, either, as I have heard nothing further from either Gray or Ruth Montgomery on this. Perhaps he has met up with his employer, Lord Keyes, in the land where missing documents don't mean a thing.

15

The Restless Ghost of Oakton, Virginia

*O*akton, Virginia, is one of those very quiet suburban communities nestling fairly close to Washington, D.C., that has changed slowly but inevitably from completely rural to slightly suburban over the years. Many people who work in Washington have bought houses in this community. The houses are fairly far apart still, and the general character is one of uncrowded, rustic environment. When one drives through Oakton, one gets a rather placid, friendly feeling. None of the houses look particularly distinguished, nor do they look sinister or in any way outstanding. It takes all of forty-five minutes to get there when you leave the center of Washington, and you pass through several other villages before reaching Oakton. Thus, the community is well buffeted from the main stream of capital life, and not given to extremes of either appearance or habit.

The house we were yet to know was owned by the Ray family. Virginia Ray and her husband, Albert, had come to friends of ours, Countess Gertrude d'Amecourt and her daughter, Nicole, now Mrs. Jackson, once they heard that I was among their friends. They had seen me on television in Washington and knew of my interest in hauntings. What they had seemed to fit into that category, and it occurred to the Rays to ask whether I could have a look at their "problem."

Nicole Jackson drove us out to Oakton—by "us" I mean my ex-wife, Catherine, and myself. As yet we were not able to bring a medium along, but then I wanted to find out firsthand what exactly had happened that had disturbed the Rays to such an extent that they needed my help. After about forty-five minutes we arrived in a pleasant-looking country lane, at the end of which the house stood. The house itself was somewhat inside the grounds, and as we drove up we noticed a large barn to the left. Later on, we were to learn how important that barn was in the goings-on at the house.

Mr. and Mrs. Ray and various children and relatives had assembled to greet us. After some handshaking we were led into the downstairs parlor and made comfortable with various juices. It was a warm day for May, and the refreshments were welcome. When the excitement of our arrival had died down somewhat, I asked that those who had had experiences in the house to come nearer so I could question them. The others I requested to keep back, so I could get my bearings without interruptions.

174

The Restless Ghost of Oakton, Virginia

In a roomful of people, young and old, this is an absolute necessity.

Albert Bartow Ray was retired, and gave the impression of a man well set in his ways, happy to live in the country, and not particularly disturbed by unusual goings-on. His pleasant tone of voice, his slow way of moving about, seemed to me indicative of an average person, not in any way an occult buff or a hysterical individual likely to manufacture phenomena that did not really exist.

Virginia Ray also gave a very solid impression, and neither of the Rays was in any way frightened by what they had experienced. It was simply a matter of wanting to know what one had in one's house, and if possible of getting rid of it. But if I had not come, they would have lived on in the house—at least, in May they felt that way.

They had been in this house for about six years at the time of our visit. They liked it; they considered it a comfortable old house. They knew nothing about its history or background, except that the timbers holding up the house were old logs, and they had wooden pegs in them. Even the rafters of the roof were made of logs. This indicated that the house must have been built at least a hundred years earlier.

When I inspected the building I found it pleasant and in no way eerie. The stairs leading to the upper story were wide and the bedrooms upstairs friendly and inviting. The land upon which the house stood was fairly substantial—perhaps two or three acres or more. About the most unusual thing outside the house was the large old barn, somewhat to the left of the house, and a stone in front of the house that looked not quite natural. Upon

175

close inspection, I wondered whether perhaps it wasn't an Indian tombstone, or perhaps an Indian altar of sorts. It looked far too regular to be completely shaped by nature. The Rays had no idea how it got into their garden, nor did they know anything particular about the history of the barn. All they knew was that both barn and house were old and that a long time before this the property had indeed been Indian territory. But so was most of the land around this area, so the fact that Indians lived there before is not terribly surprising.

The Rays had bought the house in June 1962 from a family named Staton. The Statons stayed on until October of that year before the Rays moved in. After the series of events that had caused them to seek my help had happened, the Rays quite naturally made some inquiries about their house. Mrs. Ray tried to talk to neighbors about it, but it was difficult to get any concrete information. The former owner's daughter, however, allowed that certain things did happen at the house, but she would not go into details.

Even before the Rays moved into the place, however, their experiences with the uncanny began.

"I came up one day," Mr. Ray explained, "and the house was open. I locked the house up, and because the house was still vacant I would come by here two or three times a week and check it. Frank Pannell, a friend of mine who works for the county and sells real estate on the side, called me one day and he says, would I meet him someplace, he had a contract he'd like for me to read over. I told him I would be here by 4:30, so he met me here. That was in the first part of November. We walked down to the lake—there's a lake back here—we walked around and got in the house just about dark. There were two lights over this mantel that worked from a switch, and we had that light on. I was reading the contract, and he was standing here with me, when we heard *something start to walk around upstairs.* It sounded like a person. So I looked at Frank and said, 'Frank, what is that?' He said, 'It's somebody up there.' I said, 'Couldn't be, the house is locked.' He said, 'Just the same, there's someone up there." We went upstairs, but didn't see anyone and came back down again. I started to read the contract when we heard something walking around again. We went half way up the steps, when *something* seemed to walk right by our heads there. We came down here, and Frank said he could hear voices.

"The next thing that occurred was that my son, Albert Jr., and I came by here on a Friday after that, following Thanksgiving. We had had some vandalism, kids had shot some windows out with a .22 rifle. So we had decided we'd spend the night here. We brought out some camping equipment and slept in the dining room. About 8:30, he said, 'Dad, wouldn't you like a cup of coffee or something?' He took the car and drove up to Camp Washington. Well, while he was gone, I was lying here reading, with a reading light on. All of a sudden I heard something in the kitchen that sounded like somebody suffering—making all kinds of noises. I got up and walked in, turned the light on, and it stopped. We had a little fox terrier who'd bark at any noise. When the noise started again I called her and she came directly to me, but she never barked or growled as if she were afraid. I stood it as long as I could, then I got up and went into the kitchen again, but I didn't see anything. I went down to

177

the basement. I went all over the house. I went all over the yard. I went everyplace. There was no one there."

"Did it sound human?" I interjected.

"Well, sir, it sounded like somebody *moaning*. I felt the hair standing up on the back of my neck."

"And when your son came back?"

"We ate and went to sleep. I didn't tell him about the noise I'd heard. He woke me about three o'clock in the morning telling me that he had been *hearing noises*. He had heard something moaning—the same noise, apparently, that I had heard."

"Any other experiences prior to your actually moving in?" I asked. Evidently these phenomena were not dependent on a human power source to manifest.

"My married daughter, Martha, then still in college, came here one night with me to check the house. She went upstairs, while I went in this room to check the thermostat. It was extremely cold, and I wanted to make sure the furnace would cut on and cut off. Suddenly she screamed and ran down the stairs, and said, 'Daddy, *something bumped into me!*' We went up, and every time I'd take a step, she'd take a step right behind me, almost stepping on me the whole time. So we went all over the house and didn't find anything.

"A cousin named Martin was then stationed at Fort Belvoir, and he would come up over the weekend. He was having dinner with us, and we got to talking about it. He laughed and said, 'Oh I don't believe in anything like that.' So he said to my son, 'How about you and I spending the night out there? We'll show your dad he doesn't know what he's talking about.' So they came out. About three o'clock in the morning they called me from Camp Washington up here, and they were both talking over the

178

phone at the same time. I couldn't understand what they were saying, and finally I quieted them down. Martin kept saying, 'I believe it, I believe it!' I said, 'You believe *what?*' And he said, 'There's *something* in that house.' They could hear 'things' walking around, and different noises. I was living down in Sleepy Hollow then, and so I said, 'I'll meet you there.' They said, 'We won't meet you at the house. We'll meet you at the driveway.' I locked the house up. Two weeks later, a group of boys—high school boys and my son—decided to come by and spend the night. But about three o'clock in the morning, there was a pounding on the door, and when I opened the door, in burst these five boys, all excited, all of them talking at the same time. They had meant to stay overnight, but left about 2:30 in the morning. They heard a lot of noise; they heard things walking around. There was snow on the ground at the time. But when they raised the blinds to the bay window, there was a man—a big man—with a straw hat on standing outside looking in at them. They loosened the cord and the blind fell down. In a little while they got nerve enough to look out again. They could see a man standing out *at the barn.* They saw the white doors of that barn, and right in front they could see the outline of a man standing. That was too much. They ran out, got in the car, and drove away just as fast as they could. I had to come out here and lock the house up and turn all the lights out.

"That spring, 1964, there'd been termites in the house. I had a man working for me by the name of Omar Herrington. Mr. Herrington dug a trench all around the house and worked here for about four or five days. And we put chlorodane around the foundation, the house, the barn, and garage. We removed the shrubs. I came out on

179

a Friday to pay him, just about 11:30. As I drove up, he said, 'Mr. Ray, weren't you out here a little earlier? I heard you come in. I heard you walking around.' I said, 'I'm sorry, it wasn't me.' 'That's funny,' he replied. "The other day I heard something moaning like somebody in misery.'"

"Did you ever *see* anything?" I asked Ray.

"Yes, on two occasions. One night in 1965 I stayed in this room, in the downstairs part of the house, and after watching television I went to sleep on the couch. My wife went upstairs. About two o'clock in the morning, *something* woke me up. I could hear some tingling noise. It sounded like glass wind chimes. I sat up on the couch, and I could see in the corner a bunch of little lights, floating in the air. It looked like they were trying to take on the shape of something. That's the first time I really got scared. I turned the light on, and it just faded away."

"And what was the second occasion that you saw something unusual?"

"That was in the bedroom upstairs, where my wife and I sleep, two or three months later. I woke up, and I thought it was my son standing by my bed. I said, 'Bartow, what are you doing here?' There was no answer. I said it again; I could see the outline and face of a person! I turned the light on, and there wasn't anyone there. Then I got up and went to my son's room, and there he was, sound asleep."

"Did your wife see the apparition?"

"I don't think so, but she kept telling me that there was something *out in the barn*. The barn is about a hundred and fifty feet away. I'm in the construction business, and one day I was drawing up a set of plans for a private school, working on the porch.

The Restless Ghost of Oakton, Virginia

"All of a sudden, I heard a noise like tools being handled, out in the barn, as if they were being thrown all over the place! I went out and opened the door, but everything was in place. I came back three times that afternoon. I heard noise, went out, and *everything was in place.* I have three pigs, and I put them into the lower part of the barn. Mr. Herrington would come by and feed the pigs every morning. One morning he said, 'If you don't stop following me around and standing back in the shadows and not saying anything, I'm going to stop feeding those pigs.' I said, 'Well, Mr. Herrington, I have *not* been standing out here.' He said, 'I know better, you were there!'"

"In digging around the house, have you ever found anything unusual in the soil?" I asked.

Mr. Ray nodded. "Yes, I found some things—broken old pottery, and in the garden I have found something that I think may be a tombstone. It's a black rock; weather-beaten, but it was covered over with grass and the grass kept dying at that spot."

"What did you do with it?"

"I dug down to see what it was, but I left it there. I pulled the grass off, and there's a stone there, a square, cut stone."

"Did the phenomena begin after you found this stone, or was it before?"

"Oh no, it started before that. It was two or three years later that I found that stone."

"Did it make any difference, after you found the stone?"

"No, it didn't seem to. Then, when my aunt, Alberta Barber, was visiting us, she broke her ankle. I had to sleep down here on a pallet beside her couch so that if

181

she had to go to the bathroom, I could help her. One night, about one o'clock, there was a knocking on the wall, and it woke me up. She said, 'What is it?' I got up and turned the lights on, and didn't see a thing. On two occasions my wife and I were dressing to go out for the evening, when there was a loud knock on the porch door. Virginia said to me, 'Go down and see who it is.' I went down, and there wasn't a soul. One time, not too long ago, I was sleeping in the front left bedroom upstairs, and I felt something was in there; I could hear someone *breathing*. I got up and turned the light on and I didn't see anybody. This was about three o'clock. I had some papers in the car. I went out, got the papers, and slammed the car door. At that moment *something* went up the side of the storage shed. I don't know what it was."

"It went up—which way?"

"I could hear the noise, and I saw something go up on top of that shed and then take off. That sort of scared me. I sat up and worked the rest of the night."

"Any other unusual happenings?" I asked.

"A lot of times the switch to the furnace at the head of the stairs is turned off, and the house starts to get cold. Also, often, when I step out of the car and start to walk in here, I've heard *something walking behind me.* Four or five different people have had that experience."

"Who were these other people who heard this person walking behind them?"

"My son for one. Then Bob, a friend of our nephew's. Bob would go out and work on his car when he got home, and he was late for dinner every evening. One night he came home mad and said, 'Why don't you stop coming out and walking up and down without coming in where I'm working?' We looked at him and assured him that we hadn't been doing that."

"Did he see anyone?"

"No, he never saw anyone, but he could hear them walk on the gravel, halfway between the barn and the garage where he was working."

"All right, thank you very much," I said, and turned to the Rays' daughter, who had been listening attentively.

"Mrs. Bonnie Williams, what were your experiences in this house?"

"When I was seventeen, three years ago, I was asleep one night on this same couch. It was about one o'clock in the morning, and I had just turned out the light, after reading for a while. My parents were asleep upstairs. I was lying there, and I wasn't asleep, when I noticed a light right in this corner. I didn't pay any attention to it, but rolled over. As I rolled over, I looked out the two windows which are right above the couch, and there was no light *outside*. It was a very dark night. So I became curious, and I rolled back over and I looked at the light and it was still there. I sat up, turned on the light and there was nothing. So I turned out the light and pulled the covers over my head. About five minutes later, I thought, I'd look again. This light was still here. It was a strange light, not a flashlight beam but sort of translucent, shimmering and pulsating."

"What color was it?"

"It was a bright white."

"Did it have any shape?"

"It seemed to; as it was pulsating, it would grow in size. But when it started doing that, I got scared and I turned on the light, and there was nothing."

"Anything else?"

"This was at the time when Tommy Young, my cousin, and Bob Brichard were here. Everybody was at the dinner table, and my friend Kathy Murray and I were leaving the house since we were eating dinner over at her house. We went out the back door, and we got about halfway down the walk when we heard moaning. It seemed to be coming from the bushes near the fence. I said, 'Come on,' and we started walking along but after we had taken about four steps, it started again. Well, when she heard it the second time she took off running for the house, and I decided I wasn't going to stand there by myself, so I went running into the house, too."

"Did it sound like a woman or a man?"

"A man."

"Any other visual experiences?"

"No, but I've heard something upstairs many times when I'm the only one home, sitting downstairs. There was something walking around upstairs."

"Well, was there in fact someone there?"

"I went upstairs. There was nothing."

"Did you ever feel any 'presences'?" I asked.

"One night," Bonnie replied, "at one o'clock in the morning, we wanted to have a séance. Since you get the feeling more often upstairs, we went up into my brother's room. We were sitting on the edge of the bed; my brother was nearest to the closet; Jackie Bergin, my aunt, was next to me; and I was on the other side. We were really concentrating for 'it' to appear. Then my brother spoke up and said, 'Do you see what I see?' And there was a shimmering light in the closet. It was very faint."

I thanked Bonnie and questioned her mother, Mrs. Virginia Ray, about her own experiences here.

"First of all," she said seriously, "I believe that there is a relationship between the barn and the house. The first things I heard were the noises of tools or whatever being knocked around in the barn. I heard it from inside the house. Then I had a very peculiar experience one Sunday afternoon. An acquaintance, Mrs. Ramsier, and I were standing on the front porch talking when all of a sudden it sounded as if the whole barn were collapsing. We both ran out the door and got as far as the maple tree in the side yard, but the barn was still standing. The noise took off about at the level of the eaves, where the gable comes down, and then traveled in a straight line over into the woods, and got quieter as it went away into the woods."

"I understand your mother also had an experience here?"

"My mother, Mrs. Bonnie Young, was here last July for my daughter Martha's wedding. She didn't believe anything we had said previously about this. I got up and left my room. I saw her light on and stuck my head in the door. I had intended to say absolutely nothing to her about what I had just experienced, but she said, 'Did you hear the ghost?' I asked her what she'd heard, and she said in the bedroom immediately adjoining hers she heard all the furniture moving around. She thought, what in the world is Martha doing, moving all the furniture around in the middle of the night! Then the noise left that room and moved to the side of the house, to this chimney, and then it disappeared."

"What was it, the thing that you yourself had heard at the same time your mother experienced this?"

"I was asleep in Bonnie's room, which does seem to be a center of activities, too—the barn and Bonnie's room are the centers. I became aware of a very loud noise— loud and gathering in the distance. It was coming closer together and getting louder and just moving towards the house. By the time it got to the house it seemed to be in two forms."

"What did it sound like?"

"Not like a boom; it was just a loud, *gathering* noise."

"Was it high-pitched or low-pitched?"

"I would say nearer low than high."

"Did you see any figure or any face of any kind?"

"Well, I didn't see it, but I was conscious of this noise coming into a configuration as it got to the window. All of a sudden these two noises came right through the window and up to my bed, and just went *wrrp, rrr;* hard-sounding noises. They seemed to be two separate noises. At this point I tried to get up enough courage to talk to it, but I couldn't. I was frightened by that time. I thought, I'll just go to sleep, but I couldn't. Finally, I got up, when I felt it had diminished, and left the room. Then I found out about Mother's experience."

"Have you had any unusual dreams in the house?"

"Yes, but not in this house. I went down to visit my mother once before she came up here. I woke up in the middle of the night, with this very loud, distinct voice that said, *there is something wrong, pack up and move away!* I didn't know whether it was *there* or *here.*"

"Was it a man or a woman?"

"I would say it was a man. I got up, walked the floor, and decided to pay attention. I had not planned to leave that day, but I told Bonnie about it and we went home that day."

"But it could have applied to this house."

"Yes, even though Mother's place is eleven hundred miles away, in Florida. The first night after we moved into this house, I went to bed. I had the feeling that a mouse started at the tip of the bed and ran straight to the floor. But my thought was—well, it wasn't a mouse because it didn't go *anywhere else*. I refused to worry about it. Then, a week or ten days ago, in April [1968], my husband's brother, Gilbert Ray, was here. He came out of the bathroom with the light off. He called to me, 'Ginny, do you mind coming here for a minute? Do you see anything over there?' I said, 'Yes I do.' And written on the metal cabinet above our washing machine in fluorescent light was the word L-A-R-U, in one line. And below that was sort of a smeared G, and an O. On the side of the cabinet there was one small slash. And then, between the cabinet and the window sill, in a narrow area about eight inches, there was an abstract face—eyebrows, nose, and mouth, and the face was sort of cocked on the wall. It was definitely there. We washed it off. It seemed like fluorescent paint. Two or three days afterward, in the bathroom, I did find on the cap of a deodorant a tiny bit of fluorescent paint. We have tended to say that it was *somebody* who did it, some physical person. *But we have no idea who did it.*"

"Well, did anybody in the family do it?"
"They say no."
"Were there any kids in the house?"
"No."
"There is no logical reason for it?"
"We have no logical reason for it."
"You saw the fluorescent light?"
"Three people saw it."

So there had been something more than just noises. I tried to put some meaning into the letters L-A-R-U-G-O, assuming they were of supernormal origin for the mo-

187

ment. It was a pity that the fluorescent paint was no longer available for inspection or analysis. It might have been ordinary, natural fluorescent paint, of course. But then again, the ectoplasmic substance often found in connection with materialization does have similar fluorescent qualities and upon exposure to light eventually dissolves. What the Rays had described was by no means new or unique. In photographs taken under test conditions in an experiment in San Francisco and published by me in *Psychic Photography—Threshold of a New Science*, I also have shown similar writings appearing upon polaroid film. In one particular instance, the word WAR, in capital letters, appears next to the portrait of the late John F. Kennedy. The substance seems to be greenish-white, soaplike, soft material, and there is a glow to it, although it is not as strong a glow as that of commercial fluorescent material.

I questioned all members of the household again. There was no doubt that no one had been playing tricks on any of them by painting fluorescent letters or that anyone from the outside could have gotten into the house to do so without the Rays' knowledge. Of that I became sure and quite satisfied. Under the circumstances, the supernormal origin of the writing was indeed the more probable explanation.

Who, however, was *Larugo*, or did it mean *Laru* and the word *Go?* I realized that I had to return to the house with a competent medium, preferably of the trance variety, to delve further into the personality causing the various phenomena. That there was a disturbed entity in and around the Ray house I was, of course, convinced. It would appear also that there was some connection with the barn, which, in turn, indicated that the disturbed

188

entity was not an owner but perhaps someone who just worked there. Finally, the tombstonelike stone found in the ground by the Rays indicated that perhaps someone had been buried on the grounds of the house.

We walked over to the barn, which turned out to be rather large and dark. Quite obviously it was not of recent origin, and it was filled with the usual implements, tools, and other paraphernalia found in country-house barns. There was a certain clammy chill in the atmosphere inside the barn that I could not completely account for in view of the warm weather outside. Even if the barn had been closed off for several days during the day and night, the wet chill of the atmosphere inside—especially the lower portion—was far beyond that which would have been produced under such conditions.

Unfortunately, I could not return immediately with a medium to investigate the matter further. Toward fall of 1968, word came to me through the mutual friends of the Rays and ourselves that they would eventually move from the house. Without knowing any of the details, I felt it was imperative that I get in touch with Mrs. Ray.

I called her on October 31, apologizing for the seeming connection between Halloween and their ghostly phenomena, and inquired how matters stood in house and barn. I also was able to tell Mrs. Ray that I would be at the house on November 7 at noon with a medium, Mrs. Ethel Johnson Meyers. This was good news to her indeed, for the phenomena had continued and had not been any less since my first visit.

To begin with, Mrs. Virginia Ray was forced to sleep with the hall light on and had done so for about five months because of an increasing uneasiness at night.

One afternoon during the summer two small boys living in the neighborhood came to her door inquiring about the noises that were going on in the barn. Mrs. Ray had been taking a nap and had heard nothing, but the boys insisted that something was going on in the barn. Together they investigated, only to find everything in place and quiet. "We have bats, swallows, and we were developing a colony of pigeons in the barn," Mrs. Ray explained, "the last of which we do not want. My son, who is now twenty-one, was home on vacation when he decided to use a rifle to get rid of the pigeons. When he did so, an unusual spot of light came on the walls of the barn. He took one look at it and declined to spend any time in the barn after that."

One of the most impressive experiences perhaps occurred to the Rays' new son-in-law, who had come to spend the summer. He had heard all the stories of the phenomena and didn't believe any of them. One night, he was awakened at about a quarter to four in the morning by the noise of loud knocking outside the screen. Then the noise came on into the room, and he observed that it was a high hum mixed in with what sounded like the tinkling of a wind chime. The same night Mrs. Ray herself was awakened by a sound that she at first thought was high above her outside of the house, and which she sleepily took to be the noise of an airplane. Then she realized that the noise was not moving. Independent of the son-in-law and Mrs. Ray, Mr. Ray had also heard a similar noise at the same time.

Mrs. Ray's mother came for a visit during the summer. During her stay, the hall lights were being turned off—or went off by themselves—not less than four times in one night. There was no faulty equipment to be blamed; no other explanation to be found. Lights would go on and off more frequently now, without hands touching them, and the furnace again went off. Somebody or something had turned the emergency switch.

I was all set to pay the Rays a visit on November 7. At the last moment I received a hurried telephone call from Mrs. Ray. She informed me unhappily that the new owners objected to the visit and that therefore she could not offer the hospitality of the house again. They would move from the house on December 2 and the new owner had already started to take over.

"That's nothing," I said. "Perhaps I can get permission from them to pay a short visit."

Mrs. Ray seemed even more nervous than at first. "I don't think so, but you could try," she said, and supplied me with the name and address of the new owner. And she added, cryptically, "But he is a military man and I don't think he likes what you are doing."

I wrote a polite letter requesting only that we complete what we had started earlier, both in the interests of parapsychology and the house itself. I included my credentials as a scientist and teacher, and promised not to permit any undue publicity to arise from the case. This is standard procedure with me, since it is not my intention to cause the owners of haunted houses any embarrassment or difficulty in the community. I assumed, quite rightly, that whatever it was that caused the Rays to leave would not go out with them but would remain tied to the house. There is an overwhelming body of evidence to support this view. Only once in a while, and in special cases, is a haunting attached to one particular person in a house. Clearly this is not the case in the Oakton haunt, and I had to assume that the matter was not resolved.

191

I made some inquiries about the new owner, and discovered that Colonel S. was a retired army officer who had served in nearby Washington for many years while his wife was a teacher. Since there was very little time left before my impending visit, I hoped that permission would come through prior to November 7. The day before I received a certified letter with return receipt request from Colonel S. The letter was truly the letter of a military man: curt, insulting, and full of non sequiturs. The colonel tried hard to convince me that my work wasn't worthwhile or that it made no sense whatsoever. I realized that the man was more to be pitied than scorned, so I took his letter, wrote on it that I did not accept discourteous letters because they would contaminate my files, and returned it to him. I have heard nothing further from the colonel or his wife, and if there is any phenomenon going on at his Oakton, Virginia, house, he is handling it all by himself. He is most welcome to it. Quite possibly, he is not even aware of it, for he may be gifted with a lack of sensitivity that some people have. On the other hand, one cannot be sure. It is quite possible that the noises have since continued and will continue, or that other, more stringent phenomena will follow them. I don't think that a disturbed spirit has any respect for the opinion of a military man who wishes that spirits wouldn't exist.

On November 7 we did drive by the house and Mrs. Meyers stepped out briefly and went as close to the grounds as we could without entering the house proper or violating the colonel's newly acquired property rights. Happily, the public thoroughfares in Virginia may be walked upon by parapsychologists and mediums with no need to ask permission to do so. As Ethel faced the enclosure of the house, she received the distinct impression of a troubled entity. Without having been told anything at all about the nature of the phenomenon or the location of it, she pointed at the barn farther back as the seat of all the troubles. "It's down there, whatever it is," Ethel said, and looked at me. "But I would have to be closer to do anything about it. All I can tell you is that someone is awfully mad down there." Under the circumstances, I asked her to come back with me and let the matter rest.

Nothing further was heard from either the Rays or anyone else concerning the house until April 20.

Mrs. Ray wrote us from her new address in McLean, Virginia. "I feel like we have gone off and left the 'presence.' Mr. Ray is much less tense, as we all are to a degree." But that same day at four o'clock in the morning she woke up with a start. Suddenly she knew what the troubled entity wanted. Even though they had left the house, the unfortunate one was able to reach out to her at the same hour at which most of the audible phenomena had taken place. Perhaps this was a last message from the haunt of Oakton. Mrs. Ray hoped that it would indeed be the final message, and that she would be troubled no more.

When she understood what the entity wanted, she immediately set about to fulfill his wish. Quietly and without fanfare she made arrangements with an Episcopal priest to have the house exorcised. This, of course, was done through prayer, in a very ancient ritual going back to the early days of the church. Sometimes it is effective, sometimes it is not. It depends upon the one who is being exorcised, whether or not he accepts the teachings of the church, and whether or not he is a believer in the Deity.

The Rays did not keep in touch any longer with the new owners of their property, but once in a while word came back to them about their former home. A friend who hadn't heard of their removal to McLean tried to visit them. When the gentleman drove up to the gate, he realized that something was different. The gates had always been wide open, as had the hospitality and heart of the Rays. Now, however, he found the gate was closed. A somber, almost forbidding air hung around the Oakton house. Sadly, the gentleman turned around and left. He knew then without asking that the Rays had moved on.

A tombstone unmarked in the garden, a haunted barn, and a scrawled message written by a desperate hand from beyond the grave—do they indicate someone's unavenged death? So often I have heard "pray for me" when a soul has passed over in anguish and, clinging steadfastly to the beliefs of the church, wants the final benediction, even postmortem. Could it not be that the Oakton haunt was resolved not by a parapsychologist and his medium prying further into the tangled affairs of someone long dead, but by the simple prayer of an Episcopal priest doing so at a distance? If and when the house is again for sale, we will know for sure.

16

The Hauntings at Howard Lodge

Somewhere between Washington and Baltimore is a small community called Sykesville. It is a little bit closer to Baltimore than it is to Washington, and most of the people who live there work in Baltimore. Some don't work at all. It is not what you might call a poor community but, to the contrary, is one of the last remaining strongholds of the rural hunting set whose main occupation and pride were their farms and manor houses.

Howard Lodge was built there in 1774 by Edward Dorsey. Tradition has it that it was named Howard Lodge when Governor Howard of Maryland stayed in it during the period in which the United States became independent. Tax records seem to indicate that it was owned at one time by relatives of Francis Scott Key, the author of our national anthem. Key himself visited Howard Lodge and carved his name in one of the upstairs window sills, but unfortunately, the windows were later destroyed by storms.

The house consists of two stories and is made of brick imported from England. The attic and roof beams were made by hand from chestnut wood and are held fast by pegs driven their full length. Today's owners, Mr. and Mrs. Roy Emery, have made some changes, especially in the attic. At one time the attic was two stories high, but it has been divided into storage rooms above the beams and finished rooms below. At the turn of this century dormer windows were installed by a previous owner, a Mrs. Mottu of Baltimore. The oldest part of the house is the thick-walled stone kitchen downstairs. On the ample grounds there is an old smokehouse and a springhouse, both dating from the original period when the house was built. Surrounded by tall trees, the estate is truly European in flavor, and one can very well imagine how previous owners must have felt sitting on their lawn looking out into the rolling hills of Maryland and dreaming of past glory.

The house has been furnished in exquisite taste by its present owners, the Emerys. Mr. Emery is an attorney in Baltimore, and his wife, a descendant of very old French nobility, saw service as a nurse in the late unlamented French-Indochina campaign. The furnishings include period pieces assembled with an eye toward fitting them into the general tone of the house, and French heirlooms brought into the house by Mrs. Emery. There isn't a piece out of key at Howard Lodge, and the house may well serve as an example to others who would live in eighteenth-century manor houses. When I appeared on Baltimore television I received a letter from Mrs. Emery, in which she asked me to have a look at Howard Lodge and its resident ghosts. It would appear that she had several, and that while they were not malicious or mischievous, they nevertheless bore investigation if only to find out who they were and what they wanted.

Long before Mrs. Emery had heard of me, she had invited two men, who were aware of the existence of ghosts, to come to the house. They were not private investigators or apprentice ghost-hunters, to be sure— simply two gentlemen interested in the supernatural. Barry and Glenn Hammond of Washington, D.C., coming to the house as friends, reported seeing a gentleman outside looking toward the house. The gentleman in question was not of this world, they hastily explained. They knew all about such personalities since they were accustomed to distinguishing between the flesh and blood and the ethereal kind. The Emerys had other guests at the time, so the two gentlemen from Washington were not as much at liberty to speak of the resident ghosts as if they had come alone. While they were wandering about the house in search of other phantoms, Mrs. Emery busied herself with her guests. On leaving, however, the Hammonds happily informed Mrs. Emery that Howard Lodge had not just two ghosts—as the Emerys had surmised—but a total of five. They left it at that and went back to Connecticut Avenue.

Jacqueline Emery was not particularly overtaken with worry. She was born Countess de Beauregard, and as with many old aristocratic families, there had been a family specter and she was quite familiar with it while growing up. The specter, known as the White Lady, apparently can be seen only by members of the de Montrichard family, who happened to be related to Mrs. Emery. No one knows who the White Lady is, but she appears regularly when a member of the family is about to die, very much as an Irish banshee announces the coming of death. There may be a relationship there since so many old French families are also of Celtic origin.

I met Mrs. Emery's uncle, the Baron Jean Bergier de Beauregard, who lives with his family at Chateau de Villelouet in the heartland of France. The Baron readily confirmed that many members of the Beauregard family have indeed shown the ability of second sight, and that psychic occurrences were not particularly upsetting to any of them. They took it in their stride.

Jacqueline Emery has inherited this particular talent also. She frequently knows what is in the mail or what phone calls are about to be made to her, and she is aware of the future in many small ways, but she takes it as part of her character. Nevertheless, it indicates in all the Beauregards a natural vein of psychic ability, and it is that psychic ability that made the appearances at Howard Lodge possible, in my view.

I finally managed to come out to Howard Lodge. Roy Emery picked me up in Baltimore and drove me to his house. Present were not only his wife but their two daughters, both college students. Ariane, the elder, is an avid reader of mine and wants to devote herself to psychic studies if all goes well. Proudly, Jacqueline Emery showed me about the house and around the grounds while there was still enough light to see everything. While we were walking I learned further details about Howard Lodge. For one thing, it appeared that Jerome Bonaparte had actually been to the house while he was courting Mrs. Patterson, whom he later married. Not three miles away from Howard Lodge was the estate of the Pattersons, where Napoleon's brother lived out his life in peace and harmony. All around us was plantation country, and what little was left of the old plantations could still be seen in the area.

"We now have only two hundred acres," Mrs. Emery explained, "but when we bought the property it was part of five hundred acres, and a hundred years ago it was about seven or eight hundred acres. I imagine that in the beginning it must have been about two thousand acres. That's what the plantations around here were like."

Before I went into the matter of the hauntings properly, I wanted to learn as much as possible about the house itself, its background, its structure, and since Mrs. Emery already knew these facts I saw no reason not to discuss them.

"Was this the plantation house, actually?" I asked.

"It must have been, yes. And it is a rather formal house, which is typical of the English houses, with the hall going all the way through the house, and two rooms deep on either side. The kitchen must have been an addition later, even though it is old."

"There are four rooms downstairs?"

"There are more than that, but it is two rooms deep on either side of the hall. You see, here you have the living room and the music room, my husband's library, and the dining room. The dining room has been extended going east-west, because the hall doesn't go all the way through to the door; the partition has been removed."

"And upstairs?"

"Upstairs, there are six bedrooms, and then the attic, which I will show you, was a two-story one. Now we've made it a third floor, with still a large attic on top."

"So it's actually a three-level house?"

"Well, we have the basement, we have this floor, the second floor, the third floor, and the attic; that's five stories."

"How long ago did you come here?"

"It will be ten years in December. We moved in here in 1959. The house had been lived in by hillbillies, and horribly mistreated. The kitchen, through which you came in, had pigs, with litters. This room was used—the various corners were used instead of bathrooms. It had a couch that was full of rats. The rats were so used to people that they didn't move when you came in. It was full of flies and fleas and rats and mice and smells, and chewing gum on the floors. And Roy and I spent about a month, on our knees, on this very floor, trying to remove all of this. All the walls were covered with six to seven layers of wallpaper, which were removed, and then I painted. Of course the hard part was removing the paper. Each time there had been a draft in the room, due to some hole in the masonry or something, they had put on another layer of wallpaper, thus cutting off, or hiding, the problem, rather than doing anything about it. And so forth!"

"Were they squatters or had they bought it?"

"They had bought it because they had had a farm on what is now Friendship Airport. Needless to tell you, it was a very nice thing to have. They bought this house from a man who worked in a bank in Washington. They bought it cash."

"But they didn't know how to live."

"Oh, no! See, they used a house as you would squeeze a lemon; after there was nothing left, they left and abandoned the house—went to another one. The time had come for them to leave; they had been here seven years, and it was going to pot. The plumbing was completely shot. The heating system was so dangerous that the electrician said, 'You really must believe in God'; and everything about like that."

"And you took it over then and restored it?"

"Yes, and everybody told us we were absolutely crazy. We spent the first month, five of us, in one room. I had disinfected that room, working in it for a month."

"You have three children?"

"Yes. And Chris was only two. And—well, we are *still* working on it."

I decided to come to the point.

"When was the first time you noticed anything *unusual* anywhere?"

"It was when I became less busy with doing things in the house. You know, when you are terribly busy you don't have time to realize what's going on. Three years ago I became aware of *a man on the landing*. I know it is a man, though I have never *seen* him. I'm absolutely convinced that he's a man in either his late forties or early fifties, and in addition, he's from the eighteenth century *because in my mind's eye I can see him.*"

"Was there anything for the first seven years of your occupancy here?"

"I cannot recall. Except possibly some vague sensation about steps going from the second to the third floor."

"Noises?"

"Oh yes, you always have the feeling somebody's going up the steps. Always. We've always taken it for granted it was because it was an old house, but since we have rugs I *still* hear steps."

"Now, what were the circumstances when you felt the man on the stairs? On the landing, I mean."

"Well, I was going to my room, on the second floor, and you have to go through the landing. This is the only way to go to that room. And then suddenly I had to stop, *because he was there.*"

"Did you feel cold?"

"No, I just felt he had to move and he wasn't going to move, and eventually he did, but he wasn't aware of me as fast as I was of him."

"What time of day was that?"

"Evening. It's always dusk, for some reason. You see, the landing has a southern exposure, which may have something to do with it, and it's always very sunny during the day."

"After this first experience, did you have more?"

"Oh yes, often. For quite a while he was constantly there."

"Always on that spot?"

"Always on the landing. You see, the landing has a very good vantage point, because *nobody* can go upstairs or downstairs without going through it."

"Then would you say somebody might watch from that spot?"

"You can see *everything*—originally the lane was not what you came through, but at the front of the house. From the landing you have a perfect command of the entire lane."

"After this first experience three years ago did you ever see him, other than the way you describe?"

"No. Although I have to be very careful when I say that because after a while, as you well know, it is difficult to separate something you see in your mind from something you see physically. Because I feel that I could touch him if I tried, but I never have. Even though I'm not afraid of him, I still don't feel like it."

"Did you ever walk up the stairs and run into *something*?"

"A wall. Sometimes I feel that there is a partition or something there."

"Something that you have to displace?"

"Yes. But then I wait until it displaces itself, or I move around it. But somehow I know where it is because I can move around it."

"Have you ever seen anything?"

"Often. On the landing."

"What does it look like?"

"Fog. And I always think it's my eyes."

"How tall is it?"

"Frankly I have never thought about it, because I will blink a few times. I've always thought it was *me*. You see, it's very foggy here, outside. But then I saw it in several rooms."

"Did you ever smell anything peculiar?"

"Yes, I often do. There are some smells in this house and they often take me back to something, but I don't know what."

"Do you ever hear sounds that sound like a high-pitched voice, or a bird?"

"Bird, yes. Very often."

"Where do you hear that? What part of the house?"

"Never on this floor. Upstairs."

"Have there been any structural changes in the house?"

"I think the landing."

"Only the landing? How was it affected?"

"We changed one partition, for it was much too logically altered to have been something that existed when the house was built. The way we found it, it couldn't have been that way because it was ridiculous. Anybody with a hoop skirt, for instance, or a wide dress, could never have managed the top of the steps onto the landing with the partition the way it was there. We changed it, and I will show you because the seam is in the floor. We were told that the landing *had* been changed, and for some reason everything is around that landing."

"You mean changed back to what it was originally, or changed?"

"We don't know, because we don't know how it was."

"Did you widen it or narrow it?"

"We widened it."

"Now, since living in this house have you ever had odd dreams? Have you felt as if a person were trying to communicate with you?"

"Yes. Often."

"Will you talk about that?"

"Only that I'm rather ashamed, that I usually try to block it out."

"Well, do you ever get any feeling of the communicators?"

"Because I'm negative I don't think there is any actual communication, but I've often been *aware of someone even coming in the room where I am.*"

"How does this manifest itself?"

"I'm aware of a shadow. With my eyes open."

"This is on the second floor?"

"Yes."

"At night?"

"Yes. And then, that night while I slept on the third floor—I'm sure it's my man on the landing. He came up, and why I got scared I don't know because this man is awfully nice, and there is nothing . . ."

"What do you mean, he came up?"

"I heard him come up the stairs, and he came and watched me."

"Why did you sleep on the third floor that night?"

"Because Roy had turned on the air conditioner. I cannot sleep with an air conditioner."

"So you took one of the guest rooms. Does this room have any particular connection with the landing?"

"You have to go through the landing because of the steps going up and going down. Both end up on the second-floor landing."

"And he came up the stairs, and you felt him standing by your bed?"

"Yes. Watching—probably wondering what I was doing there. But originally this was not a floor used for bedrooms. We did that."

"What was it used for?"

"It was a two-story attic, and we divided it in two by putting in a ceiling, and I don't believe it could have been used except, possibly, for servants."

"When was the last time you had a sense of this being?"

"In the fall."

"Is there any particular time when it's stronger?"

"Yes, in the summer."

"Any particular time of day?"

"Dusk."

"Is it always the same person?"

"Well, I always thought it was, but I never gave it too much thought."

"Is there more than one?"

"Yes."

"When did you notice the second 'presence'?"

"It was about two years ago, when Chris, my boy, was moved up to the third floor, that I heard *breathing*. It was in the master bedroom. I can show you exactly where because the breathing came from the right side of the bed, below, as if a child would have slept in a trundle bed or in a low cradle or something, and that breathing came from below me. The bed is fairly high."

"On the second floor?"

"Yes. And it was very definitely a child, and I can explain that very readily—there is not a mother in the world who will not recognize the breathing of a child, when it's sick and has a fever."

"Did your husband hear this?"

"No. He never hears anything of this."

"But was he present?"

"No. He was in his library, downstairs."

"Was this late at night?"

"No—I go to bed much earlier than Roy. It must have been around eleven, or maybe midnight."

"The first time you heard this, did you wonder what it was?"

"Well, I knew what it was, or what it had to be, since I couldn't possibly hear my children breathe from where I was. I was aware that it must be something which had occurred in that very room before."

The Hauntings at Howard Lodge

"Did you ever hear any other noise?"

"Yes. That child cries, and there is pain."

"How often have you heard it?"

"The breathing more often than the crying. The crying only a couple of times."

"In the same spot?"

"Yes."

"Is there a woman around? Do you have a feeling of a woman when that happens?"

"Yes, and she would be on my side of the bed. And this is the part that bothers me!"

"What do you mean?"

"Because I have the feeling her bed was where mine is. I'm sure she slept on the right, because the child is on the right."

"The furniture in the bedroom is yours—you brought this in yourself?"

"Oh yes, there wasn't anything that belonged to this house."

I thought all this over for a moment, then decided to continue questioning my psychic hostess.

"Was there anything else, other than what we have just discussed?"

"Yes, the portrait of my ancestor that I brought back from France. I was born in 1923, and she was born in 1787."

"And what was her name?"

"I don't remember her maiden name, but she was an Alcazar. She married a Spaniard."

"What is special about the portrait?"

"Of course, the eyes—you will find those eyes in any well-painted portrait—they are eyes that follow you everywhere. But I wouldn't refer to that because this is very common in any museum or in any home where they have family portraits. This is not so much that, but the moods she goes through. She definitely changes her expression. When she disapproves of someone she shows it. And every once in a while, if you glance at her rapidly, she is not the woman you now see in the portrait, but somebody else."

"Does anyone other than you see this?"

"Yes, two other people—my English friend of whom I talked before, and another English friend who is married to an American friend. They both saw it."

"Have you ever felt anything outside the house, on the grounds?"

"You think there is a branch that's going to hit your face, and yet there is no branch. I thought that people always felt like that when they walked outside, but they *don't*. Also I can't walk straight in the dark."

"What do you mean?"

"I don't know! I could walk on a straight line, painted line, on the roof without the slightest difficulty, but in the dark I never walk straight."

"You have two dogs. Have they ever behaved strangely?"

"All the time. They bark when there is absolutely nothing there."

Mrs. Emery interrupted my thoughtful pause.

"There is also something about a room on this floor, Mr. Holzer."

"The one we're sitting in?"

"No—the next one, where the piano is. Every night before I go to bed I have to have a glass of orange juice. And sometimes I'll *race* downstairs—I'll feel there is somebody in that rocking chair and I'm afraid to go and check."

"Do you have a feeling of a presence in that room?"

"Yes—oh yes, yes, very strong. Almost every day, I'd say."

"It's *that* room, and the landing, then?"

"Yes."

At this point I had to change tapes. I thought again about all I had heard and tried to make the various elements fall into place. It didn't seem to add up as yet—at least not in the same time layer.

"To your knowledge," I asked Mrs. Emery, "has anything tragic ever happened here in the house?"

"We don't know. This is the thing that is so disappointing in this country, that so few records are kept. In France you have records for six hundred years. But here, past fifty years people wonder why you want to know."

"Is there any legend, rumor, or tradition attached to the house?"

"There are several legends. They also say that Governor Howard, who gave his name to Howard County, which until 1860 was part of Anne Arundel County, lived in this house. But it's extraordinary, at least to me it is, coming from France, that people cannot be sure of facts which are so recent, really."

"What about the people who lived here before? Have you ever met anybody who lived here before?"

"Yes. I met a man named Talbot Shipley, who is seventy-eight and was born here."

"Did he own the house at one time?"

"His parents did, and—he was the kind, you know, who went, '*Oh!* where you have that couch, this is where

209

Aunt Martha was laid out'; and, 'Oh, over there, this is where my mother was when she became an invalid, and this was made into a bedroom and then she died in there'; and, 'Oh, Lynn, you sleep in that room? Well, this is where I was born!' And that's the kind of story we got, but he's a farmer, and he would perhaps not have quite the same conception of a house as we do. To him, a house is where people are born and die. And perhaps to me a house is where people *live*."

"What about servants? Did you ever have a gardener or anyone working for you?"

"Oh, I have people work for me once in a while. I have discarded all of them because everything is below their dignity and nothing is below mine, so it's much easier to do things myself!"

"Did they ever complain about anything?"

"I had a woman once who said she wouldn't go to the third floor. There is something else," Mrs. Emery said. "There are two niches on either side of where there must have been a triangular porch, which would go with the style of the house. They seem to be *sealed*. The man who is remodeling the smokehouse into my future antique shop, is dying to open them up and see what's inside them, because really they *don't make any sense*."

"Do you have any particular feelings about the two niches?"

"They are on each side of my desk on the landing, but on the outside. As a matter of fact, I never thought of that! It's toward the ceiling of the landing but on the outside."

"What could possibly be in them?"

"I don't know. We thought perhaps the records of the house."

210

"Not a treasure?"

"They say that during the Civil War people buried things, and also during the Revolution, so there could be treasures. Somebody found a coin—1743—on the lane."

"An English coin?"

"Yes."

"Who found it?"

"A young girl who came to see us. So we let her keep it. And a windowsill was replaced in the dining room, and quite a few artifacts were found in that windowsill. Buttons and coins."

After dinner I went with Mrs. Emery through the house from top to bottom, photographing as I went along. None of the pictures show anything unusual, even in the area of the landing upstairs—but that, of course, does not prove that there is not a presence there lurking for the right moment to be recognized. Only on rare occasions do manifestations of this kind show up on photographic film or paper. It would have taken a great deal more time and patience to come up with positive results.

I talked to the two girls, Ariane and Lynn, now in their early twenties, and to Chris, the little boy, but none of the children had had any unusual experiences as far as the specter on the landing was concerned, nor were they frightened by the prospect of having a ghost or two in the house. It was all part of living in the country. I took a good look at the portrait of the maternal ancestor, and could find only that it was a very good portrait indeed. Perhaps she didn't disapprove of me, or at any rate didn't show it if she did.

But when I stood on the landing, on the spot where most of the manifestations had taken place, I felt rather strange. Granted that I knew where I was and what had occurred in the spot I was standing. Granted also that suggestion works even with professional psychic investigators. There was still a residue of the unexplained. I can't quite put into words what I felt, but it reminded me, in retrospect, of the uneasy feeling I sometimes have when an airplane takes a quick and unexpected dive. It is as if your stomach isn't quite where it ought to be. The feeling was passing, but somehow I knew that the spot I had stepped into was not like the rest of the house. I looked around very carefully. Nothing indicated anything special about this landing. The ceiling at this point was not very high, since the available room had been cut in two when the floor was created. But there was a sense of coziness in the area, almost creating an impression of a safe retreat for someone. Could it be then, I reasoned afterward, that the spectral gentleman had found himself his own niche, his own retreat, and that he very much liked it? Could it not be that he was pleased with the arrangement; that perhaps when the Emerys created an extra floor out of part of the old attic, they had unconsciously carried out the designs of those who had lived in the house before them? Usually hauntings are due to some structural change which does not meet with the approval of those who had lived before in the house. Here we might have the reverse: a later owner doing the bidding of someone who did not have the time or inclination to carry out similar plans. For it must be recalled that a good house is never finished, but lives almost like a human being and thrives on the ministrations of those who truly love it.

It was quite dark outside by now. Nevertheless, I stepped to the nearest window and peered out onto the land below. A sense of calmness came over me, and yet a certain restlessness as if I were expecting something or someone to arrive. Was I picking up the dim vibrations left over from a past event? I don't fancy myself a medium or even remotely psychic, but when I stood on the second-floor landing at Howard Lodge, there was a moment when I, too, felt something uncanny within me.

A little later, Roy Emery drove me back to Baltimore and dropped me off at my hotel. Coming back into town was almost like walking into a cold shower, but twenty-four hours later I had again grown accustomed to the rough and materialistic atmosphere of big-city life. I had promised the Emerys to come back someday with a trance medium and see whether I could perhaps let the unknown man on the landing have his say. In the meantime, however, I promised to look up the de Beauregards in France, and Mr. and Mrs. Emery promised to keep me informed of any further developments at Howard Lodge should they occur.

I had hardly returned from Europe when I received an urgent note from Mrs. Emery:

A friend of mine recently lost her mother and I invited her for the weekend. She was brought here by a mutual friend who also spent the weekend. I was very tired that evening, and shortly before midnight I had to excuse myself. Barbara wanted to stay up and Don stayed with her, feeling that she wanted to talk.

The following morning they told me that they had been sitting in the living room, and that Barbara had turned off the lights because she wanted to enjoy the country peace to the utmost. They then both heard footsteps coming down the steps and assumed that I'd changed my mind

213

*and had joined them. They heard the steps cross the thresh-
old and the love seat creaked under the weight of someone
sitting there. Barbara became aware that it was not I there
with them, and she could hear someone breathing very
regularly. Holding her own breath, she then asked Don if
he could hear anything. He had, and had also been holding
his breath, to hear better. Barbara and Don both commented on how friendly they felt this presence to be. They
are both absolutely convinced that there was someone with
them in that room.*

It is perhaps a good thing that the unknown gentleman
on the second-floor landing does not have to leave his
safe retreat to go out into the countryside and search for
whatever it is that keeps him on the spot. He would find
his beloved countryside vastly changed beyond a few
miles. As it is, he can remember it the way he loved it, the
way Howard Lodge still reflects it. And the Emerys, far
from being upset by the additional inhabitant in their old
house, consider it a good omen that someone other than
flesh and blood stands guard and peers out, the way a
night watchman stands guard over precious property. It
assures them of one more pair of eyes and ears should
there be something dangerous approaching their house.
In this day and age such thoughts are not entirely without reason.

As for the child whose breathing Mrs. Emery heard
time and again, we must remember that children died far
more often in bygone years than they do today. Child
mortality rates were very high because medicine had not
yet reached the point where many diseases could be prevented or their death toll sharply reduced. A child then
was often a far more fragile human being than it is today.

Perhaps it was one of the children belonging to a former owner, who fell ill from a fever and died.

But the gentleman on the landing is another matter. Since it was the lady of the house primarily who felt him and got his attention, I assume that it was a woman who concerned him. Was he, then, looking out from his vantage point to see whether someone were returning home? Had someone left, perhaps, and did part of the gentleman go with her?

One can only surmise such things; there is no concrete evidence whatsoever that it is a gentleman whose lady had left him. Without wishing to romanticize the story, I feel that that may very well have been the case. It is perhaps a bit distressing not to know how to address one's unseen guest other than to call him the "presence on the second-floor landing." But Mrs. Emery knows he is friendly, and that is good enough for her.

17

The Indian Girl Ghost
of Kentucky

*F*rontier states have per-
haps more colorful, unusual ghosts than other U.S. re-
gions. The same may also be said of the people who
encounter the ghosts.

Mrs. D. and her son, Bucky, lived in a comfortable
house on a hilltop in suburban Kentucky, not far from
Cincinnati, Ohio. It is a pleasant white house, not much
different from other houses in the area. The surroundings are lovely and peaceful, and there's a little man-
made pond right in front of the house. Nothing about the
house or the area looks in the least bit ghostly or unusual. Nevertheless, Mrs. D. needed my help in a very
vexing situation.

Six months after Mrs. D. had moved into the house,

she began to hear footsteps upstairs, when there was no one about, and the sound of a marble being rolled across the hall. Anything supernatural was totally alien to Mrs. D.

Nevertheless, she has a questioning and alert mind, and was not about to accept these phenomena without finding out what caused them. When the manifestations persisted, she walked up to the foot of the stairs and yelled, "Why don't you just come out and show yourself or say something instead of making all those noises?"

As if in answer, an upstairs door slammed shut and then there was utter silence. After a moment's hesitation, Mrs. D. dashed upstairs and made a complete search. There was no one about and the marble, which seemingly had rolled across the floor, was nowhere to be seen.

When the second Christmas in the new house rolled around, the D.s were expecting Bucky home from the army. He was going to bring his sergeant and the sergeant's wife with him, since they had become very friendly. They celebrated New Year's Eve in style and high spirits (not the ethereal kind, but the bottled type).

Nevertheless, they were far from inebriated when the sergeant suggested that New Year's Eve was a particularly suitable night for a séance. Mrs. D. would have no part of it at first. She had read all about phony séances and remembered what her Bible said about such matters. But later, after her husband had gone to bed, the four of them decided to have a go at it.

They joined hands and sat quietly in front of the fireplace. Nothing much happened for a while. Then Bucky, who had read some books on psychic phenomena, suggested that they needed a guide or control from the other

218

side of life to help them, but no one had any suggestions concerning to whom they might turn.

More in jest than as a serious proposal, Mrs. D. heard herself say, "Why don't you call your Indian ancestor, Little White Flower!" Mr. D. is part Cherokee, and Bucky, the son, would, of course, consider this part of his inheritance, too. Mrs. D. protested that all this was nonsense, and they should go to bed. She assured them that nothing was likely to happen. But the other three were too busy to reply, staring behind her into the fireplace. When she followed the direction of their eyes she saw what appeared to be some kind of light similar to that made by a flashlight. It stayed on for a short time and then disappeared altogether.

From that day on, Mrs. D. started to find strange objects around the house that had not been there a moment before. They were little stones in the shape of Indian arrows. She threw them out as fast as she found them. Several weeks later, when she was changing the sheets on her bed, she noticed that a huge red arrow had been painted on the bottom sheet by unseen hands.

One afternoon she was lying down on the couch with a book, trying to rest. Before long she was asleep. Suddenly she awoke with a feeling of horror that seemed to start at her feet and gradually work its way up throughout her entire body and mind. The room seemed to be permeated with something terribly evil. She could neither see nor hear anything, but she had the feeling that there was a presence there and that it was very strong and about to overcome her.

For a few weeks she felt quite alone in the house, but then things started up again. The little stone arrowheads appeared out of nowhere again, all over the house. Hysterical with fear, Mrs. D. called upon a friend who had dabbled in metaphysics and asked for advice. The friend advised a séance in order to ask Little White Flower to leave.

Although Little White Flower was not in evidence continually but seemed to come and go, Mrs. D. felt the Indian woman's influence upon her at all times. Later the same week, Little White Flower put in another appearance—this time visual. It was almost four o'clock in the morning, when Mrs. D. woke up with the firm impression that her tormentor was in the room. As she looked out into the hall, she saw on the wall a little red object resembling a human eye, and directly below it what seemed like half a mouth. Looking closer, she discerned two red eyes and a white mouth below. It reminded her of some clowns she had seen in the circus. The vision remained on the wall for two or three minutes, and then vanished completely.

After several postponements, I was finally able to come to Kentucky and meet with Mrs. D. in person. On June 20, 1964, I sat opposite the slightly portly, middle-aged lady who had corresponded with me so voluminously for several months.

As I intoned my solemn exorcism and demanded Little White Flower's withdrawal from the spot, I could hear Mrs. D. crying hysterically. It was almost as if some part of her was being torn out and for a while it seemed that *she* was being sent away, not Little White Flower.

The house has been quiet ever since; Little White Flower has presumably gone back to her own people and Mrs. D. continues living in the house without further disturbances.

18

A Crime of Passion in New Orleans

Jean Hatton comes from a family in which the psychic has been in evidence for many generations, such as precognitive dreams and clairvoyance. Foreknowledge of events or places has been rampant on her mother's side of the family, and as a preteen-ager Jean had some ESP experiences. Around forty years of age at the time the events related here occurred, she and her husband live in the heart of New Orleans. She was a professional musician for a while and taught music in high school for five years. Her mother's family is Irish, Dutch, and Indian, while her father's side of the family came from Wales, England, and Ireland. Thus a predominance of Celtic elements in her background may be responsible for her readiness to accept

221

the reality of psychic phenomena. At any rate, when she moved from her childhood home in San Antonio, Texas, to New Orleans she made friends with a married couple living on Decatur Street in the French Quarter. The very first time she tried to enter their apartment she almost tripped. She felt a kind of elastic force trying to keep her out as if she were not welcome. The house in which the couple's apartment was located was a very old house. That one and some of the adjoining ones were among the few that hadn't been destroyed in the fires so common in this part of town. At least two hundred years old, the house in question was one of the finest examples of colonial architecture.

Forcing her way through the invisible curtain, Jean then entered the apartment. She saw an old fireplace against one wall facing a bedroom door. The entrance was to the right. To the left were the living room and a long narrow room probably used as a pantry or wardrobe. The owner of the apartment tried to tell her that something very tragic had occurred in the apartment, but before he could do so Jean herself told him the story. How she could know this was as much a mystery to her as it was to her host. But she pointed at a clock and insisted that it would always stop at three o'clock in the morning because it was then that "something had happened." Before she knew what she was doing, Jean found herself standing by the fireplace looking at the clock. Then she turned toward the door, resting her hands on the mantelpiece. She seemed to be wearing a white gown with full sleeves, probably a nightgown. At this moment she clearly heard steps. A door was opened and through it came the "wrong man." The man she saw now clairvoyantly was tall, with unruly gray hair and a deepsettype face. He wore a silk hat and black cape. She knew then that the woman was trying to express herself through her; that she had been stabbed where she stood and had fallen in front of the fireplace.

At this moment she came out of her semi-trance. It was all she could get, but her host assured her that the impression was not fantasy. He explained that he had seen just such a woman walk at night, her bloody hands crossed on her breasts. Both he and his wife had frequently heard the footsteps of someone coming up the stairs to their third-floor apartment. One night when Sheri, the wife, was home alone playing old English folk songs on her guitar, she looked up and saw the two entities standing there in the door. She was not afraid so she kept on looking at them before they faded away.

It became clear to the owner of the apartment that something very drastic had occurred at a previous time. But they could not figure it out and learned to live with their spectral visitors. One day the husband was up in the attic, above their apartment, clearing up some flooring. To his horror he discovered two human skeletons underneath. Hastily closing the door to the attic behind him, he took the two skeletons and quietly buried them. He decided not to report the matter to the police after all since it might have been something that had occurred a long time ago and calling attention to it now might draw unfavorable publicity to himself and the house. From that moment the psychic phenomena stopped abruptly. But the owner of the apartment was not satisfied until he knew what had caused the two skeletons to be buried in so unusual a place as the attic of the apartment. He started to dig into the past of the house and asked questions around the area. As far as he could determine, the woman in the nightgown had lived in the apartment, and once while she was waiting for her lover the door had opened and instead of her lover her husband had come through it. He had discovered the relationship and had come to kill her. After he murdered her he waited until the lover arrived and killed him, too, then hid the bodies in the attic.

Silently the host handed Jean a knife to touch and psychometrize, that is to say, read from it what could be gleaned of its past. As if she had been handed a glowing piece of coal she dropped it immediately. She could not touch it no matter how often she tried. The knife was an old knife of nondescript appearance, with a discolored blade and of no particular merit. Almost hysterical and sobbing, Jean assured her host that it was the knife that had been used to murder the woman. He nodded. He himself had found the blade among the bricks of the fireplace.

19

The Piano-Playing Ghost

*I*n the old days, owning a piano was a major achievement—an object of pride—and someone who could actually play it was a person to be much admired. In rural areas of the Southwest and the South, where pianos were not so common in those days, this talent was especially revered.

Hollygrove is only a small town in eastern Arkansas, but to Sharon Inebnit it is the center of her world. She lives there with her farmer husband in quiet, rural Arkansas far from metropolitan centers. Little Rock is a long way off and not a place she is likely to visit often. Her mother lives in Helena close to the Mississippi state line. Traveling east on Highway 86 and then on 49, Sharon has gone back and forth a few times in her young

225

life. She knows the area well. It is not an area of particular merit but it has one advantage: It's very quiet. About halfway between Hollygrove and Helena stands an old house that attracted Sharon every time she passed it. There was no reason for it, and yet whenever she passed the old house something within her wondered what the house's secret was.

Sharon is now in her early twenties. She has lived with an extraordinary gift of ESP since infancy. That is a subject one doesn't discuss freely in her part of the world. People either ridicule you or, worse, think you're in league with the devil. So Sharon managed to keep her powers to herself even though at times she couldn't help surprising people. She would often hear voices of people who weren't even within sight. If she wanted someone to call her, all she had to do was visualize the person and, presto, the person would ring her. Whenever the telephone rings she knows exactly who is calling. Frequently she has heard her neighbors talking five hundred yards from her house. She is so sensitive she cannot stand the television when it is turned on too loud.

Her husband, a farmer of Swiss extraction, is somewhat skeptical of her powers, though he is less skeptical now than he was when he first met her. Back in the summer of 1963, when they first kept company, she was already somewhat of a puzzle to him. One day, the fifteen-year-old girl insisted they drive into Helena, which was about five miles from where they were then. Her boyfriend wanted to know why. She insisted that there was a baseball game going on and that a private swimming party was in progress at the municipal pool. She had no reason to make this statement, however, nor any proof that it was correct, but they were both very

226

much interested in baseball games, so her boyfriend humored her and decided to drive on to Helena. When they arrived at Helena they found that a baseball game was indeed going on and that a private swimming party was in progress at the municipal pool just as Sharon had said. Helena has a population of over ten thousand people. Sharon lives twenty-five miles away. How could she have known this?

In March 1964 her maternal grandmother passed away. She had been close to her but for some reason was unable to see her in her last moments. Thus the death hit her hard and she felt great remorse at not having seen her grandmother prior to her passing. On the day of the funeral she was compelled to look up, and there before her appeared her late grandmother. Smiling at her, she nodded and then vanished. But in the brief moment when she had become visible to Sharon the girl understood what her grandmother wanted her to know. The message was brief. Her grandmother understood why she had not been able to see her in her last hours and wanted to forgive her.

In April 1964, when she was just sixteen years old, she married her present husband. They went to Memphis, Tennessee, for four days. All during their honeymoon Sharon insisted on returning home. She felt something was wrong at home, even though she couldn't pinpoint it. Though it wasn't a hot period of the year she felt extremely warm and very uncomfortable. Eventually her husband gave in to her urgings and returned home with her. Assuming that her psychic feelings concerned an accident they might have on the road, she insisted that they drive very carefully and slowly. There was no accident. However, when they entered the driveway of her home she found out what it was she felt all that distance away. A large fertilizer truck had hit a gasoline truck in front of her mother's house. A tremendous fire had ensued, almost setting her mother's house on fire. The blaze could be seen clearly in towns over five miles away. Both trucks burned up completely. It was the heat from the fire she had felt all the way to Memphis, Tennessee.

The house outside of Hollygrove, however, kept on calling her and somehow she didn't forget. Whenever she had a chance to drive by it she took it, looking at the house and wondering what its secret was. On one such occasion it seemed to her that she heard *someone play a piano inside the vacant house.* But that couldn't very well be; she knew that there was no one living inside. Perhaps there were mice jumping up and down the keyboard, if indeed there was a piano inside the house. She shook her head, dismissing the matter. Perhaps she had only imagined it. But somehow the sound of songs being played on an old piano kept on reverberating in her mind. She decided to do some research on the house.

Tom Kameron runs an antique shop in Hollygrove, and since the old house was likely to be filled with antiques he would be the man to question about it. That at least was Sharon's opinion. She entered the shop pretending to browse around for antiques. A lady clerk came over and pointed at an old lamp. "I want to show you something that you'll be interested in," she said. "This came from the old Mulls house here." Sharon was thunderstruck. The Mulls house was the house she was interested in. She began to question the clerk about the antiques in the Mulls house. Apparently a lot of them had been stolen or had disappeared during the last few years. Since then a caretaker had been appointed to guard the house. At this point the owner of the shop, Tom Kameron, joined the conversation. From him Sharon learned that the house had belonged to Tom Mulls, who had passed away, but Mrs. Mulls, although very aged, was still alive and living in a sanitarium in Little Rock. Kameron himself had been a friend of the late owner for many years.

The house had been built by a Captain Mulls, who had passed away around 1935. It was originally built in St. Augustine, Florida, and was later moved to Hollygrove.

The captain wasn't married, yet there was a woman with him in the house when it stood in Hollygrove. This was an Indian girl he had befriended and who lived with him until her death. The man who later inherited the house, Tom Mulls, was an adopted son. Apparently Captain Mulls was very much in love with his Indian lady. After her death he had her body embalmed and placed in a glass casket, which he kept in a room in the house. It stayed there until he died, and when Tom took over the house he buried the casket in the cemetery not far away. Her grave still exists in that cemetery. There were many Indian relics and papers dealing with Indian folklore in the house during her lifetime, but they have all disappeared since. The Indian girl played the piano very well indeed, and it was for her that the captain had bought a very fine piano. Many times he would sit listening to her as she played song after song for his entertainment.

The house has been vacant for many years but people can't help visiting it even though it is locked. They go up to the front steps and peer in the windows. Sharon was relieved to hear that she was not the only one strangely attracted to the old house. Others have also been "called" by the house as if someone inside were beckoning to them. Over the years strangers who have passed by the house have come to Mr. Kameron with strange tales of music emanating from the empty house. What people have heard wasn't the rustling of mice scurrying over a ruined piano keyboard but definite tunes, song after song played by skilled hands. Eventually the house will pass into the hands of the state since Mrs. Mulls has no heirs. But Sharon doubts that the ghost will move out just because the house changes hands again. She feels that her presence is very much alive and wholly content to live on in the old house. True, she now plays to a different kind of audience than she did when Captain Mulls was still alive, but then it is just possible that the captain has decided to stay behind also—if only to listen to the songs his Indian lady continues to play for his entertainment.

Part V

Ghosts in California

20

The Little Old Lady of
the Garden

Gardening is one of the finest expressions of humankind's cultural heritage, for it stems back to the early Greek and Roman cultures, if not beyond that into Babylonian and Chaldean realms. The hanging gardens of Nineveh were far more elaborate than anything moderners can dream up no matter how green their thumbs, and the rose gardens of Emperor Diocletian at Salonae, among which he spent his declining years, were a great deal more elaborate than the gardens we are apt to have for our own.

Gardening is also a health measure for it serves two purposes admirably well: It provides people with physical exercise, and it cleanses the air through the chemical process of photosynthesis, the miraculous arrangement whereby carbon dioxide is changed into oxygen naturally.

Americans in the Eastern states often consider gardening a hard-to-find pleasure especially if they live in the cities. But in the sunny West, it comes as a natural adjunct to one's house and is often the most desirable feature of it. Many of the citizens of the small communities of California have gone there, usually from the East or Midwest, to have an easier life in their later years. To them, having a garden to putter in is perhaps one of the chief attractions of this unhurried way of life.

The western climate is very kind to most forms of flowers, to fruit trees, and to almost all the plants usually found in both moderate and tropical climates, so it is small wonder that some of the California gardens turn into veritable show places of color and scent for their loving owners.

Naomi S. is a widow who has lived in California most of her life. Since the passing of her second husband, she has lived quietly in the southern California community of Huntington Park, and nothing of great importance happens to her now. That is as it should be, for she has had a glimpse into a world that has at once amazed and frightened her and she prefers that the excursion into it remain a veiled memory that will eventually be indistinguishable from the faded pictures of other past experiences in her busy and full life.

At the time, in 1953, she and her husband had been house hunting in Lynwood for a suitable place. She did not care for the run-of-the-mill houses one often finds in American communities and when they both saw this strangely attractive old house on Lago Avenue, they knew at once that that was *it*.

It was almost as if the house had *invited* them to come and get it, but so eager were they to investigate its possibilities, they never thought of this until much, much later.

The house was built in Norman style, almost European in its faithful copying of such old houses, and it was covered with all kinds of greens and vines going up and down the stone walls. Since it was surrounded by shrubbery and trees in the manner of a fence, it was most secluded, and one had the feeling of complete privacy. There was sufficient land around it to make it even more remote from the surrounding community, and as the zoning laws in Lynwood were quite carefully worded, chances of a new building going up next door to them were remote. They immediately went past the shrubbery and looked around, possibly to see if anyone could show them the house. The sign outside had read FOR SALE and given the name of a real estate firm, but it did not state whether or not the house was currently inhabited. As they approached the house across the soft lawn they came to realize immediately that it could not be. All around them were signs of neglect and apparently long periods of no care at all. What had once been a beautifully landscaped garden was now a semi-wilderness in which weeds had overgrown precious flowers and the shrubbery grew whichever way it chose.

The paths, so carefully outlined by a previous owner, were hardly recognizable now. The rains had washed them away and birds had done the rest.

"Needs lots of work," her husband mumbled apprehensively, as they observed the earmarks of destruction all around them. But they continued toward the house. They did not enter it but walked around it at first in the manner in which a wild animal stalks its prey. They wanted to take in all of the outside grounds first, before venturing inside.

On the other side of the house was a fine patio that had apparently served as a breakfast and dining patio at one time. A forlorn broken cup and a rusty spoon lay on the ground, but otherwise the patio was empty and still.

"Boy, they sure let this place run downhill," Mr. S. remarked and shook his head. He was a businessman used to orderly procedures and this was anything but good sense. Why would anyone owning so lovely a place let it go to pot? It didn't make sense to him.

All over the neighborhood, down Elm Street, the houses were aristocratic and well kept. It would seem *someone* would care enough to look after this little jewel of a house, too. Why hadn't the real estate man sent someone around to clean things up once in a while? He decided to question the man about it.

From the patio on down to the end of the property, clearly marked by the shrubbery, there was almost nothing but roses. Or rather, there had been at one time. One could still see that some loving hand had planted rows upon rows of rose bushes, but only a few of them were flowering now. In between, other plants had grown up and knowledgeable eyes could tell at once what was left of the roses needed careful and immediate pruning. Still, there was hope for the roses if a lot of work were put into them.

They entered the house through the patio door, which was ajar. Inside they found further proof of long neglect.

236

The furniture was still there, so it was a furnished house for sale. This was a pleasant surprise for it would make things a lot easier for them, financially speaking, even if some of the things they might buy with the house had to be thrown out later.

The dust covering the inside and an occasional spider's web drove home the fact that no one had lived here for years. But this did not disturb them, for there are lots of nice houses in California standing empty for years on end until someone wants them. They felt a strange sensation of being at home now, as if this had already been their house and they had just now reentered it only after a long summer vacation.

Immediately they started to examine each room and the gray, almost blackened windows. No doubt about it, it would take months of cleaning before the house would be livable again. But there was nothing broken or inherently beyond repair in the house and their courage rose, especially when they realized that most of the Victorian furniture was in excellent condition, just dirty.

After a prolonged stay in the house, during which they examined every one of the rooms, every nook and cranny, and finally went out into the garden again, they never doubted for a moment that this would be their future home. It never occurred to them that perhaps the sign had been out there for months even though someone had already bought the place or that it might be available but priced beyond their means.

Somehow they knew immediately that the house was right for them, just the size they wanted—they had no children—not too big to manage, but yet spacious and above all quiet, as it sat in the midst of what might once again become a fine garden.

"Well, what do you say, Naomi?" Mr. S. inquired. It was more of a rhetorical question since he, and she, knew very well what they were to do next. "Yes, it will do," she nodded and smiled at him. It was a good feeling to have found one's home.

They carefully closed the patio door and locked it as best they could—after all, it was *their* home now, practically, and not just a neglected, empty old house for sale. As they walked up the garden path toward Elm Street, they had the distinct feeling of being followed by a pair of eyes. But they were so preoccupied with thoughts of how to make this place into a livable home that they paid no heed. They didn't even turn around when they heard a rustling sound in the leaves that covered the path. It was the kind of sound the wind would make, had there *been* a wind.

After they left the place, they immediately drove down to the real estate office.

Yes, the place was still for sale. They sighed with relief, too noticeably to escape the glance of the real estate man. It bemused him, since he was only too glad to unload the white elephant the house on Lago Avenue represented to him. After some small talk, they agreed on a price and move-in date, and then Mrs. S. began to wonder about the people who had lived there before.

But the real estate man, either by design or ignorance, could not tell them much. The house had been there for about thirty years or so, but even that was not certain. It might have been sixty years, for all he knew. It could not be more than that, for Lynwood wasn't much older. Who had built it? He didn't know their names, but a couple had built it and lived in it originally, and after them a number of other people had either bought or rented it,

238

but somehow nobody stayed very long. His company had just recently taken over its sale, he believed, in the name of some absentee heir, across the country somewhere, but he really could not tell them more than that.

"It's just an old house, you know," he finally said and looked at them puzzled. "Why do you want to know more?"

Why indeed? The man was right. Resolutely, they signed the contract and a few weeks later, when their affairs elsewhere had been wound up, they moved into the house.

The first few days were grim, reminiscent of the pioneering days of early Americans as the S.s worked from early in the morning to late in the evening to get their bedroom into livable condition. After that, the kitchen and so forth needed to be redone until gradually, with much sweat and effort, the house changed. In the spring, they turned their attention to the garden, and since Mr. S. had gone into semiretirement from his business he had a little more time on his hands to help. Now and then they used the services of a local gardener, but by and large, it was their own effort that made the garden bloom again. Carefully pruning the roses, and whenever they found a gap, replanting a rose bush, they managed to bring back a new life to the beautiful place. Inside the house the old furniture had been dusted and repaired where necessary and they had augmented the pieces with some of their own, interspersing them where suitable. So the house took on a strange mixture of their old house and what must have been the former owner's own world, but the two did not seem to clash, and intermingled peacefully for their comfort.

They never tried to change anything in either house or

garden just for change's sake: If they could find what had stood on the spot, they would faithfully restore it, almost as if driven by a zeal to turn the clock back to where it had stood when the house had first been built. They felt themselves motivated by the same loyalty a museum curator displays in restoring a priceless masterpiece to its original appearance. Their efforts paid off, and the house became a model of comfortable, if somewhat Victorian, living.

As they became acquainted with their garden, they became aware of the fact that it contained lots more than roses or ordinary flowers. Apparently the previous owners liked rare plants for there were remnants of unusual flowers and green plants they had never seen before outside of museums or arboretums. With some of them, the original label had remained, giving the name and origin. Whenever they were able to, they fixed these labels so that much of the old flavor returned to the garden. They even went to the local florist and asked him to explain some of the rare plants, and in turn they bought some replacements for those that had died of neglect, and put them where they would have been before.

With all this work taking up most of their time, they found no opportunity to make friends in the community. For a long time, they knew no one except the real estate man and the gardener who had occasionally worked for them, neither of whom became social acquaintances.

But one morning Mrs. S. noticed a nice woman pass her as she was working in the front garden, and they exchanged smiles. After that, she stopped her in the street a day or so later and inquired about shops in the area and it turned out the woman was a neighbor living across the street from them, a certain Lillian G., who had been a longtime resident of the area. Not a young woman any longer, Mrs. G. knew a great deal about the community, it appeared, but the two women never talked about anything but current problems of the most mundane nature—on the few occasions that they did meet again. It was almost as if Naomi did not *want* to discuss the story of her house any longer, now that she owned it.

A year went by and the S.'s were finally through with all their restorations in the house and could settle back to a comfortable and well-earned rest. They liked their home and knew that they had chosen well and wisely. What had seemed to them at the time a beckoning finger from the house itself now appeared merely as an expression of horse sense upon seeing the place and they prided themselves on having been so wise.

It was summer again and the California sky was blue and all was well with the house and themselves. Mr. S. had gone out and would not be back until the afternoon. Mrs. S. was busy working in the rose garden, putting some fine touches on her bushes. Despite the approaching midday, it was not yet too hot to work.

Naomi had just straightened out one of the tea roses, when she looked up and realized she had a visitor. There, on the path no more than two yards away stood a rather smallish lady. She was neatly dressed in a faded house dress of another era, but in California this is not particularly unusual. Lots of retired people like to dress in various old-fashioned ways and no one cares one way or another. The lady was quite elderly and fragile, and Naomi was startled to see her there.

Her surprise must have been obvious, for the visitor

241

immediately apologized for the intrusion. "I didn't mean to scare you," she said in a thin, high-pitched voice that somehow went well with her general appearance and frailty.

"You didn't," Naomi bravely assured her. She was nothing if not hospitable. Why should a little old lady scare her?

"Well then," the visitor continued tentatively, "would it be all right if I looked around a bit?"

This seemed unusual, for the place was scarcely a famous showplace, and Naomi did not feel like turning it into a public park. Again her thoughts must have shown on her face, for the lady immediately raised her hand and said, "You see, my husband and I originally built this place."

Naomi was flabbergasted. So the owners had decided to have a look at their house after all these years. At the same time, a sense of accomplishment filled her heart. Now they could see how much had been done to fix up the house!

"It's a beautiful place," Naomi said and waved her visitor to come with her.

"Yes, isn't it?" the lady nodded. "We took great pride in it, really."

"Too bad it was in such bad shape when we bought it, though," Naomi said succinctly. "We had to put a lot of work into it to bring it back to its old state."

"Oh, I can see that," the lady commented and looked with loving eyes at each and every shrub.

They were on the garden path in the rear now.

"Oh, you've put pink roses where the tea roses used to be," she suddenly exclaimed. "How thoughtful."

Naomi did not know that the tea roses had been on

that spot for there had been nothing left of them. But she was glad to hear about it. The visitor now hopped from flower to flower almost like a bird, inspecting here, caressing a plant there, and pointing out the various rare plants to Naomi, as if *she* were the hostess and Naomi the visitor.

"I am so glad you have brought life back into the house, so glad," she kept repeating.

It made Naomi even happier with her accomplishment. Too bad her husband couldn't be here to hear the lady's praise. Mr. S. had sometimes grumbled about all the hard work they had had to put in to make the place over.

"The begonia over there . . . oh, they are still missing, too bad. But you can fix that sometime, can you not?" she said and hurried to another part of the garden, as if eager to take it all in in whatever time Naomi allowed her to visit with her.

"Wouldn't you like to have a look at the inside of the house, too?" Naomi finally suggested. The lady glowed with happiness at the invitation.

"Yes, I would like that very much. May I?" Naomi pointed at the garden door and together they stepped inside the house. The cool atmosphere inside was in sharp contrast to the pleasant, warm air in the garden.

"Over there, that's where the grandfather clock used to be. I see you've moved it to the den."

Naomi smiled. They had indeed. The lady surely must have an excellent memory to remember all that, for they had not yet entered the den. It never occurred to Naomi that the visitor knew the clock had been moved prior to seeing it in the den. So much at home was the little old lady in what used to be her house, that it seemed perfectly natural for her to know all sorts of things about it.

"The table is nice, too, and it fits in so well," she now commented. They had brought it with them from their former home, but it did indeed blend in with the furniture already in the house. The visitor now bounced gaily to the other end of the long room which they were using as a day room or parlor.

"That chair," she suddenly said, and pointed at the big, oaken chair near the fireplace, and there was a drop in her voice that seemed to indicate a change in mood.

"What about the chair?" Naomi inquired and stepped up to it. The visitor seemed to have difficulty in holding back a tear or two, but then composed herself and explained—

"My husband died in that chair."

There was a moment of silence as Naomi felt compassion for the strange lady.

"He was raking leaves one morning . . . it was a nice summer day just like today . . . just like today . . . he always liked to do a little work around the garden before breakfast. I was still in bed at that hour, but I was awake and I heard him come into the house when he had finished his chores in the garden."

Naomi had not said anything, but her eyes were on the lady with interest. She noticed how frail and ethereal she looked, and how old age had really rendered her thin and somehow tired. And yet, her eyes had an unusual, bright sparkle in them that belied her frail and aged appearance. No, this woman was all right, despite her advanced age. Probably lives alone somewhere in the area, too, now that her husband is dead, Naomi mused.

"My husband came into the house and a little later I

got up to fix him breakfast as I always did," the visitor continued, all the while holding the back of the chair firmly with one hand.

"When I called out to him to come and get it, I received no reply. Finally I thought this odd and went into the room—this room—and there, in this chair, I found him. He was dead."

The account had given Naomi a strange chill. It suddenly occurred to her how little she knew about the former owners. But the icy hush that had settled over the two women was broken when the lady let go of the chair and turned toward the door.

"I'd like another look at the patio, if I may," she said and as if she wanted to make up for her seriousness before, now she chatted interminably and lightly about the pleasures of living in such a house as this.

They had arrived at the rose beds again and the visitor pointed at a particularly full-blown dark red bush Naomi had fancied all along more than any other rose bush in the garden.

"They were always my favorites," the lady said, almost with a whisper.

"Then let me give you some to take home with you," Naomi offered and since the visitor did not protest her offer, she turned around to reach for the scissors, which she kept at the foot of the patio.

Her back was not turned more than a second. But when she looked up at her visitor again, the little lady was gone.

"That's rude of her," Naomi thought immediately. Why had she suddenly run away? Surely, the offer of roses from her former home was no reason to be offended. But then it occurred to Naomi that perhaps the lady's emotions at being back in her old home, yet no longer mistress of it, might have gotten the upper hand with her and she simply could not face having a stranger give her roses from *her* favorite bush.

"I wonder which way she went, though," Naomi said out loud. She heard no car drive off, so the lady must have come on foot. Perhaps she could still catch her, for surely she could not have gotten far. It was plain silly of her not to take the proffered roses.

Naomi quickly went down the garden path and looked there and then looked at the driveway but the woman was not on the property any longer. She even ran out onto the street and looked down Elm Street but the visitor was nowhere in sight.

"But this is impossible," Naomi thought. "She can't just disappear." So little time had elapsed between their last words and Naomi's pursuit that no human being could have disappeared without trace.

Still puzzled, Naomi went back into the house. The whole episode took on a certain dreamlike quality after a while and she forgot about it. Surely there must be some explanation for the lady's quick disappearance, but Naomi had other things to do than worry about it.

For reasons of her own she felt it best not to tell her husband about the visit, for she was not at all sure herself now that she had not dreamed the whole thing. Of course, she hadn't. The lady's footprints were still visible in the soft soil of the lawn several days after the visit. Such small feet, too. But somehow she felt reluctant to discuss it further. Besides, what of it? A former tenant wants to visit the old home. Nothing special or newsworthy about that.

The Little Old Lady of the Garden

*   *   *

Several weeks later she happened to have tea with the neighbor across the street. Over tea and cookies, they talked about the neighborhood and how it had changed over all the years Mrs. G. had lived there. Somehow the visitor came to mind again, and Naomi felt free to confide in Mrs. G.

"I had a visitor the other day, only person I've talked to except for you," Naomi began.

"Oh?" Mrs. G. perked up. "Anyone I might know?"

"Perhaps . . . it was the lady who built our house . . . who lived there before us."

Mrs. G. gave Naomi a strange look but said nothing.

"She was a little lady with a faded pink dress and kind of sparkling eyes, and she told me she and her husband had built the house," Naomi said, and described what the visitor had looked like in minute detail. When she had finished, Mrs. G. shook her head.

"Impossible," she finally said. "That woman has been dead for years."

Naomi laughed somewhat uncertainly.

"But how could she be? I saw her as plainly as I see you. She looked just like any little old lady docs."

"Maybe it was someone else," the neighbor said, half hoping Naomi would readily agree to her suggestion.

"I don't think so," Naomi said firmly, however. "You see she also pointed out the chair her husband died in. He had been raking leaves before breakfast, and when she called out to him to come and get it, he didn't answer, and then she went into the parlor and there he was, dead in that big oaken chair."

Mrs. G. had suddenly become very pale.

"That is absolutely true, I mean, the story how he

died," she finally managed to say. "But how would *you* know about it?"

Naomi shrugged helplessly.

"I didn't know it until the lady told me about it," she repeated.

"Incredible. But you've described her to a tee and he did die the way she said. They've both been dead for years and years, you know."

Naomi finally realized the implication.

"You mean I've been visited by a ghost?"

"Seems that way," Mrs. G. nodded gravely.

"But she seemed so very real . . . so solid. I'd never have known she was just a ghost. Why, we even shook hands and her hand felt fine to me."

The woman went over the experience once more, detail for detail. There was one thing that was odd, though. On recollection, Mrs. S. did recall that she had not *heard* the woman enter her garden. She had looked up from her chores, and there the woman stood, smiling at her from in front of the roses. No sound of footsteps on either entering or leaving. Then, too, her intimate knowledge of each and every plant in the garden.

"She even knew the Latin names of everyone of them," Naomi pointed out.

"No doubt she did," Mrs. G. explained, and added, "she and her hubby were great horticulturists and took enormous pride in creating a genuine arboretum in their garden."

But why had she visited her old home?

After some thought, Naomi felt she knew the answer. They had just finished restoring the house and garden to their original appearance and probably the same flavor they had had in the years when the original owners had the place. The ghostly lady felt they should be rewarded for their efforts by an approving gesture from *them*. Or had she simply been homesick for her old home?

Naomi was quite sure, now, that she had never really left it. In her mind's eye it had never fallen into disrepair and the lovely roses never ceased to bloom even when the garden had become a wilderness.

She never discussed the matter again with her neighbor or with anyone else for that matter. Her husband, whom she later divorced, never knew of the incident, for Mrs. G. also kept the secret well.

The house may still be there amid the roses, and the little lady in the faded dress no doubt still delights in skipping along its paths enjoying her beloved flowers.

21

The Wild Party Ghost

*T*his is the true story of a nice, average house on Hollywood's quiet Arden Boulevard—the furthest appearance from what a haunted house is supposed to look like.

The house itself, barely thirty years old, was being plagued by the noises of a wild party going on at night, during which someone was apparently killed, and by other uncanny noises, including footsteps where nobody was seen walking as well as voices resounding in the dark, telling the current owners to get out of *their* house!

I had been to this house several times, and on one occasion I brought along Maxine Bell, a local psychic. That visit proved memorable not only because material obtained by Miss Bell, in semi-trance proved accurate to a large degree, but because of my own photographic work.

Left alone in the most haunted part of the house, I took at random a number of black-and-white pictures of a particular bedroom, which of course was empty, at least to my eyes.

On one of the pictures, taken under existing daylight conditions and from a firm surface, the figure of a young girl dressed in a kind of negligee appears standing near the window. As my camera is double-exposure proof and both film and developing are beyond reproach, there is no other rational explanation for this picture. Since that time, I have succeeded in taking other psychic photographs, but the "girl at the window" will always rank as one of my most astounding ones.

The whistling noises, the popping of a champagne bottle in the dark of night followed by laughter, the doors opening by themselves, and all the other psychic phenomena that had been long endured by the owner of the house, Helen L., would not yield to my usual approach: a trance session and an order to the ghost to go away. There were complications in that Miss L. herself had mediumistic talents, although unsought and undeveloped, and there was present in the household a mentally handicapped sister, often the source of energies with which poltergeist phenomena are made possible.

Nevertheless, when we left the house on Ardmore Boulevard I had high hopes for a more peaceful atmosphere in the future. For one thing, I explained matters to Miss L., and for another, I suggested that the garden be searched for the body of that murder victim. We had already established through neighbors that a fight had actually occurred some years ago in the house. It was entirely possible that the body of one of the victims was still on the grounds.

In July of 1964 the noises resumed, and thuds of falling bodies, footfalls, and other noises started up again in the unfortunate house. Quite rightly, Helen L. asked me to continue the case. But it was not until the spring of 1965 that I could devote my energies toward this matter again.

All I had accomplished in the interim was a certain lessening of the phenomena, but not their elimination.

On March 14, 1965, Helen L. communicated with me about a matter of great urgency. For the first time, the ghost had been seen! At 3:00 A.M. on March 13, her mother had been awakened by strange noises, and looking up from the bed, she saw the figure of a man beside the bed. The noise sounded to her as if someone were tearing up bedsheets. Frightened, the old lady pulled the covers over her head and went back to sleep. Helen L. also heard heavy footsteps all over the house that same night. Needless to say, they had no visitors from the flesh-and-blood world.

"Are you going to be here in April? Help!!" Helen L. wrote. I answered I would indeed come and bring Sybil Leek with me to have another and, hopefully, final go at this ghost. But it would have to be in June, not April. During the first week of May, Helen awoke on Sunday morning to hear a man's voice shushing her inches away from her pillow. She could hardly wait for our arrival after that. Finally, on June 28, I arrived at the little house with Sybil to see what she might pick up.

"I know there is a presence here," Sybil said immediately as we seated ourselves in the little office that was situated in back of the bedroom where most of the disturbances had occurred. I turned out the light to give Sybil a better chance to concentrate, or rather, to relax, and immediately she felt the intruder.

"It is mostly in the bedroom," she continued. "There are two people; the man dominates in the bedroom area, and there is also a woman, a young girl."

I decided Sybil should attempt trance at this point, and invited the ghost to make himself known. After a few moments, Sybil slipped into a state bordering on trance, but continued to be fully conscious.

"Morton," she mumbled now, "there is something terribly intense . . . have a desire to *break* something . . . Morton is the last name."

I repeated my invitation for him to come forward and tell his story.

"The girl goes away," Sybil intoned, "and he says he comes back to find her. And she isn't here. He was going to celebrate. He must find her. Wedding party, celebration . . . for the girl. She wasn't happy here; she had to go away. This man is a foreigner."

"You're right." The booming voice of Helen L. spoke up in the dark across the room. Evidently Sybil had described someone she recognized.

"Jane Morton," Sybil said now, flatly, "something to do with building, perhaps he had something to do with building this house . . . he's an older man. Jane . . . is young . . . I'm trying to find out where Jane is . . . that's what *he* wants to know . . . I will tell him it didn't matter about the party . . . she would have gone anyway . . . she hated the old man . . . this man fell . . . head's bad . . . fell against the stable. . . ."

"Did he die here?" I pressed.

"Eighteen thirty-seven," Sybil said, somewhat incongruously. "Eighteen thirty-seven. Came back . . . went out again, came back with people, was drunk, hurt his head, left-hand side. . . ."

Despite my urging, the entity refused to speak through Sybil in trance. I continued to question her nevertheless.

The ghost's name was Howell Morton, Sybil reported, although I was not sure of the spelling of the first name, which might have been Hawall rather than Howell.

"He came here to do some building, someone was accidentally killed and buried in the garden. . . ."

"Who buried this person?"

"Boyd Johnson . . . Raymond McClure . . . Dell . . . Persilla. . . ." The voice was faltering now and the names not too clear."

"Is the girl dead, too?"

"Girl's alive. . . ."

"Is there anyone dead in this house outside of Morton?"

"Morton died here."

"Who was the figure I photographed here?"

"Jane . . . he wants to draw her back here . . . but I think she's alive . . . yet there are things of hers buried. . . ."

Sybil seemed confused at this point.

"Meri . . . Meredith. . . ." she said, or she could have said. "Married her." It just was not clear enough to be sure. Morton and some of his friends were doing the disturbing in the house, Sybil explained. He died at the party.

"There was violence outside," Sybil added and Helen L. nodded emphatically. There was indeed.

"Drunk . . . four o'clock . . . he died accidentally. . . ."

Where is he buried in the garden, Helen L. asked anxiously.

"Straight down by the next building," Sybil replied. "It wasn't built completely when he died."

Later we all went into the garden and identified the building as the garage in back of the house.

But Helen was not yet ready to start digging. What would the neighbors think if we found a body? Or, for that matter, what would they think if we didn't? There we left it, for her to think over whether to dig or not to dig—that was the question.

I returned to New York in the hope that I would not hear anything further from Helen L. But I was mistaken. On July 5, I heard again from the lady on Ardmore Boulevard.

Her other sister, Alma, who lives in Hollywood but has stayed at the house on Ardmore on occasion, called the morning after our visit. It was then that she volunteered information she had been holding back from Helen L. for two years for fear of further upsetting her, in view of events at the house. But she had had a dreamlike impression at the house in which she "saw" a man in his middle years, who had lived in a lean-to shack attached to the garage.

She knew this man was dead and got the impression that he was a most stubborn person, difficult to dislodge or reason with. What made this dream impression of interest to us, Miss L. thought, was the fact that her sister could not have known of Sybil Leek's insistence that a man lay buried at that very spot next to the garage! To the best of Helen L.'s knowledge no shack ever stood there, but of course it may have stood there before the present house was built.

Also, Helen reminded me that on those occasions when her mother and sister slept in the garage, when they had company in the main house, both had heard heavy footsteps coming up to the garage and stopping dead upon reaching the wall. Helen L.'s mother had for years insisted that there was "a body buried there in the garden" but nobody had ever tried to find it.

Nothing more happened until May 8, 1966, when Sybil Leek and I again went to the house because Helen L. had implored us to finish the case for her. The disturbances had been continuing on and off.

With us this time was Eugene Lundholm, librarian and psychic researcher. Trance came quickly. Perhaps Sybil was in a more relaxed state this time than during our last visit, but whatever the reason, things seemed to be more congenial.

"I'm falling," her voice whispered, barely audible, "I'm hungry. . . ."

Was someone reliving moments of anguish?

"Who are you?" I demanded.

"Can't breathe. . . ."

"What is your name?"

"Ha . . . Harold. . . ."

He had great difficulties with his breathing and I suggested he relax.

"Kill her . . ." he now panted, "kill her, kill the woman. . . ."

"Did you kill her?"

"NO!"

"I've come to help you. I'm your friend."

"Kill her before she goes away. . . ."

"Why?"

"No good here . . . where's he taken her? Where is she?"

The voice became more intelligible now.

"What is her name?"

"Where is she? . . . I'll kill her."

"Who's with her?"

"Porter."

"Is he a friend of yours?"

"NO!"

"Who are you?"

"Harold Howard."

"Is this your house?"

"My house."

"Did you build it?"

"No."

"Did you buy it?"

Evidently my questioning got on his nerves, for he shouted, "Who are *you?*" I explained, but it didn't help.

"Too many people here . . . I throw them out . . . take those people out of here!"

Strangely enough, the voice did not sound like Sybil's at all; it had lost all trace of a British flavor and was full of anger. Evidently the ghost was speaking of the revelers he had found at his house, and he wanted them out.

"His friends . . . take them away . . . she brought them. . . ."

"While you were away?" He was somewhat calmer now.

"Yes," he confirmed.

"Where were you?"

"Working."

"What do you do?"

"Miner."

"Where do you work?"

"Purdy Town." He may have said Purgory Town, or something like it.

"What happened when you came home?"

Again he became upset about the people in his house, and I asked that he name some of them.

"Margaret . . ." he said, more excited now. "Mine . . . twenty-five . . . I came home . . . they were here . . . too many people . . . party here. . . ."

"Did you hurt anyone?"

"I'm going to kill her," he insisted. Evidently he had not done so.

"Why?"

"Because of him." Jealousy, the great ghostmaker.

"Who is he?"

"Porter."

"Who is he?"

"He took my place. Eric Porter."

"What year is this?"

It was high time we got a "fix" on the period we were in.

" 'Forty-eight."

"What happened to you . . . afterward?"

"People went away . . . Porter . . . outside . . . I want to go away now. . . ."

It became clear to me that the girl must have been killed, but that a shock condition at the time of the crime had prevented this man from realizing what he had done, thus forcing him to continue his quest for the girl. I told him as much and found him amazed at the idea of his deed.

"Why did he follow me . . . he followed me . . . then I hit him in the guts. . . ."

259

"What did you do with him then?"

"Put him away."

He became cagey after that, evidently thinking I was some sort of policeman interrogating him.

"I watch him," he finally said. "I look after him . . . in the garden. I won't let him in the house."

I asked him further about himself, but he seemed confused.

"Where am I?"

He asked me to leave the other man in the garden, in the ground. He would never go away because he had to watch this other man.

"Margaret comes back," he said now. Was there a foursome, or were we dealing with more than one level of consciousness?

"Keep him away from her," the ghost admonished me.

"I will," I promised and meant it.

I then told him about his death and that of the others, hoping I could finally rid the house of them all.

"She'll come back," his one-track mind made him say. "I'll wait till she is in bed and then I'll kill her."

I explained again that killing the other man wouldn't do any good since he was already dead.

"My head's bad," the ghost complained.

"You cannot stay at this house," I insisted firmly now.

"Not leaving," he shot back just as firmly. "My house!"

I continued my efforts, explaining also about the passage of time.

" 'Forty-eight . . ." he insisted, "I fight . . . I fight . . ."

"You've been forgiven," I said and began the words that amount to a kind of exorcism. "You are no longer guilty. You may go."

260

"Carry him," he mumbled and his voice weakened somewhat. "Where is she? Who'll clean up?"

Then he slipped away.

I awakened Sybil. She felt fine and recalled nothing. But I recalled plenty.

For one thing, it occurred to me that the ghost had spoken of the year '48 but had not indicated whether it was 1948 or 1848, and there was something in the general tone of the voice that made me wonder if perhaps we were not in the wrong century. Certainly no miner worked in Los Angeles in 1948, but plenty did in 1848. Eugene Lundholm checked the records for me.

In the '40s, mines sprang up all over the territory. In 1842 Francisco Lopez had discovered gold near the San Fernando Mission, and in 1848 a much larger gold deposit was found near Sacramento.

The famous gold strike at Sutter's Mill occurred in 1848. But already in the early 1840s mining existed in southern California, although not much came of it.

After we went back to New York, Helen L. reached me again the last week of July 1966.

Her mother refused to leave the house, regardless of the disturbances. Thus a sale at this time was out of the question, Miss L. explained.

Something or someone was throwing rocks against the outside of the house and on the roof of their patio—but no living person was seen doing it. This, of course, is on par with the poltergeist course. Just another attention-getter. Loud crashes on the patio roof and nobody there to cause them. Even the neighbors now heard the noises. Things were getting worse. I wrote back, offering to have another look at the haunted house provided she was willing to dig. No sense leaving the corpus delicti there.

But on September 18 Miss L. had some more to tell me. Rocks falling on the driveway behind the house brought out the neighbors in force, with flashlights looking for the "culprits" who could not be found. Nor could the rocks, for that matter. They were invisible rocks, it would seem.

This took place on numerous occasions between 6:15 and 7:30 P.M. and only at that time. To top it off, a half-ripe lemon flew off their lemon tree toward Miss L. with such force that it cracked wide open when it landed on the grass beside her. It could not have fallen by itself and there was no one in the tree to throw it.

I promised to get rid of the lemon-throwing ghost if I could, when we came to Los Angeles again in October. But when I did, Miss L.'s mother was ill and the visit had to be called off.

I have not heard anything further about this stubborn ghost. But the area was populated in 1848 and it could be that another house or camp stood on this site before the present house was erected. There is a brook not far away. So far, neither Mr. Morton nor Mr. Howard has been located and Jane and Margaret are only ghostly facts. A lot of people passed through the house when Miss L.'s family did not own it, and of course we know nothing whatever about the house that preceded it.

One more note came to me which helped dispel any notion that Helen L. was the only one bothered by the unseen in the house on Ardmore.

It was signed by Margaret H. Jones and addressed *To Whom It May Concern*. It *concerned* the ghost.

Some years ago, when I was a guest in Miss L.'s home at ——— Ardmore Boulevard, in Los Angeles, I heard what

*seemed to be very heavy footsteps in a room which I knew
to be empty. Miss L. was with me at the time and I told her
that I heard this sound. The footsteps seemed to advance
and to recede, and this kept up for several minutes, and
though we investigated we saw no one. They ceased with
the same abruptness with which they began.*

I fondly hoped the manifestations would behave in a
similar manner. Go away quietly.

But on October 6, 1967, Helen L. telephoned me in
New York. She had spent a sleepless night—part of a
night, that is.

Up to 4:00 A.M. she had been sleeping peacefully. At
that hour she was awakened by her cat. Putting the animal down, she noticed a strange light on her patio, which
was located outside her bedroom windows. She hur-
riedly threw on a robe and went outside.

In the flower bed on her left, toward the rear of the
garden, she noticed something white. Despite her dislike
for the phenomena that had for so long disturbed her
home, Helen L. advanced toward the flower bed.

Now she could clearly make out the figure of a woman,
all in white. The figure was not very tall and could have
been that of a young girl. It seemed to watch her intently,
and looked somewhat like the conventional white bed-
sheet type of fictional ghost.

At this point Miss L.'s courage left her and she ran
back to her room.

The next morning, her eyes red with exhaustion, she
discussed her experience with her aged mother. Until
now she had been reluctant to draw her mother into
these matters, but the impression had been so overpowering that she just had to tell *someone.*

To her surprise, her mother was not very upset. Instead, she added her own account of the "White Lady" to the record. The night before, the same figure had apparently appeared to the mother in a dream, telling her to pack, for she would soon be taking her away!

When Helen L. had concluded her report, I calmed her as best I could and reminded her that *some* dreams are merely expressions of unconscious fears. I promised to pay the house still another visit, although I am frankly weary of the prospect: I know full well that you can't persuade a ghost to go away when there may be a body, once the property of said ghost, buried in a flower bed in the garden.

After all, a ghost's got rights, too!

22

The Haunting at Newbury Park

I am indebted to Mrs. Gwen Hinzie, an amateur psychic, for some of the most interesting and bizarre cases of genuine hauntings in the area of northern California. One such case was the haunted house and barn at Newbury Park, California.

Mrs. Hinzie wanted my opinion on her "problem."

"I have been disappointed that you have not yet commented on our situation here," she wrote me regarding "the uncomfortable atmosphere around the barn and the voice I've heard saying 'Hi.' But I do have, I believe, additional information on that which we think is interesting.

"First I will tell you about our town, Newbury Park. It *is* on the map and up to five years ago had a population of about five thousand or less. We now have about eleven thousand people, I believe. My husband and I have lived here since June 1961, but in another part of town 'til last February. The town's only claim to fame is its stagecoach inn, a hostelry which, I understand from Mrs. Michael Hagopejion, the president of the Conejo Valley Historical Society, was used as a hotel and stopover for the stage-coach traveling between Santa Barbara and Los Angeles from 1876 to 1915. The inn is now being moved from its location, the equivalent of about two city blocks from us, to another location a few hundred feet away, as the free-way overpass will pass through the original site of the inn. It is a two-story frame building of nineteen rooms.

"Up to 1960, Newbury Park, except for a very small residential section, was all ranch land. These ranches were in size from hundreds to thousands of acres. Many of the owners were related to each other, and so for the past ninety years it has been a small ranching commu-nity.

"I have learned from our friend Martin Bettin that sometime in the late 1800s there was a boy staying at the inn who, probably in exploring the hilly country close by, became lost. The boy was never found. I cannot help wondering if it's the child's voice we have heard, and if it *is* the voice of a young boy, could it be the ghost of this lost child?

"Martin Bettin got his information from a fireman at the Lake Sherwood fire station. His name is Simeon Dyke and he got the story from his father, an old-timer in the Conejo Valley.

"Another thing of interest to the barn area (which I find uncomfortable): This property, belonging to Allen Hays, our landlord, was purchased by his father some-time between 1910 and 1920, I understand. We live on about 2½ acres of land, but the Hays ranch consisted of hundreds of acres and, after old Mr. Hays's death, was divided between his children, Allen Hays and Reba Jeffries.

"Through Simeon Dyke, Martin learned that in about 1920 there were a house and barn in the pasture adjacent to our present barn. They were torn down years ago. But at that time the people who lived in that house had a little girl, aged two or three, who fell into an open well or cesspool and was drowned. Could this, I wonder, have anything to do with my feeling about the barn area? Actually, however, my feeling is not around the pasture but the barn itself, outside that fenced pasture and also the road—part of it—above the barn closer to the house.

"I overheard a conversation between Martin and Sharon Bettin and Sharon's mother, Mrs. Davies, while I was at Mrs. Davies's house, and asked them about it. Apparently they didn't want to say anything in front of me, but Martin and Sharon have admitted to Mrs. Davies they have an uncomfortable feeling in our barn. I had always felt myself *like a trespasser there,* and seldom visit the barn, but Martin has about a hundred rabbits there and he is there frequently. He says he feels as if someone might come around the corner at any time. He says it's almost as if you expect someone to suddenly come up from nowhere and tap you on the shoulder—and Martin isn't timid. Sharon said she felt uncomfortable there, too."

By now I thought I knew Newbury Park pretty well without ever having set foot on this little speck of land. Mrs. Hinzie had a way of describing her world that had authenticity, and I decided to let her be our guide if and when we could go there in person.

REAL HAUNTINGS

*　*　*

Meanwhile I asked her to report further unusual happenings to me when they took place. Mrs. Hinzie was a bit worried about my postponing our visit to the fall of 1966.

"We expect to move from here in about a year, and it is unlikely that the place will be tenanted again after that, as Mr. Hays, our landlord, wants to sell this property for commercial use and undoubtedly this little house will be torn down. It is ten years old and made of cement blocks.

"There have been three occurrences that I have not mentioned, over the past two months. The most recent was a weird 'singing' or 'whistling' noise that I heard a few nights ago. I am reasonably sure this was not my imagination, as my son, David, has told me of hearing such a noise about two months ago while he was in the bathroom. He was frightened, but no one else heard it and I could not imagine what it could be other than a little air in the pipes. But when I heard what I assume was the same noise it was while I sat up alone in our living room–kitchen area.

"The other thing that happened was the day I saw the ghost. I knew from the voice that it was a boy of about ten or twelve. But this day (in late January), while I was washing the windows, I saw through the window pane clearly standing by the fence a young boy *and you could see the fence through him!* It was in the morning and that side of the house was shaded, but the yard behind it was in brilliant sunlight. I wasn't sure I could believe my eyes and when I turned around he was gone.

"Another hard-to-explain thing that happened was one evening at least a month ago—maybe more—when my husband and I were sitting in the living room and the

268

room was fairly quiet. We both heard a sound that could only be called a whimpering near the door. I had heard this several months before but no one else had."

The experiences of young children are generally considered unworthy of belief when one investigates scientifically phenomena of this kind, and yet no one dares say that all children make up stories and that there are not keen observers among the very young.

I did not attach importance to the testimony of the Hinzie children by itself, but coming on the heels of so much *adult* evidence, it seemed to reinforce the whole case and therefore I am reporting it. Mrs. Hinzie carefully wrote down what her children reported seeing in the house.

"David told me about some misty shapes he had seen, and said the other kids also saw them some time ago in their bedroom. He said it was dark in the room and these 'things' were light.

"Near the ceiling he saw three misty shapes and they seemed to be looking down at the children. They were vague but he thought they were people. He called me and when I came in and opened the door they disappeared.

"Until June of 1965 (that is, in reference to our staying in this house), my husband, Don, worked nights (2:00 p.m. to 10:30 p.m.). It was during that period (between late February and mid-June) that one night there was an uproar in the bedroom and the children all called me and I rushed in, after removing books, etc., from my lap in the living room and opened the door and the kids pointed to the *ceiling* near the end of the bedroom partition and said, 'See it, Mom—see it.' But I saw nothing.

"I turned around to turn on the light and it was gone.

"The kids said, that night, they 'saw something' in that

spot. They said it was 'horrible' and could not describe it. Said it was not misty and had, according to them, no definite shape. They asked me to leave the door open, which I did after first closing it and telling them it was nonsense. But they were nearly hysterical when I closed the door, so I immediately reopened it. They settled down almost immediately after that and slept. There was no reoccurrence of that particular night.

"The children sleep in a room that is on the north side of the house and has two windows on that side. There are no windows in the east wall or the south or west wall and the two bedrooms I mentioned are really one room partitioned to within about three feet of the door.

"The 'shapeless, horrible' thing the kids saw was on my mind for a while after that, and when I saw something in there later on, I was not sure it was not subconscious suggestion on my part and never mentioned it to anyone, but it was about three weeks later that it happened. The children were insisting upon the door being left open and I allowed it for several weeks after they saw this thing.

"The night I saw *something,* the door was, therefore, open. I was sitting across from the door by the windows and looked up to see a *misty, whitish shape in the doorway* next to the partition and partly over it—above floor level some six feet, I would say. It seemed to move slightly and I really thought the kids must have seen something. I went in, but all was silence. There was no odor of smoke, and the thing must have gone farther up on the wall because it seemed higher. Also, it did not move now as I looked at it. I left the door open and went back to my chair, but when I had sat down again it was no longer visible.

"At least once, after we had been in the house about a

270

month, my son John asked me if fog could come in the house and into the bedroom. He was in bed at the time and asked me if I could see the 'fog in the room.' I told him that if fog came in (we had much rain and fog at the time) it would not be visible, as the house is warm and would make this vapor disappear. However, he insisted there was fog in the room. I could not see it.

"John, too, has been subject to nightmares in the past five to six years and I am beginning to wonder about them. He is not a particularly fearful child when awake—he is, as a matter of fact, braver than our other two children and very matter-of-fact. He is highly intelligent and is always seeking answers to things. He will be ten in June. Many times my husband or I have had to call out loudly and sharply to John during the night when he has been shouting in his sleep—sometimes sitting up—to jolt him out of his dream, as he doesn't hear you when you speak to him in a normal tone and are beside his bed while he is having one of these nightmares. I have found he is not as bad lately but have also found touching him or being by his side will often frighten him greatly even with the light on. I sometimes find, though, that calling out to him only half awakens him, and I have to go into the room, turn on the light and go up to his bed talking all the time before he knows who spoke to him. Then he settles down. But children do have nightmares, and I did not give it really serious thought until about Christmas time last year (1965) when one night, after I had gone to bed and all the family was asleep, I heard John start talking as if he were awake, making comments and talking (apparently) to David.

"Then I thought I heard a patient voice answering him *and* calling him by name saying to the effect 'no, John.'

271

Then John began to get excited and I, thinking it was David, heard finally an irritable 'Oh, John, go to sleep, shut up!' There was just a moment or two of silence and then John started very excitedly: 'What? *What?* Who's there? Who *are* you?' I called to John, 'It's Dave,' and then went into the bedroom and turned on the light. John was as close to hysterics as I've ever seen him, huddled in his bed, alternately covering his head and pulling out. He began to relax when he saw me, and Dave was sprawled out on the bed looking very much asleep—and I'm sure he was, as he was face up and made no effort to shield his eyes from the light when I came in. I went up to John's bed and said to him, 'John, you're dreaming,' but am sure he was not asleep because he looked at me, *seeing me,* and said he wasn't. He said he thought some-one was asking him questions but he didn't know who it was. I told him it must have been Dave, but he said it didn't sound like Dave and I must admit it really didn't—the voice was somewhat slurred at times and different from Dave's. John insisted there was someone else in the room, but I told him this could not be. He was sure it was a boy.

"There hasn't been much else happening around here recently other than my hearing outdoors, apparently on the hill behind the clothesline, a whimpering sound, quite loud, that lasted for several minutes at a time.

"Also, yesterday afternoon, my daughter and I were sitting on the patio and we both heard distinctly two car doors slam on the other side of the house. She went to see if the truck doors had slammed shut, but they were both open and there were no cars out there. On many occasions, particularly after we had lived here only about a month or so, when I was here alone in the afternoon, I would hear a car stop on the gravel by the carport and a door slam shut—not very loud but distinct—and not so loudly as we heard them outside yesterday. Yesterday, however, I heard no crunching of gravel.

"At first, when I heard the car pull up and the door slam I would get up and go look out the kids' bedroom window, but I never saw anything.

"I forgot to mention that one day, three months after we had moved in here, I was sitting at the table in the living room–dining room–kitchen area and *saw the door open*. The handle was turned gently. I heard a little sound and it opened—about six inches. I went and closed it and that was all."

The incidents in the little house at Newbury Park seemed to point out some pretty curious things: For one thing, the white form was seen well above ground level, near the ceiling, as it were. After we looked over the house in person, I realized *why*. The house had been built onto the hillside, artificially terracing it, so that the ceiling level coincided with what was formerly the ground level. Any ghosts appearing at the ceiling were really walking on what was *to them*, at least, still ground level!

I had not yet been to the house when the children's report was sent to me by Mrs. Hinzie, although we had met in San Francisco. But at that time I specifically asked Mrs. Hinzie not to talk of the events in her house at Newbury Park so that Sybil could not "tune in" on them, and nothing pertaining to Newbury Park was discussed. When we finally did go there in October of 1966, it came as a great surprise to Sybil to meet the ghost lady from San Francisco again—in her own surroundings this time!

REAL HAUNTINGS

On May 18, Mrs. Hinzie was further disturbed by occurrences of a paranormal nature.

"Last week I walked into the house from outdoors and closed the door behind me. There was no one in the house and no animals in the house, but I distinctly heard a few feet from me a cat hiss sharply. I looked around to be sure that no cats were in the house. This had also happened last summer.

"Twice in the past month—only a few days apart—I thought *I was touched by someone.* The first time I was washing dishes at the sink and felt, I thought, two small hands lightly on my back at the waistline. I turned around thinking John had sneaked up on me (the children were in bed) but there was no one there. A few days later I walked outside in front of the front window, to the door. There is a bench in front of the window. As I walked by the bench I distinctly felt the *back of my skirt and my slip being pulled* firmly. I reached down to touch my clothes but they were in place and the pressure immediately stopped.

"Perhaps I should have known there was something odd about this place when we moved in.

"The day my husband brought me to the house to see the place I had a strange experience. Don, my husband, had just painted the house inside and it was clean and when he asked me what I thought of it, I said, 'Well, it's all right, but don't you think Mr. Hays ought to fix *that hole in the wall?*' To me it looked as if, above the stove, there was a cement block neatly removed from the wall. He said, 'Where?' and I said, 'Why, right there where that red light is coming through.' He said there wasn't one and yet I thought there was a red light glowing there, not fire but more like an electric light. It faded out and the block was, of course, in place. My family laughed at me, so I thought I had imagined it, but last week as I sat with my back to the window, facing the stove, I was watching television. For some reason I looked up and saw the calendar on the wall to the left of the stove lighted up as if someone had thrown a beam of red light on it. The curtains were opened behind the couch where I sat but no one could have stood outside and played a beam of light on the calendar. It encompassed only the calendar."

The skirt-pulling incident reminded me of similar attention-getters in other cases of hauntings, except that I felt a certain pathetic helplessness here, as we were apparently dealing with the ghost of a child, and there is nothing sadder.

On May 31, Mrs. Hinzie had further developments to report, for as so often happens, the nearer one gets to visit a haunted place, the more frantic do the restless ones become, to make sure, perhaps, that you don't overlook them!

"The last occurrence—which I had not told you about —happened within a few days of my return home from San Francisco. I walked between the dining table and the fireplace and felt small gentle tugs at the side of my skirt. There was nothing there to catch the skirt on and I was, for once, *not* alone in the room. But I didn't mention it to anyone then. *It would seem that someone wants to get my attention.*

"The night after I returned from seeing you (Tuesday, May 17) I was sitting alone in the living room and the children and my husband were all asleep in bed. I heard a *loud* slam of a door in the bedroom (there is only one leading outside) and went in. Everyone was still asleep, apparently undisturbed, and I found the door ajar—I

275

mean by that closed but not firmly latched—a slight push would have opened it. Yet a slam as hard as I heard would surely have latched the door firmly, as there is nothing wrong with the catch.

"The last thing that happened was the day before yesterday when my son John, who was reading in the bedroom, heard a car pull up on the gravel. There was no one there, but there was a distinct crunching sound as tires passed over gravel. This, strangely enough, is the only really consistent thing that happens here. I have heard a car's tires on the gravel so many times since we moved in that I usually simply ignore it. Only when it is *very* distinct (I mean really loud) do I look outside. When I hear it, I am not aware of the sound of a motor—just the sound of the tires as the car comes to a stop.

"The first time I ever noticed this house, I felt a Model T Ford car, open sedan type, coming up the front road to the house. This makes no sense as the road has been here only about four years.

"That particular day I was sitting in the car with the children at the foot of the hill, in the parking lot there, and one of the children brought the house to my attention. Few people notice it—although we are not isolated —possibly because you can see only the rooftop from the parking lot below.

"The house was built ten years ago. The hill was excavated to make room for the house and no one else had ever lived on the spot. There was another road, now not in use, on the other side of the house from the road now used near the front of the house, but it was closed off by part of the hill being excavated only about four years ago. The road generally used now goes through the parking lot at the foot of the hill. There is also another road connected to the road not now in use that goes to the barn."

The business about the Model T Ford puzzled me, of course. But there are cases on record where ghost cars have been observed by psychically gifted people. Anything touched by human emotions may have an etheric double, and if such a car had been part of an emotional experience, a ghost of that car might very well still be part of the atmosphere around the house!

It was plain to me that Mrs. Hinzie was able to see simultaneously into both halves of our world, and that events impressed upon the psychic ether around us were just as clear to her as events in the physical world.

On recollection, Mrs. Hinzie admitted to still another incident involving clairvoyance, which seemed to me particularly relevant because it concerned another ghost car.

"This happened about 1945 or 1946. Fremont Place is a small walled section of Los Angeles—a few blocks only in size, on the south of Olympic Boulevard opposite Los Angeles High School. It was an affluent district in the '20s and the early '30s.

"My mother and her husband, W. A. Anderson, were on a visit to Los Angeles and they had rented a house for a month on a street in the area.

"I sat in the back seat of the car—my brother-in-law drove and my sister and mother and W. A. Anderson were all present. As we drove up the street, I looked into the rearview mirror and saw behind us and gaining on us (we were going slowly) an old sedan (1920s), very high and narrow—a closed car. I could clearly see a woman sitting in the backseat. It looked a little dusty and muddy as I recall but not particularly worn out, or shiny and

277

well-cared-for either. As my brother-in-law eased the car toward the curb, this old sedan passed us *very* closely on the left side and turned closely in front of us in to the curb. It stopped or had almost stopped—that was more my impression (there was no sound of a motor, by the way)—and the door in the rear right side opened immediately and a woman got out. Her face I did not see but she wore a black dress, with a '30s hemline, rather long, and a widow's veil on her head. It was thrown back from her face in front and hung over her arms and back to about her elbows. She was walking quickly up toward a house—I think it was the house we entered—when my attention was called away from her by someone in the car. I did not see her again. As my brother-in-law rolled to a stop he hit the old car and we *felt a jar*. I told him what we had hit, but apparently *no one else had seen the car* as they all laughed.

"We then walked up to the house and opened the door. My hair, I was told, stood on end *all* the time we were there, which was less than ten minutes.

"There was a large entry hall and lounge room to the right, which we went into. I kept feeling as if someone were going to rush out of the butler's pantry behind the dining room to the left all the time I was there, but never really saw that part of the house so I don't even know if there *was* a pantry!

"Mother and W. A. Anderson had been there since the day before—rented the house sight unseen. They had, Mother said, quarreled the night before in the house and her husband slapped her—this I think was significant—the place had such an air of tension as if suddenly a fist fight would start. I asked if it was the house in which a

278

man had committed suicide in the '30s; he was a well-known business and society figure, as I recall."

When I was in Hollywood in October 1966, I passed through the area. It is indeed an aristocratic-looking "compound," where the politically great and the movie stars had made their homes. It still has an air of mystery around it.

On October 5, shortly before our planned visit, Mrs. Hinzie had had another brush with the uncanny.

"The thing I'm about to tell you happened about two to four weeks ago. I was outside. The children were just out of school (about 3:30 P.M.) but none had come up the hill. Our dog, Penny, was with me. I heard a child's voice; it sounded like a little girl five to six years old. She called out something very clearly but I do not remember what. It sounded as if she were not exactly on the road but *above it* near the trees at the bend of the road. The dog heard it, too, and went over near the road and then came back.

"The other thing that happened was a week ago Saturday about 6:00 P.M. I was standing at the sink fixing something for dinner. The kids were down at the school and Don, my husband, was at the barn. The bedroom and bathroom doors were open but the front door was closed. I heard the front door close—*not open*—not loudly but not stealthily—and saw from the corner of my eye a child, *a boy wearing a white shirt,* go from the direction of the door toward the bedrooms or bathroom. I was so certain I had seen and heard someone I went in search of him because I knew it was not one of my boys. They don't ever wear white shirts, except on Sunday. But there was no one there. That same night I saw a streak of light on our bedroom partition—about two feet long and about four inches at one end, two inches at the other—a pointed thing like an arrow.

"It was very white and low on the wall—about three and one-half feet up—I don't know where it could have come from; it was quickly gone."

Finally, the great day arrived. Everything had been prepared for our coming by Mrs. Hinzie—by everything I mean not only her own house and "case," but two other hauntings not far away which she had brought to my attention and which we intended to look into on the same day prior to returning to Los Angeles.

It was an unusually warm day in October 1966 when we started out from Sybil Leek's apartment near Western Avenue. Catherine, my ex-wife, was driving, I was doing the piloting with a map, and Sybil was snoozing in the backseat, tired out from an avalanche of radio and TV appearances in connection with her latest book.

Thanks to Mrs. Hinzie's exact instructions, we made the trip over sundry freeways in about an hour, going toward Ventura and finally veering off the freeway when we reached the little town of Newbury Park. With some maneuvering we managed to find the parking lot through which we were to drive in search of the dirt road leading up to the knoll on which the house stood.

It was the kind of road perfectly suited to a Model-T, and not really to a modern no-shift car, but we made it and arrived at the Hinzie house around noon, with the sun blazing down at us at something like 95° Fahrenheit. Our hostess came out to greet us, and we quickly entered the neatly kept little house. The children were still at school and only Mrs. Hinzie and her friend Mrs. Bettin were in the house. Sybil took a chair near the window and I started to work with her almost immediately.

The Haunting at Newbury Park

As always, I first asked Sybil if she had any feelings about the house as she came upon it for the first time.

"Not about the house," Sybil replied, "but about the ground . . . the side of the house. I don't think it is a road now. The land is more important than any building here. There is a spot outside the house. . . ."

She did not feel particularly restless *inside* the house, however.

"Outside, there must have been a great deal of coming and going," Sybil continued. "More than one person is connected with it, a communal feeling. This, I am sure, was a meeting place."

She felt that the spot went back three hundred years, and that more than a single restless personality was in evidence. With that, she began to relax and her state of trance became more pronounced.

"Two different periods," Sybil mumbled now. "Sixty years ago, beginning of the century, and then . . . two different nationalities. . . ."

"Who is present here now?"

"Daniel . . . Walker . . ."

For a few minutes there was heavy breathing, and then another personality appeared to be in command of Sybil's lips. At first, the voice was faint, and I had to strain to hear at all, but gradually, as we paid attention, it became stronger until it was heard clearly for all of us to understand—except that it was in Spanish, a language Sybil did not speak fluently; she knows only a few phrases and words, about as much as a tourist might pick up on a casual visit to Spain.

It was a man's voice that came through her now.

"No gusta," it said, and repeated, as if to impress us

with the fact that there was something he did not like, *"no gusta."*

"What is your name?"

"Rafael."

"What?"

"Rafe . . ."

"Why are you here?"

"Wait."

"Whom are you waiting for?"

"Man . . . Pietro . . . *frater.* . . ."

"What is your brother's name?"

"My—brother—Darshee—Darshin—"

"Where does he live?"

"Valley. . . ." He pronounced it *"Valle,"* the Spanish way.

Then he seemed to become cognizant of my presence.

"Who are you?"

"I'm a friend," I replied softly, "who would like to help you."

"I shall kill you. Go away quickly!"

"Is this your property?"

"Mine."

"How long have you been here?"

"Don't know."

"What year is this?"

"Eighteen eighty-two," he said haltingly.

"What day?"

"Day?"

"What is your birthday?"

"June . . . birthday. . . ."

"What is your father's name?"

"Daschee." I could not be sure if he said Darshee, Dashee, Dasche, or something sounding like it.

282

"First name?"

"Dashee Hermanos." Did he perhaps mean "Taje" pronounced in the Spanish way?

"Your mother's name?"

"Maria Garcia . . . Graciella."

"Where did you go to school?"

"School . . . *escuela.* . . ."

"Do you understand English? What I am asking you?"

A moment of silence.

"No . . . I am married . . . Melita. . . ."

"What was her maiden name before she married you?"

"Doran."

"Where was she from?"

"*Escuela . . . hablo . . . escuela . . .*"

I decided to try to get the information, which had been very confusing up to now, by using what Spanish I knew.

"Do you understand English?" I said in Spanish.

No reaction.

"*¿Estan ustedes Español?*" I tried.

"*Sí.* . . ."

"*¿Por que razón está usted aquí?*" I inquired again. (Why was he here?)

"*Me . . . hermano . . . muerte . . .*"

How old was his brother who died? "Ten," he said in Spanish, becoming very emotional now.

What was his brother's name? "Dan . . . Dana . . . Dajo. . . ."

What could we do to help? "Where is my son?"

Evidently he was looking for his son. I asked where he would like to go now.

"*No gusta,*" he repeated, and we were back where we started, not much wiser.

"*¿Qué desira usted?*"

283

"Mi hijo," he pleaded, "I want my son."

The son, it seemed, was only two years old.

I asked him now what was his profession, what did he do. But I did not get an answer. He slipped away before I could get him to tell me, and Sybil returned to her own body—and senses. But before she was entirely "out," I sent her back, this time to observe while entranced, and to describe to me, still in trance, what she saw in the nonphysical world around her.

"Four people . . . child and two men . . . little child, not baby, died suddenly here . . . two men are digging . . . for the child is dead . . . also a woman . . . she is watching me . . . disturbance here . . . children play . . . I don't think she likes the men . . . very uneasy feeling between the people here . . . children playing will disturb the little one . . . this is a bad spot for children . . . child can't move . . . hot, no water . . . spirits in the mountains . . . spirits protect this ground, this is not for people to live on . . . should respect the land . . . this land belongs to the spirits . . . sacred to the great . . . from the mountain. . . ."

"Are the four people still here?"

"Feathers and food . . . for spirits . . . lot of people here . . . dancing quietly . . . dark hair . . . nothing at the top and trousers . . . Homayo is the name . . . spirit . . . from the mountains to this spot . . . Homayo the great one . . . eagle feathers. . . ."

I promised we would "sacrifice" in their honor.

"No animals here . . ." Sybil continued, "this is Homayo's place. Do not disturb. Children should not be here."

I assured the Indian spirit that his memory would be

respected and then I recalled Sybil to the year 1966. But Sybil stayed "with it" a while longer, it appeared.

Homayo was still on her mind. Nothing would grow here, she felt. There was a plague here, and the child was a victim of it.

"The child is buried under the tree," she now said. The only tree, we later found, was in back of the house, an ancient tree indeed.

"By the little road," the entranced Sybil added. That, too, was correct. The little road in back of the house did go by the tree. There was a house there once that no longer exists.

What did the parents want done about their child?

"Don't disturb it," Sybil reported, "leave the tree."

"What are they looking for in the house?"

"Digging. . . ."

"What was here before?"

"Wooden house. Child died here. No water."

The men were fighting over the land, she added. "Too many people coming here, Homayo strikes them down. Thirst."

"What does the child look like?"

"Thin, brown child."

"Male or female?"

"Can't tell. Perhaps ten . . . nine . . . ten. Walking, riding. Has a cloth over it. On the ground. Long hair."

"What is its name?"

"Raffi. . . ."

Evidently the two layers confused Sybil, for she was not sure which was which—the Indians or the later settlers.

Finally, Sybil came back to her own self. While she rested up from all that had come through her the past hour, I turned to Gwen Hinzie and asked for her comments concerning the material that had now been added to our knowledge of the case.

"Well, of course, we've seen a ten-year-old boy several times here, and yesterday I saw a man, too, outside this window, in his middle fifties, with kind of a humped back—and there were Spanish-speaking settlers here and it is a fact that the Chumash Indians lived here . . . also, there was a house behind the school over there, where people lived until about 1920. They had a child, a little girl, who fell into a well and died. There certainly were people out here in 1882, and many of them spoke Spanish."

"What about the name Daniel that was mentioned early in the session?"

Mrs. Hinzie nodded.

"A family named Borchardt owned much of the land here for many years . . . and Daniel was Mr. Borchardt's first name, I think. But I'm not sure."

"What about the child being buried under the tree?"

"Well, there is this big tree behind the house, and I did see a child—a ghost child, that is, about a year and a half ago, behind that tree."

"Was it male or female?"

"Male, but it looked older than the one I had seen on the lawn at the house. I thought at first it had gone down the hill, but it could not have disappeared from view at that spot—unless it had sunk into the ground. There just is no way to go."

I agreed that this would have been impossible, after inspecting the spot.

"About those Indians," Mrs. Hinzie said, as an afterthought, "it sounds like a ceremonial ground rather than

286

a burial ground. Women would never do in a ceremonial area."

Mr. Hinzie, who had come in at the onset of the trance session and had sat quietly watching it all, now spoke up.

"There is an Indian burial ground being excavated right now nearby."

I then talked to the three children, ages nine to twelve, and they reiterated their stories substantially as told to me by their mother. They seemed like bright, normal youngsters, no more imaginative than ordinary children and not too eager to talk about it.

When they pointed to the ceiling of their room as the haunted spot, Sybil, who had stepped into the room now, nodded assent.

"That would be the original land level," she remarked, "and *they* would walk on that level."

We then went outside, as Sybil felt an urge to "putter around" despite the great heat.

Sybil insisted that there was an Indian trail leading from the hills to the sea directly through the house—in fact, over the spot where the children had seen the apparitions. Mr. Hinzie confirmed that there was such a trail although he did not know its exact location.

We returned to the car now, as Mrs. Hinzie had other points of psychic interest in store for us.

Since then, Mrs. Hinzie has tried to check up on some of the Indian doings in the area. In nearby Agoura, in the San Fernando Valley, archaeologists from the University of California were busy digging up a Chumash Indian burial ground. These Indians, Mrs. Hinzie discovered, had been converted to Christianity by Spanish Franciscan priests. This area was within the ground covered by the mission at San Buenaventura, now Ventura. The Indians have disappeared and there is but one survivor living in Newbury Park now who is half Chumash and half Mexican.

I haven't heard anything further about any disturbances at the Hinzie house since our return from California. With so many layers of psychic consciousness in the spot, it seems a little difficult to sort out the ghosts. But the fact remains that Mrs. Gwen Hinzie has a prolific talent for seeing and hearing them, and our own Sybil was able to give information that dovetails with the earlier testimony. Indian ceremonial grounds are a little hard to pin down, as there is no written literature among the Indians, but the little lost boy, between two states of being, as it were, must surely be guided across the threshold. Perhaps as the flesh-and-blood children in the Hinzie house grow older and their available energies cannot be drawn upon any longer for some of these psychic manifestations, the ghost of the boy will also fade away into the "land of the great spirit" where red or white skins no longer matter.

A few days before, as we were flying toward Los Angeles, Sybil had suddenly turned to me with a puzzled expression.

"What a strange occupation," she said, "to be a worm rancher!"

I was nonplussed. What had brought on that remark? Sybil was not sure. It had just entered her mind.

I dismissed the strange thought, but when we met Mr. Hinzie, he took us to the back of the house where the barn stood.

"I've got a little business on the side going in there," he explained lightly. *"I'm a worm rancher!"*

I had never heard of anyone raising worms for fishermen, but apparently this occupation was not unique, though admittedly rare.

Sybil evidently had a premonition of all this. It makes me feel that our mission to Newbury Park was indeed "in the cards" long before we set foot there.

Mrs. Hinzie kept looking for possible confirmations of some of the things that had come through in trance. For one thing, the business about Indians at her house wanted further elucidation.

In January 1967, Mrs. Hinzie was able to send excerpts from proper sources on the local Indians, the tribes Sybil had referred to in trance.

"I have researched the Chumash Indians out here to some extent and have found out a little bit bearing out Sybil's description of religious rites, which I'll quote here. This information comes from a book called *San Buenaventura: The Mission by the Sea,* by Father Zephyrin Engelhardt, O.F.M., printed in 1930 for the author by the Schauer Printing Studio, Inc., Santa Barbara, California.

"The following (pp. 33–40) was written by Father José Señan between 1812 and 1823 during his term of office as Presidente at Mission San Buenaventura, in Ventura. It was in answer to a list of questions proposed by the Spanish Government and sent to the priests at each mission with regard to the Indians of their area who lived and worked at the particular mission. They were called *neophytes* and all were of the Chumash tribe. The quotes are numbered apparently as they were in Fr. Señan's *Requesta* (reply).

12. No inclination to idolatry is observed in our neophytes; nor can it be said that in savagery they

289

practiced any formal idolatry. In the vicinity of their rancherias (small villages) *and on the mountain,* they used to have some places which they kept very clean, swept, and adorned *with beautiful plumage* put on poles. To these places they would go as to their sacred places. Here they would *assemble* in time of need and conduct a sort of pilgrimage. One of their number, in the name of all the rest, who observed profound silence would pray for rain, offering an abundance of acorns, seeds, and wild fruits which constituted their daily sustenance. They would catch fish or kill deer in order that no bear might catch them or the bite of a rattlesnake might not afflict them. They would pray also for health and other good things. At the end of the supplication, they would in their simplicity and crude veneration offer beads, acorns, and various seeds, in order that they might be regarded with favor by the invisible one, whom they pictured to themselves according to their rude notions as the author and giver of rains, seeds, fruits, and other good things. The first part of this petition was always uniform. It was preceded by a salutation which in our language (Spanish) means as much as "Grand Captain or Captain of Captains, behold us and hear what we say."

19. The gentiles (pagans) of this vicinity have not adored the sun nor the moon.

28. They never offered human sacrifices to gods.

33. [I]n paganism they used only a flute-like thing made of elderwood, as also a bone *whistle,* with which the players produce a shriek and violent trill, at the same time making strange and ridiculous

contortions of the body. Their songs are weird, more adapted to arouse sadness than gladness.

36. The dress of the male neophytes consists of a short overall, called *cotón*, or a breechcloth, in place of breeches, and of a blanket. All this clothing is made at the mission. The pagans know nothing of dress, except that women wear the hide of a deer or fringes of grass to meet the demands of natural decency.

"This, above, is shown to have been written August 11, 1815, at Mission San Buenaventura, by Father José Señan."

"As to our own house, all is peaceful and serene, except that twice in the past month I've heard someone humming (kind of tunelessly) outside the door or at least close to it. It is the voice of either a child or a woman. We have no more lights or opening of doors and cars arriving on the gravel or slamming of car doors.

"There is no longer the feeling of little cat feet on our bed. My husband used to feel a cat walk across his feet whether he was sleeping on his lunch hour or at night. I had always felt it walking up toward me on my side of the bed, but until he told me he felt the little feet I really thought it must be my imagination. It never walked *on* me, just beside me. This was true almost from the time we moved in here. It is a very light step, almost weightless but not quite."

To sum it all up: Sybil, a stranger to those parts, had correctly described the ghost of a young child, the presence of Indians on the very spot where I had taken her, and a number of small but significant details, such as the ridiculous bit of information concerning Mr. Hinzie's worm-ranching activities. More important even, Mrs. Gwen Hinzie's own place in our psychically oriented world of study and knowledge seems pretty secure to me. She is, to borrow from Gilbert and Sullivan, the very model of a modern amateur medium!

In July 1967 Mrs. Hinzie contacted me again. All had been serene at the house for several months, except for a couple of gentle reminders that perhaps one of the ghosts, the child, had not yet left, even though the father had gone on.

A door opened by itself on one occasion; then a small white cloud appeared next to Mrs. Hinzie's bed that she at first mistook for cigarette smoke, until she convinced herself that the ashtray was cold. But the clincher came a few days after, when she was awakened in bed by the touch of a hand taking hers! The unseen hand felt soft and warm, but very firm. When it clasped Mrs. Hinzie's own hand, she naturally tried to withdraw it. The ghost hand tightened, and at the same time Mrs. Hinzie felt a strong pain in her armpits, as if fingers were pressing there.

In desperation, Mrs. Hinzie moved her own hand, with the ghost hand holding on to it, to her face and *bit into it.*

"It felt as though I had bitten into foam rubber," she said, but the ghost hand let go now and soon sleep returned to the "ghost lady of Newbury Park."

I advised Mrs. Hinzie to speak to the little ghost, should it ever return, as a mother would—to have the little one join his father out there in the great beyond.

But then some children, even ghostly ones, are notoriously bad at taking orders.

23

The San Bernardino
Murder Ghosts

*I*t all started in 1964 when I was lecturing for the American Society for Psychic Research in Los Angeles, and a good many people came forward to tell me of their own psychic experiences, especially those involving ghosts and apparitions. One of the people who could not get to hear me speak was a woman named Verna Kunze. She had seen a ghost and I asked her to make a written statement about her experience. A practical and factual woman, Mrs. Kunze did not hesitate to do so.

"I had purchased an apartment building in San Bernardino, California, on G Street, which had formerly been a nun's home on E Street closer in town. Undoubtedly it had been a single-dwelling mansion at one time.

293

"The upper right-hand apartment was more suited to my needs and the one I was occupying during the time— September 1957 to October 1960.

"After I had lived there for some months I came in from a shopping trip and, going to the closet in the front bedroom, opened the door to hang up my coat. There I saw very clearly, standing inside the closet in front of the door, a man of medium height (about five feet eight inches), round face, fair complexion, dressed in clothing about the style of the early 1900s, pink-and-white striped shirt, no coat, high stiff turned-over collar, sailor straw hat on his head, nondescript tan trousers and button shoes—I think they were brown with white trim. Garters to hold up his sleeves were on his arms.

"At first I was so startled (not scared) that I couldn't say anything but while I was staring at him, the picture faded from sight.

"I saw him again in the same position, same clothing, in exactly the same manner on three other occasions.

"Being rather psychic but not a medium, I asked the Supreme Deity for protection and thought nothing of it. After about the third appearance, I asked that he depart, asked God's blessing on him and saw him no more. However, on the last impression, it seemed to me that he might have been murdered and stood in the closet to be hidden—or had committed a murder and was hiding in the closet. He was as clear in picture as though he were real. I told a medium friend about it who visited me a short time later but no one else.

"Later I sold the apartment and returned to Santa Ana to live. I do not know who owns the apartment building now as it has changed hands since."

I travel a great deal and it was not until the fall of 1966

that I finally got around to the ghost in San Bernardino. I got in touch with Mrs. Kunze to see if anything had happened, or at any rate if she could arrange for us to visit her old apartment.

Mrs. Kunze went to see the current owners of the house and found them somewhat hesitant about the whole business. They had not received any complaints from anyone about ghosts and would just as well let sleeping ghosts lie. But Mrs. Kunze is a persuasive person, having spent many years working for the immigration service. She promised not to divulge the exact address of the house or the name of the current owners, and finally an appointment was made for us to have a look at the house in October 1966. Fortunately, the tenant of the corner apartment we were interested in had just vacated and the new owner had not yet moved in, so we would find an empty flat.

After we arrived in Los Angeles, I phoned Mrs. Kunze again to make sure we had access to the apartment, for the drive to San Bernardino takes two hours and it was one of the periodic hot spells the area suffers—so I wanted to be sure we were welcome. All was in readiness, and we arrived at the house on schedule, at four in the afternoon on a hot October day.

The house sat back from the street, a modest yellow stucco building of two stories that belied its age, which was, I later discovered, considerable for this part of the world.

A dark-haired lady received me at the door, while Catherine, my ex-wife, and Sybil Leek remained in the car, out of earshot. Mrs. Kunze also came out to greet me. I then fetched the others, and without saying anything pertaining to the house, we left the dark-haired lady, who was the landlady, downstairs and walked up to the second floor where we followed Sybil into the "right" apartment. She knew just where to go.

Mrs. Kunze sat down in one of the chairs, Sybil stretched out on the bed and we waited for what might happen now. We did not have to wait long, for Sybil instantly got the scent of things.

"Death and destruction," she said, "comparatively recent. This is an absolutely horrible place."

She shivered, though the temperature outside was above ninety degrees. I, too, felt a chill and it wasn't the power of suggestion, either.

"I think death has hung over this place for some time," Sybil elaborated now. "If there was anyone in it I would warn them not to be here."

"Is any entity present?" I asked casually, for I already knew the place was haunted. What I did not know of course was the story behind the haunting or anything more than what Mrs. Kunze had originally written me. And Sybil had no knowledge of that, either.

"I seem to be attracted to the bathroom and that little door there," Sybil commented. "The bathroom has some significance in this. Stomach feels irritated."

"What about any structural changes?" I interjected.

"I haven't paid attention to that, for the overwhelming influence is of terribly brooding, resentful . . . death. Like having my head in a piece of *black velvet*. Something hanging right over me."

"Does it involve violent death?"

"Yes. Suffocation. But then again, I have this sickness of the stomach, but that may be associated with someone here. . . ."

"Is it murder, suicide, or accidental death?"

296

"Two people are involved. A murder, because of the resentfulness. Connection with the door. Not clear yet. A usurper, a person who should not be here."

"How far back do we go here?"

"It could be now . . . it seems very close. Recent."

"Describe the person you feel present here."

"A slightly round-faced lady . . . funny, I keep getting another house!"

Sybil interrupted herself. She knew nothing of the fact that this house had been moved to its present site from another place.

"Where is the other house?" I asked.

"The person who is here was involved with *another* house. Tall, thin trees nearby. Two houses . . . the other is a pleasant house . . . light-colored car. . . ."

I asked Sybil to look at the woman again, if she could.

"Hair short in neck . . ." Sybil said, gradually becoming more and more in trance, "I can't find the body, though . . . one part of her is here and one part of her is there. . . ."

"Is she present now?"

"I follow her. . . ."

"Is she in this room?"

"Yes . . . and then she goes . . . D . . . Don . . ."

"What is her occupation?"

"The voice . . . voice . . . she runs away . . . somebody mustn't know, she says . . . she is very vain. . . ."

"How is she dressed?"

"Black head," Sybil said. It struck me suddenly that Sybil might be describing a nun's habit.

"Why is the black head here?" Sybil now demanded to know.

But Sybil was speaking of a black *face.*

"Light car, black face," she mumbled.

"Why is she here?" I wanted to know.

"Waiting for . . . this isn't her home. Waiting for relief. Somebody came to take her away from here. A woman. Because she did not live here."

"How did she get here then?"

"She needed to stay here to wait for things . . . to come to her."

"Whose place is this?"

"Don't know . . . knew someone here. The little car, light car. D-o-n."

"What happened to her here?"

"She—was—suffocating—sick to stomach—head and neck—"

"Did she commit suicide?"

"No."

"Was she murdered?"

"Don't say that!"

"Was she killed?"

"Yes. . . ."

"By whom?"

"D-o-n."

I then brought Sybil quickly to herself, but for some time after, she kept feeling quite uncomfortable and sighed with relief when we left the place.

Mrs. Kunze, who had witnessed all this, had nodded several times during the hour. I now wanted to find out if there was anything she could add to the brief testimony she had given me originally.

"Did this apparition you told me about ever look at you?" I inquired. The man with "the German face" in the straw hat must have been quite a sight greeting her from the open closet door—very dead.

298

"No, he did not," Mrs. Kunze replied. "I immediately got the impression that he was dead. His eyes did not move. A minute later he was gone and I hung up my coat."

A month later, when he reappeared to her, he did not stay as long, she explained, but the view was the same.

The third time she started to pray for him, and instead of fading away as on the previous occasions, he disappeared like a flash.

"Weren't you curious about the apartment? I mean, didn't you make some inquiries about its previous occupants?"

"I did not. I knew when I bought the place that it had been the home of nuns, and moved here after some years from another location—where now the Junior High School stands. The building is at least sixty years old. There may have been two or three other owners before I purchased it. It was remodeled around 1953 or '54. Until then it belonged to the nuns."

Again I questioned her about the appearance of the ghost. She stuck to her story. The man was more 1903 than 1953.

"At that time there were certainly nuns here," she commented.

Had she had other uncanny experiences in this haunted apartment?

"Only this," Mrs. Kunze replied. "In my inspirational work, I found I could not work here. My guides told me this was an evil house. But I haven't heard anything."

"How long have you yourself been psychic?"

"When I was about thirteen, I was invited to a Sunday school party, and I was a stranger in the neighborhood, not knowing anyone there. That was in Columbus, Ohio.

About a week before the party I told my mother that I had dreamt of and had seen this party, the girls there and even the pictures on the wall—in great detail. A week later I went and recognized it all."

"Have you had any other premonitions?"

"A number of them. I do automatic writing, and a lot of predictions have thus been dictated to me by what I call my masters, my spiritual guides."

I decided we should leave metaphysics alone, and turn to the business at hand.

"About the material obtained just now through Sybil Leek," I said, "does any of it ring a bell with you?"

"Well, she certainly got the business with the two houses," Mrs. Kunze commented. "This house was in two locations, as you know."

"What about the trees surrounding the house?" In this part of California, trees are not common and would naturally be a landmark.

"Probably so," Mrs. Kunze said, "and she mentioned a face covered with black velvet—could that not be a nun covered with a coif?"

"Could be," I agreed. "It seems strange, though, that you haven't felt a female influence here, or have you?"

"Not at all," Mrs. Kunze confirmed, "but I felt from the looks of the *man* that he had either committed a murder or done something very wrong. I just felt it as I saw him there in the closet. I suppose he had jumped in there to avoid detection."

Evidently Mrs. Kunze had seen the ghost of the murderer while Sybil found the ghost of the victim. Now if Mrs. Kunze's prayer had indeed freed the ghost from the spot where his crime had been committed, then it was only natural that Sybil did not feel him any longer there.

At the same time, if Mrs. Kunze felt the overpowering tragedy of the murderer tied to the spot of the crime, it would have blotted out the comparatively weaker presence of the victim, who after all, was not guilty of *anything!*

I discovered that the building in its original site faced a Catholic school and that San Bernardino has a high percentage of Catholics among its inhabitants. Thus a convent would not have been out of place here.

On November 5, 1960, Mrs. Kunze moved out of the haunted apartment to a new house in nearby Santa Ana. The ghost, of course, did not move along with her, for the new apartment was free from any and all psychic influences, pleasant, in fact, in every sense of the word.

While she lived at the San Bernardino address, the evil atmosphere of the place seemed to have taken its toll of her day-to-day life. Everything she seemed to touch went wrong; her personal life was a shambles—apparently for no logical reason. The moment she moved away from the apartment, all went well. Suggestion? Not really. The facts were quite solid.

As for the empty apartment in San Bernardino, it is all ready for the new tenant to move in.

"I wouldn't take this place for nothing," Sybil mumbled, as she rushed past me down the stairs and into the street.

Considering the fact that Sybil had been apartment-shopping with a vengeance at the time, the victim of the ghost in the closet must have made quite an impression on her.

At any rate, the restless nun doesn't live there anymore.

301

24

The Phantom Boy of Santa Ana

Ghosts can be frightening, though they never harm anyone—but fearing the unknown causes people to be upset without realizing that they bring on their own problems in that way.

But when the ghost is but a little child, the matter is more frustrating than dangerous, because the child is likely unable to communicate properly. Still, an experienced investigator will have to find a way to contact and put to rest the little one, no matter how difficult.

Little did I know when I had successfully investigated the haunted apartment of Mrs. Verna Kunze in San Bernardino that Mrs. Kunze would lead me to another case equally as interesting as her own, which I reported on in my book *Ghosts of the Golden West.*

Mrs. Kunze is a very well-organized person, and as a former employee in the passport division of the State Department she is used to sifting facts from fancy. Her interest in psycho-cybernetics had led her to a group of like-minded individuals meeting regularly in Orange County. There she met a gentleman, formerly with the FBI, by the name of Walter Tipton.

One day, Mr. Tipton asked her help in contacting me concerning a most unusual case that had been brought to his attention. Having checked out some of the more obvious details, he had found the people involved truthful and worthy of my time.

So it was that I first heard of Mrs. Carole Trausch of Santa Ana.

What happened to the Trausch family and their neighbors is not just a ghost story. Far more than that, they found themselves in the middle of an old tragedy that had not yet been played out fully when they moved into their spanking new home.

Carole Trausch was born in Los Angeles of Scottish parentage and went to school in Los Angeles. Her father is a retired policeman and her mother was born in Scotland. Carole married quite young and moved with her husband, a businessman, to live first in Huntington Beach and later in Westminster, near Santa Ana.

She was in her early twenties, a glamorous-looking blonde who belied the fact that she has three children ages eight, six, and two, all girls.

Early the previous year, they moved into one of two hundred two-story bungalows in a new development in Westminster. They were just an ordinary family, without any particular interest in the occult. About their only link with the world of the psychic were some peculiar dreams Carole had had.

The first time was when she was still a little girl. She dreamed there were some pennies hidden in the rose bed in the garden. On awakening, she laughed at herself, but out of curiosity she did go to the rose bed and looked. Sure enough, there were some pennies in the soil below the roses. Many times since then she has dreamed of future events that later came true.

One night she dreamed that her husband's father was being rolled on a stretcher, down a hospital corridor by a nurse, on his way to an operation. The next morning there was a phone call informing them that such an emergency had indeed taken place about the time she dreamed it. On several occasions she sensed impending accidents or other unpleasant things, but she is not always sure what kind. One day she felt sure she or her husband would be in a car accident. Instead it was one of her little girls, who was hit by a passing car.

When they moved into their present house, Mrs. Trausch took an immediate disliking to it. This upset her practical-minded husband. They had hardly been installed when she begged him to move again. He refused.

The house is a white-painted two-story bungalow, which was built about five years before their arrival. Downstairs is a large, oblong living room, a kitchen, and a dining area. On the right, the staircase leads to the upper story. The landing is covered with linoleum, and there are two square bedrooms on each side of the landing, with wall-to-wall carpeting and windows looking onto the yard in the rear bedroom and onto the street in the front room.

There is a large closet along the south wall of the rear bedroom. Nothing about the house is unusual, and there was neither legend nor story nor rumor attached to the house when they rented it from the local bank that owned it.

And yet there was something queer about the house. Mrs. Trausch's nerves were on edge right from the very first when they moved in. But she accepted her husband's decision to stay put and swept her own fears under the carpet of everyday reason as the first weeks in their new home rolled by.

At first the children would come to her with strange tales. The six-year-old girl would complain of being touched by someone she could not see whenever she dropped off for her afternoon nap in the bedroom upstairs. Sometimes this presence would shake the bed, and then there was a shrill noise, somewhat like a beep, coming from the clothes closet. The oldest girl, eight years old, confirmed the story and reported similar experiences in the room.

Carole dismissed these reports as typical imaginary tales of the kind children will tell.

But one day she was resting on the same bed upstairs and found herself being tapped on the leg by some unseen person.

This was not her imagination; she was fully awake, and it made her wonder if perhaps her intuition about this house had not been right all along.

She kept experiencing the sensation of touch in the upstairs bedrooms only, and it got to be a habit with her to make the beds as quickly as possible and then rush downstairs where she felt nothing unusual. Then she also began to hear the shrill, beeplike sounds from the

306

closet. She took out all the children's clothes and found nothing that could have caused the noise. Finally she told her husband about it, and he promptly checked the pipes and other structural details of the house, only to shake his head. Nothing could have made such noises.

For several months she had kept her secret, but now that her husband also knew, she had Diane, the oldest, tell her father about it as well.

It was about this time that she became increasingly aware of a continuing presence upstairs. Several times she would hear footsteps walking upstairs, and on investigation found the children fast asleep. Soon the shuffling steps became regular features of the house. It would always start near the closet in the rear bedroom, then go toward the stair landing.

Carole began to wonder if her nerves weren't getting the better of her. She was much relieved one day when her sister Kathleen Bachelor, who had come to visit her, remarked about the strange footsteps upstairs. Both women knew the children were out. Only the baby was upstairs, and on rushing up the stairs, they found her safely asleep in her crib. It had sounded to them like a small person wearing slippers.

Soon she discovered, however, that there were two kinds of footsteps: the furtive pitter-patter of a child, and the heavy, deliberate footfalls of a grown-up.

Had they fallen heir to two ghosts? The thought seemed farfetched even to ESP-prone Carole, but it could not be dismissed entirely. What was going on, she wondered. Evidently she was not losing her mind, for others had also heard these things.

Once she had gone out for the evening and when she returned around 10:00 P.M., she dismissed the baby-

307

sitter. After the girl had left, she was alone with the baby. Suddenly she heard the water running in the bathroom upstairs. She raced up the stairs and found the bathroom door shut tight. Opening it, she noticed that the water was on and there was some water in the sink.

On January 27 of the next year, Carole had guests for lunch, two neighbors named Pauline J. and Joyce S., both young women about the same age as Carole. The children were all sleeping in the same upstairs front bedroom, the two older girls sharing the bed while the baby girl occupied the crib. The baby had her nap between 11:00 and 2:00 P.M. At noon, however, the baby woke up crying, and, being barely able to talk at age two, kept saying "Baby scared, Mommy!"

The three ladies had earlier been upstairs together, preparing the baby for her crib. At that time, they had also put the entire room carefully in order, paying particular attention to making the covers and spread on the large bed very smooth, and setting up the dolls and toys on the chest in the corner.

When the baby cried at noon, all three women went upstairs and found the bed had wrinkles and an imprint as though someone had been sitting on it. The baby, of course, was still in her crib.

They picked up the child and went downstairs with her. Just as they got to the stairway, all three heard an invisible child falling down the stairs about three steps ahead of where they were standing.

It was after this experience that Mrs. Trausch wondered why the ghost child never touched any of the dolls. The footsteps they kept hearing upstairs always went from the closet to the toy chest where the dolls are kept. But none of the dolls was ever disturbed. It occurred to

308

her that the invisible child was a boy, and there were no toys for boys around.

The sounds of a child running around in the room upstairs became more and more frequent; she knew it was not one of her children, having accounted for her own in other ways. The whole situation began to press on her nerves, and even her husband—who had until now tended to shrug off what he could not understand—became concerned. Feelers were put out to have me come to the house as soon as possible, but I could not make it right away and they would have to cope with their unseen visitors for the time being, until I arrived on the scene.

All during February the phenomena continued, so much so that Mrs. Trausch began to take them as part of her routine. But she kept as much to the downstairs portion of the house as she could. For some unknown reason, the phenomena never intruded on that part of the house.

She called in the lady who managed the development for the owners and cautiously told her of their problem. But the manager knew nothing whatever about the place, except that it was new and to her knowledge no great tragedies had occurred there in her time.

When the pitter-patter of the little feet continued, Carole Trausch decided she just had to know. On March 16, she decided to place some white flour on the linoleum-covered portion of the upstairs floor to trap the unseen child. This was the spot where the footsteps were most often heard, and for the past two days the ghost child had indeed "come out" there to run and play.

In addition, she took a glass of water with some measuring spoons of graduated sizes in it, and set it all down in a small pan and put it into her baby's crib with a cracker in the pan beside the glass. This was the sort of thing a little child might want—that is, a living child.

She then retired to the downstairs portion of the house and called in a neighbor. Together the two women kept watch, waiting for the early afternoon hours when the ghost child usually became active upstairs.

As the minutes ticked off, Carole began to wonder how she would look if nothing happened. The neighbor probably would consider her neurotic, and accuse her of making up the whole story as an attention-getter in this rather quiet community.

But she did not have to worry long. Sure enough, there were the footsteps again upstairs. The two women waited a few moments to give the ghost a chance to leave an impression, then they rushed upstairs.

They saw no child, but the white flour had indeed been touched. There were footmarks in the flour, little feet that seemed unusually small and slender. Next to the prints there was the picture of a flower, as if the child had bent down and finger-painted the flower as a sign of continuing presence. From the footprints, they took the child to be between three and four years of age. The water and pan in the crib had not been touched, and as they stood next to the footprints, there was utter silence around them.

Mrs. Trausch now addressed the unseen child gently and softly, promising the child they would not hurt it. Then she placed some toys for boys, which she had obtained for this occasion around the children's room and withdrew.

There was no immediate reaction to all this, but two days later the eight-year-old daughter came running down the stairs to report that she had seen the shadow of a little boy in front of the linen closet in the hall. He wore a striped shirt and pants, and was shorter than she.

When I heard by telephone of the footprints, I set the week of June 2 aside for a visit to the house. Meanwhile I instructed the Trausches to continue observing whatever they could.

But the Trausches had already determined to leave the house, even if I should be able to resolve their "problem." No matter what, they could never be quite sure. And living with a ghost—or perhaps two ghosts—was not what they wanted to do, what with three living children to keep them on their toes.

Across from the Trausch apartment, and separated from it by a narrow lane, is another house just like it and built about the same time, on what was before only open farmland—as far as everyone there knows. A few years before, the area was flooded and condemned, but it dried out later. There is and always has been plenty of water in the area, a lowland studded with ponds and fishing holes.

The neighbor's name was Bonnie Swanson and she, too, was plagued by footsteps that had no human causing them. The curious thing is that these phenomena were heard only in the upstairs portion of her house, where the bedrooms are, just as in the Trausch house.

Twice the Swansons called in the police, only to be told that there was no one about causing the footsteps. In April, the Swansons had gone away for a weekend, taking their child with them. When they returned, the husband opened the door and was first to step into the house. At this moment he distinctly heard footsteps running very fast from front to rear of the rooms, as if someone had been surprised by their return. Mrs. Swanson,

311

who had also heard this, joined her husband in looking the house over, but there was no stranger about and no one could have left.

Suddenly they became aware of the fact that a light upstairs was burning. They knew they had turned it off when they left. Moreover, in the kitchen they almost fell over a child's tricycle. Last time they saw this tricycle, it had stood in the corner of their living room. It could not have gotten to the kitchen by itself, and there was no sign of anyone breaking and entering in their absence. Nothing was missing.

It seemed as if my approaching visit was somehow getting through to the ghost or ghosts, for as the month of June came closer, the phenomena seemed to mount in intensity and frequency.

On the morning of May 10, at 9:30, Mrs. Trausch was opening her front bedroom window to let in the air. From her window she could see directly into the Swanson house, since both houses were on the same level with the windows parallel to each other. As she reached her window and casually looked out across to the Swanson's rooms, which she knew to be empty at this time of day (Mr. Swanson was at work, and Mrs. Swanson and a houseguest were out for the morning) she saw to her horror the arm of a woman pushing back the curtain of Mrs. Swanson's window.

There was a curiously stiff quality about this arm and the way it moved the curtain back. Then she saw clearly a woman with a deathlike white mask of a face staring at her. The woman's eyes were particuarly odd. Despite her excitement, Mrs. Trausch noticed that the woman had wet hair and was dressed in something filmy, like a white nylon negligee with pink flowers on it.

312

For the moment, Mrs. Trausch assumed that the houseguest must somehow have stayed behind, and so she smiled at the woman across from her. Then the curtain dropped and the woman disappeared. Carole Trausch could barely wait to question her neighbor about the incident, and found that there hadn't been anyone at the house when she saw the woman with the wet hair.

Now Mrs. Trausch was sure that there were two unseen visitors, a child and a woman, which would account for the different quality of the footsteps they had been hearing.

She decided to try and find out more about the land on which the house stood.

A neighbor living a few blocks away on Chestnut Street, who had been in her house for over twenty years, managed to supply some additional information. Long before the development had been built, there had been a farm there.

In the exact place where the Trausches now lived there had been a barn. When the house was built, a large trench was dug and the barn was pushed into it and burned. The people who lived there at the time were a Mexican family named Felix. They had a house nearby but sold the area of the farm to the builders.

Because of the flooded condition of the area, the houses stood vacant for a few years. Only after extensive drainage had taken place did the houses become inhabitable. At this time the Trausches were able to move into theirs.

The area was predominantly Mexican and the development was a kind of Anglo-Saxon island in their midst.

All this information was brought out only after our

visit, incidentally, and neither Sybil Leek, who acted as my medium, nor I had any knowledge of it at the time.

Mrs. Trausch was not the only adult member of the family to witness the phenomena. Her husband finally confessed that on several occasions he had been puzzled by footsteps upstairs when he came home late at night. That was around 1:00 A.M., and when he checked to see if any of the children had gotten out of bed, he found them fast asleep. Mr. Trausch is a very realistic man. His business is manufacturing industrial tools, and he does not believe in ghosts. But he heard the footsteps, too.

The Trausches also realized that the shuffling footsteps of what appeared to be a small child always started up as soon as the two older girls had left for school. It was as if the invisible boy wanted to play with their toys when they weren't watching.

Also, the ghost evidently liked the bathroom and water, for the steps resounded most often in that area. On one occasion Mrs. Trausch was actually using the bathroom when the steps resounded next to her. Needless to say, she left the bathroom in a hurry.

Finally the big day had arrived. Mr. Trausch drove his Volkswagon all the way to Hollywood to pick up Mrs. Leek and myself, and while he did not believe in ghosts, he didn't scoff at them either.

After a pleasant ride of about two hours, we arrived at Westminster. It was a hot day in June, and the Santa Ana area is known for its warm climate. Mr. Trausch parked the car, and we went into the house where the rest of the family was awaiting our visit.

I asked Sybil to scout around for any clairvoyant impressions she might get of the situation, and as she did so, I followed her around the house with my faithful tape recorder so that not a word might be lost.

As soon as Sybil had set foot in the house, she pointed to the staircase and intoned ominously, "It's upstairs."

Then, with me trailing, she walked up the stairs as gingerly as a trapeze artist while I puffed after her.

"Gooseflesh," she announced and held out her arm. Now whenever we are in a haunted area Sybil does get gooseflesh—not because she is scared but because it is a natural, instant reaction to whatever presence might be there.

We were in the parents' room now, and Sybil looked around with the expectant smile of a well-trained bird dog casing the moors.

"Two conflicting types," she then announced. "There's anger and resentfulness toward someone. There's something here. Has to do with the land. Two people."

She felt it centered in the children's room, and that there was a vicious element surrounding it, an element of destruction. We walked into the children's room and immediately she made for the big closet in the rear. Behind that wall there was another apartment, but the Trausches did not know anything about it except that the people in it had just recently moved in.

"It's that side," Sybil announced and waved toward the backyard of the house where numerous children of various ages were playing with the customary racket.

"Vincent," Sybil added, out of the blue. "Maybe I don't have the accent right, but it is Vincent. But it is connected with all this. Incidentally, it is the land that's causing the trouble, not the house itself."

The area Sybil had pointed out just a moment before

315

as being the center of the activities was the exact spot where the old barn had once stood.

"It's nothing against this house," Sybil said to Mrs. Trausch, "but something out of the past. I'd say 1925. The name Vincent is important. There's fire involved. I don't feel a person here but an influence . . . a thing. This is different from our usual work. It's the upper part of the building where the evil is."

I then eased Sybil into a chair in the children's room and we grouped ourselves silently around her, waiting for some form of manifestation to take place.

Mrs. Trausch was nervously biting her lips, but otherwise bearing up under what must have been the culmination of a long and great strain for her. Sybil was relaxing now, but she was still awake.

"There's some connection with a child," she said now, "a lost child . . . 1925 . . . the child was found here, dead."

"Whose child is it?" I pressed.

"Connected with Vincent . . . dark child . . . nine years old . . . a boy . . . the children here have to be careful. . . ."

"Does this child have any connection with the house?"
"He is lost."

"Can you see him; can he see you?"

"I see him. Corner . . . the barn. He broke his neck. Two men . . . hit the child, they didn't like children, you see . . . they left him . . . until he was found . . . woman . . . Fairley . . . name . . . Pete Fairley. . . ."

By now Sybil had glided into a semi-trance and I kept up the barrage of questions to reconstruct the drama in the barn.

"Do they live here?" I inquired.

"Nobody lives here. Woman walked from the water to find the boy. He's dead. She has connection with the two men who killed him. Maniacs, against children."

"What is her connection with the boy?"

"She had him, then she lost him. She looked after him."

"Who were the boy's parents then?"

"Fairley. Peter Fairley. Nineteen twenty-five."

Sybil sounded almost like a robot now, giving the requested information.

"What happened to the woman?" I wanted to know.

"Mad . . . she found the boy dead, went to the men . . . there was a fight . . . she fell in the water . . . men are here . . . there's a fire. . . ."

"Who were these men?"

"Vincent . . . brothers . . . nobody is very healthy in this farm . . . don't like women. . . ."

"Where did the child come from?"

"Lost . . . from the riverside. . . ."

"Can you see the woman?"

"A little . . . the boy I can see clearly."

It occurred to me how remarkable it was for Sybil to speak of a woman who had fallen into the water when the apparition Mrs. Trausch had seen had had wet hair. No one had discussed anything about the house in front of Sybil, of course. So she had no way of knowing that the area had once been a farm, or that a barn had stood there where she felt the disturbances centered. No one had told her that it was a child the people in the house kept hearing upstairs.

"The woman is out of tempo," Sybil explained. "That makes it difficult to see her. The boy is frightened."

Sybil turned her attention to the little one now and, with my prodding, started to send him away from there.

"Peter go out and play with the children . . . outside," she pleaded.

"And his parents . . . they are looking for him," I added.

"He wants the children here to go with him," Sybil came back.

Mrs. Trausch started to swallow nervously.

"Tell him he is to go first," I instructed.

"He wants to have the fair woman come with him," Sybil explained and I suggested that the two of them go.

"She understands," Sybil explained, "and is willing, but he is difficult. He wants the children."

I kept pleading with the ghost boy. Nothing is harder than dealing with a lost one so young.

"Join the other children. They are already outside," I said.

There was a moment of silence, interrupted only by the muffled sounds of living children playing outside.

"Are they still here?" I cautiously inquired a little later.

"Can't see them now, but I can see the building. Two floors. Nobody there now."

I decided it was time to break the trance, which had gradually deepened and at this point was a full trance. A moment later Sybil Leek was "back."

Now we discussed the matter freely and I researched the information just obtained.

As I understood it, there had been this boy, age nine, Peter Fairley by name, who had somehow gotten away from his nanny, a fair woman. He had run into a farm and gone up to the upper story of a barn where two brothers named Vincent had killed him. When the

318

woman found him, she went mad. Then she looked for the men, whom she knew, and there was a fight during which she was drowned. The two of them are ghosts because they are lost; the boy lost in a strange place and the woman lost in guilt for having lost the boy.

Mrs. Kunze and Mrs. Trausch volunteered to go through the local register to check out the names and to see if anything bearing on this tragedy could be found in print.

Unfortunately the death records for the year 1925 were incomplete, as Mrs. Trausch discovered at the *Santa Ana Register;* and this was true even at the local Hall of Records in the Court House. The County Sheriff's Office was of no help either. But they found an interesting item in the *Register* of January 1, 1925:

> Deputies probe tale of "burial" in orange grove. Several Deputy Sheriffs, in a hurried call to Stanton late last night, failed to find any trace of several men who were reported to be "burying something" in an isolated orange grove near that town, as reported to them at the Sheriff's office here.
>
> Officers rushing to the scene were working under the impression that a murder had been committed and that the body was being interred, but a thorough search in that vicinity failed to reveal anything unusual, according to a report made by Chief Criminal Deputy Ed McClellan, on their return. Deputy Sheriffs Joe Scott and Joe Ryan accompanied McClellan.

Mrs. Kunze, a longtime resident of the area and quite familiar with its peculiarities, commented that such a

319

burial in an isolated orange grove could easily have been covered up by men familiar with the irrigating system, who could have flooded that section, thus erasing all evidence of a newly-made grave.

I wondered about the name Peter Fairley. Of course I did not expect to find the boy listed somewhere, but was there a Fairley family in these parts in 1925?

There was.

In the Santa Ana County Directories, S. W. Section, for the year 1925, there is a listing for a Frank Fairley, carpenter, at 930 W. Bishop, Santa Ana. The listing continues at the same address the following year also. It was not in the 1924 edition of the directory, however, so perhaps the Fairleys were new to the area then.

At the outset of the visit Mrs. Leek had mentioned a Felix connected with the area. Again consulting the County Directories for 1925, we found several members of the Felix family listed. Andres Felix, rancher, at Golden West Avenue and Bolsa Chica Road, post office Westminster, Adolph and Miguel Felix, laborers, at the same address—perhaps brothers—and Florentino Felix, also a rancher, at a short distance from the farm of Andres Felix. The listing also appears in 1926.

No Vincent or Vincente, however. But of course not all members of the family need to have been listed. The directories generally list only principals, that is, those gainfully employed or owners of business or property. Then again, there may have been two hired hands by that name, if Vincente was a given name rather than a Christian name.

The 1911 *History of Orange County,* by Samuel Armor, described the area as consisting of a store, church, school, and a few residences only. It was then called

Bolsa, and the main area was used as ranch and stock land. The area abounds in fish hatcheries also, which were started around 1921 by a Japanese named Akiyama. Thus was explained the existence of water holes in the area along with fish tanks, as well as natural lakes.

With the help of Mrs. Kunze, I came across still another interesting record.

According to the Los Angeles *Times* of January 22, 1956, "an ancient residence at 14611 Golden West Street, Westminster, built 85 years ago, was razed for subdivision."

This was undoubtedly the farm residence and land on which the development we had been investigating was later built.

And there we have the evidence. Three names were given by our psychic friend: Felix, Vincent, and Peter Fairley. Two of them are found in the printed record, with some difficulty, and with the help of local researchers familiar with the source material, which neither Mrs. Leek nor I had access to prior to the visit to the haunted house. The body of the woman could easily have been disposed of without leaving a trace by dumping it into one of the fish tanks or other water holes in the area, or perhaps in the nearby Santa Ana River.

About a month after our investigation, the Trausch family moved back to Huntington Beach, leaving the Westminster house to someone else who might someday appear on the scene.

But Carole Trausch informed me that from the moment of our investigation onward, not a single incident had marred the peace of their house.

So I can only assume that Sybil and I were able to help the two unfortunate ghosts out into the open—the boy to find his parents, no doubt also on his side of the veil, and the woman to find peace and forgiveness for her negligence in allowing the boy to be killed.

It is not always possible for the psychic investigator to leave a haunted house free of its unseen inhabitants, and when it does happen, the success is its own reward.

25

Mr. Wasserman's Ghost

One wouldn't think a brand-new modern home perched on a hill at Millbrae, a sunny little town outside San Francisco, could harbor a poltergeist case, one of those sinister disturbances, usually Germanic, involving a teenager or otherwise emotionally unabsorbed person in the household of the living. *Poltergeist* only means "noisy ghost," and a ghost it is—the youngster is not playing any pranks; the youngster is being used to play them by a disturbed person no longer in possession of a physical body.

I heard of the Millbrae case from a young girl who used to live in that house before she decided she was old enough to have a place of her own and consequently moved out to a nearby town called Burlingame. Jean

Grasso has a high school education and a big curiosity about things she cannot explain, such as ESP.

In 1964, she had an experience that particularly upset her because it did not fit in with the usual experiences of life she had been taught in school.

She was in bed at the time, just before falling asleep, or, as she puts it so poetically, "just before the void of sleep engulfs you." Miss Grasso is not at a loss for words, and is as bright a young girl as you want to meet. Her world is very real to her and has little or no room for fantasies.

Still, there it was. Something prevented her from giving in to sleep. Before she knew what she was doing, she saw her own bare feet moving across the floor of her bedroom; she grabbed the telephone receiver and blurted into it—"Jeannie, what's wrong? Did you get hurt?" The telephone had *not* rung. Yet her best friend, who was almost like a sister to her, was on the line. She had been in an automobile accident in which she had been run off the road and collided with a steel pole, but except for being shook up, she was all right.

What made Jean Grasso jump out of a warm bed to answer a phone that had not yet rung, to speak by name to someone who had not yet said "hello," and to inquire about an accident that no one had told her about as yet?

The dark-haired girl is of Italian and Greek background and works as the local representative of a milk company. She is neither brooding nor particularly emotional, it seemed to me, and far from hysterical. The uncanny things that happened in her life intrigued her more in an intellectual way than in an emotional, fearful way.

When she was sixteen, she and five other girls were

playing the popular parlor game of the Ouija board in one of the bedrooms. Jean and Michele di Giovanni, one of the girls, were working the board when it started to move as if pushed by some force stronger than themselves.

Still very skeptical about Ouija boards, Jean demanded some sign or proof of a spiritual presence. She got a quick reply: four loud knocks on the wall. There was nobody in back of the walls who could have caused them. Suddenly, the room got very cold, and they panicked and called the "séance" off then and there.

Ever since, she has heard uncanny noises in her parents' house. These have ranged from footsteps to crashing sounds as if someone or something were thrown against a wall or onto the floor. There never was a rational explanation for these sounds.

After Jean moved out to her own place in Burlingame, she returned home for occasional weekends to be with her mother. Her mother sleeps in the living–dining room area upstairs to save herself the trouble of walking up and down the stairs to the bedroom level, since she has a heart condition.

On the occasions when Jean spent a weekend at home, she would sleep in her mother's former bedroom, situated directly beneath the one her mother now used.

One night, as Jean lay awake in bed, she heard footsteps overhead. They walked across the ceiling, "as if they had no place to go."

Thinking that her mother had breathing difficulties, she raced upstairs, but found her mother fast asleep in bed. Moreover, when questioned about the footsteps the next morning, she assured her daughter she had heard nothing.

"Were they a man's footsteps or a woman's?" I asked
Jean Grasso when we discussed this after the investigation was over.

"A man's," she replied without hesitation.

Once in a while when she is in the dining area upstairs, she will see something out of the corner of an eye
—a flash—something or somebody moving about—and
as soon as she concentrates on it, it is not there. She had
chalked all that up to her imagination, of course.

"When I'm coming down the steps, in the hall, I get a
chill up my spine," the girl said, "as if I didn't want to
continue on. My mother gets the same feelings there, too,
I recently discovered."

That was the spot where I later took my psychic photographs. Did these two psychic people, mother and
daughter, act like living cameras?

"Do you ever have a feeling of a presence with you
when you are all alone?"

"Yes, in my mother's bedroom, I feel someone is
watching me and I turn but there's no one there."

I questioned her about the garden and the area around
the basement. Jean confessed she did not go there often
since the garden gave her an uneasy feeling. She avoided
it whenever she could for no reason she could logically
explain.

One night when she spent the weekend at her parents'
house and was just falling asleep a little after midnight,
she was awakened by the sound of distant voices. The
murmur of the voices was clear enough but when she sat
up to listen further, they went away. She went back to
sleep, blaming her imagination for the incident. But a
week later, to the day, her incipient sleep was again interrupted by the sound of a human voice. This time it

was a little girl's or a woman's voice crying out, *"Help . . . help me!"*

She jumped up so fast she could hear her heart beat in her ears. Surely, her mother had called her. Then she remembered that her mother had gone to Santa Cruz. There was nobody in the house who could have called for help. She looked outside. It was way after midnight and the surrounding houses were all dark. But the voice she had just heard had not come from the outside. It was there, right in the haunted room with her!

I decided to interview Jean's mother, Mrs. Adriana Grasso, a calm, pleasant woman whose skepticism in psychic matters has always been pretty strong.

"We've had this house since 1957," she explained, "but it was already five years old when we bought it. The previous owners were named Stovell and they were about to lose it when we bought it. I know nothing about them beyond that."

The very first night she went to bed in the house, something tried to prevent her from doing so. Something kept pushing her back up. On the first landing of the stairs leading down to the bedroom level, something kept her from continuing on down. She decided to fight it out. Every time after that first experience she had the same impression—that she really *shouldn't* be coming downstairs!

"I hear footsteps upstairs when I'm downstairs and I hear footsteps downstairs when I'm upstairs, and there never is anyone there causing them," she complained.

On several occasions, she awoke screaming, which brought her daughter running in anxiously. To calm her, she assured her she had had a nightmare. But it was not true. On several different occasions, she felt something grabbing her and trying to crush her bones. Something held her arms pinned down. Finally, she had to sleep with the lights on, and it seemed to help.

The sound of a big crash also made the family wonder what was wrong with their house. Mrs. Grasso heard it *upstairs* and her son, Allen, upstairs at the same time, thought it was *downstairs*—only to discover that it was neither here nor there!

"Many times the doorbell would ring and there was no one outside," Mrs. Grasso added, "but I always assumed it was the children of the neighborhood, playing tricks on us."

Loud noises as if a heavy object had fallen brought her into the garage to investigate, but nothing had fallen, nothing was out of place. The garage was locked and so was the front door. Nobody had gotten in. And yet the noises continued; only three days before our arrival, Mrs. Grasso awoke around one in the morning to the sound of "someone opening a can in the bathroom," a metal container. In addition, there was thumping. She thought, why is my son working on his movies at this hour of the night? She assumed the can-opening noises were those of motion picture film cans, of which her son has many. But he had done nothing of the sort.

Soon even Allen and Mr. Grasso heard the loud crashes, although they were unwilling to concede that it represented anything uncanny. But the family that hears ghosts together also finds solutions together—and the Grassos were not particularly panicky about the whole thing. Just curious.

It was at this point that I decided to investigate the case and I so advised Jean Grasso, who greeted us at the door of her parents' house on a very warm day in Octo-

328

ber 1966. In addition to Sybil and Catherine, my ex-wife, two friends, Lori Clerf and Bill Wynn, were with us. We had Lori's car and Bill was doing the driving.

We entered the house and I immediately asked Sybil for her psychic impressions. She had not had a chance to orient herself nor did I allow her to meet the Grassos officially. Whatever she might "get" now would therefore not be colored by any rational impressions of the people she met or the house she was in.

"There is something peculiar about the lower portion of the house," Sybil began, referring to the bedroom floor. The house *was* built in a most peculiar manner. Because the lot sloped toward a ravine, the top floor reached to street level on the front side of the house only. It was here that the house had its living room and entrance hall. On the floor below were the bedrooms, and finally, a garage and adjoining work room. Underneath was a basement, which, however, led to ground level in the rear, where it touched the bottom of the ravine.

At this point, however, Sybil and I did not even know that there was a lower portion to the house, but Jean Grasso assured us there was. We immediately descended the stairs into the section Sybil had felt was invaded by psychic influences.

We stopped at the northeast corner of the bedroom floor where a rear entrance to the house was also situated, leading to a closed-in porch whence one could descend to the ground level outside by wooden stairs.

"What do you feel here, Sybil?" I asked, for I noticed she was getting onto something.

"Whatever I feel is below this spot," she commented. "It must have come from the old foundations, from the land."

Never let it be said that a ghost hunter shies away from dusty basements. Down we went, with Catherine carrying the tape recorder and one of the cameras. In the basement we could not stand entirely upright—at least I couldn't.

"That goes underneath the corridor, doesn't it?" Sybil said as if she knew.

"That's right," Jean Grasso confirmed.

"Somebody was chased here," Sybil commented now, "two men . . . an accident that should never have happened . . . someone died here . . . *a case of mistaken identity.*"

"Can you get more?" I urged her.

"There is a lingering feeling of a man," Sybil intoned. "He is the victim. He was not the person concerned. He was running from the water's edge to a higher part of land. He was a fugitive."

Anyone coming from the San Francisco waterfront would be coming up here to higher ground.

"Whom was he running from?"

"The Law . . . I feel uniforms. There is an element of supposed justice in it, but . . ."

"How long ago was he killed?"

"Eighteen eighty-four."

"His name?"

"Wasserman . . . that's how I get it. I feel the influence of his last moments here, but not his body. He wants us to know he was Wasserman but not the Wasserman wanted by the man."

"What does he look like to you?"

"Ruddy face, peculiarly deep eyes . . . he's here but not particularly cooperative."

"Does he know he is *dead?*" I asked.

330

"I don't think he knows that. But he notices *me.*"

I asked Sybil to convey the message that we knew he was innocent.

"Two names I have to get," Sybil insisted and started to spell, "Pottrene . . . P-o-t-t-r-e-n-e . . . Wasserman tells me these names . . . P-o-v-e-y . . . Povey . . . he says to find them . . . these people are the men who killed him."

"How was he killed?"

"They *had* to kill him. They thought that he was someone else."

"What was the other one wanted for?"

"He doesn't know. He was unfortunate to have been here."

"What is his first name?"

"Jan. J-a-n."

Upon my prodding, Sybil elicited also the information that this Jan Wasserman was a native of San Francisco, that his father's name was Johan or John, and he lived at 324 Emil Street.

I proceeded then to exorcise the ghost in my usual manner, speaking gently of the "other side" and what awaited him there.

Sybil conveyed my wishes to the restless one and reported that he understood his situation now.

"He's no trouble," Sybil murmured. She's very sympathetic to ghosts.

With that we left the basement and went back up the stairs into the haunted bedroom, where I took some photographs; then I moved into the living room area upstairs and took some more—all in all about a dozen black-and-white photographs, including some of the garage and stairs.

Imagine my pleased reaction when I discovered a week later, when the film came back from the laboratory, that two of the photographs had psychic material on them. One, taken of the stairs leading from the bedroom floor to the top floor, shows a whitish substance like a dense fog filling the front right half of my picture. The other remarkable photograph taken of Mrs. Grasso leaning against the wall in the adjoining room shows a similar substance with mirror effect, covering the front third of the area of the picture.

There is a reflection of a head and shoulders of a figure that at first glance I took to be Mrs. Grasso's. On close inspection, however, it is quite dissimilar and shows rather a heavy head of hair whereas Mrs. Grasso's hairdo is close to the head. Mrs. Grasso wears a dark housecoat over a light dress but the image shows a woman or girl wearing a dark dress or sweater over a white blouse.

I asked Jean Grasso to report to me any changes in the house after our visit.

On November 21, 1966, I heard from her again. The footsteps were gone all right, but there was still something strange going on in the house. Could there have been *two* ghosts?

Loud crashing noises were heard, as well as the slamming of doors and noises similar to the thumping of ash cans. No sensible explanation for the noises could be observed by either Jean Grasso or her mother since we were there, nor by her brother and his fiancée nor even the nonbelieving father. No part of the house seemed to be immune from the disturbance.

To test things, Jean Grasso slept at her mother's house soon after we left. At 11:00 P.M., the thumping started. About the same time Mrs. Grasso was awakened by three

332

knocks under her pillow. These were followed almost immediately by the sound of thumping downstairs and movements of a heavy metallic can.

Before I could answer Jean, I had another report from her. Things were far from quiet at the house in Millbrae. Her brother's fiancée, Ellen, was washing clothes in the washing machine. She had closed and secured the door to the laundry room so that the noise would not disturb her intended, who was asleep in the bedroom situated next to that room.

Suddenly she distinctly heard someone trying to get into the room by force, and then she felt a "presence" with her that caused her to run upstairs in panic.

About the same time, Jean and her mother had heard a strange noise from the bathroom below the floor they were then on. Jean went downstairs and found a brush on the tile floor of the bathroom. Nobody had been downstairs at the time. The brush had fallen by itself—into the middle of the floor.

When a picture in brother Allen's room lost its customary place on the wall, the thumbtack holding it up disappeared, and the picture itself somehow got to the other side of his bookcase. The frame is pretty heavy, and had the picture just fallen off it would have landed on the floor behind the bookcase; instead it was neatly leaning against the wall on top of it. This unnerved the young man somewhat, as he had not really accepted the possibility of the uncanny up to this point, even though he had witnessed some pretty unusual things himself.

Meanwhile, Jean Grasso managed to plow through the microfilm files at the San Mateo County library in Belmont. There was nothing of interest in the newspapers for 1884, but the files were far from complete.

However, in another newspaper of the area, the *Redwood City Gazette,* there was an entry that Jean Grasso thought worth passing on for my opinion. A Captain Watterman is mentioned in a brief piece, and the fact that the townspeople were glad that his bill had died and they could be well rid of it.

The possibility that Sybil heard Wasserman when the name was actually Watterman was not to be dismissed— at least not until a Jan Wasserman could be identified from the records somewhere.

Since the year 1884 had been mentioned by the ghost, I looked up that year in H. H. Bancroft's *History of California,* an imposing record of that state's history published in 1890 in San Francisco.

In Volume 7, on pages 434 and 435, I learned that there had been great irregularities during the election of 1884 and political conditions bordered on anarchy. The man who had been first Lieutenant Governor and later Governor of the state was named R. W. Waterman!

This, of course, may only be conjecture and not correct. Perhaps she really did mean Wasserman with two s's. But my search in the San Francisco Directory (Langley's) for 1882 and 1884 did not yield any Jan Wasserman. The 1881 Langley did, however, list an Ernst Wassermann, a partner in Wassermann brothers. He was located at Twenty-fourth Street and *Potrero Avenue.*

Sybil reported that Wasserman had been killed by a certain Pottrene and a certain Povey. Pottrene as a name does not appear anywhere. Could she have meant Potrero? The name Povey, equally unusual, does, however, appear in the 1902 Langley on page 1416.

A Francis J. Povey was a foreman at Kast & Company

and lived at 1 Beideman Street. It seems rather amazing that Sybil Leek would come up with such an unusual name as Povey, even if this is not the right Povey in our case. Wasserman claimed to have lived on Emil Street. There was no such street in San Francisco. There was, however, an Emma Street, listed by Langley in 1884 (page 118).

The city directories available to me are in shambles and plowing through them is a costly and difficult task. There are other works that might yield clues to the identity of our man. It is perhaps unfortunate that my setup does not allow for capable research assistants to help with so monumental a task, and that the occasional exact corroboration of ghostly statements is due more to good luck than to complete coverage of all cases brought to me.

Fortunately, the liberated ghosts do not really care. They know the truth already.

But I was destined to hear further from the Grasso residence.

On January 24, 1967, all was well—except for one thing, and that really happened back on Christmas Eve.

Jean's sister-in-law, Ellen, was sleeping on the couch upstairs in the living room. It was around two in the morning, and she could not drop off to sleep because she had had too much coffee. While she was lying there, wide awake, she suddenly noticed the tall, muscular figure of a man, somewhat shadowy, coming over from the top of the stairs to the Christmas tree as if to inspect the gifts placed near it. At first she thought it was Jean's brother, but as she focused on the figure, she began to realize it was nobody of flesh and blood. She noticed his face now, and that it was bearded. When it dawned on her what she was seeing, and she began to react, the stranger just vanished from the spot where he had been standing a moment before. Had he come to say good-bye and had the Christmas tree evoked a long-ago Christmas holiday of his own?

Before Ellen could tell Jean Grasso about her uncanny experience, Jean herself asked if she had heard the footsteps that kept *her* awake overhead that night. They compared the time, and it appeared that the footsteps and the apparition occurred in about the same time period.

For a few days all was quiet, as if the ghost were thinking it over. But then the pacing resumed, more furiously now, perhaps because something within him had been aroused and he was beginning to understand his position.

At this point everybody in the family heard the attention-getting noises. Mrs. Grasso decided to address the intruder and to tell him that I would correct the record of his death—that I would tell the world that he was not, after all, a bad fellow, but a case of mistaken identity.

It must have pleased the unseen visitor, for things began to quiet down again, and as of February 6, at least, the house had settled down to an ordinary suburban existence on the outskirts of bustling San Francisco.

But the Grassos still were not completely at ease since there is always a chance that the ghost will decide I am not telling the world fast enough, though that would seem patently unreasonable. After all, he had to wait an awfully long time before we took notice of him, and I've jumped several ghosts to get him into print as an emergency case. So be it: Mr. Wasserman of Millbrae is not *the* Mr. Wasserman they were looking for, whoever they were. They just had themselves a wild-ghost chase for nothing.

A Few Last Words . . .

*A*nyone who thinks ghosts are what rattles around medieval castles in England surely will know better after reading these accounts of American hauntings.

The tragedy of a human being turning into what we have come to call a ghost is universal and extends across all time and location. Perhaps I have shown that what we are dealing with is the essential part of a personality that survives the physical death of the outer body.

We should neither be frightened nor disrespectful of those who are trapped by their emotional turmoils beyond death, since it can happen to just about anyone. . . .